THE ROAD TO FATIMA GATE

the road to
fatima
gate

THE BEIRUT SPRING, THE RISE OF HEZBOLLAH, AND THE IRANIAN WAR AGAINST ISRAEL

by Michael J. Totten

Encounter Books New York • London

First American edition published in 2011 by Encounter Books,
an activity of Encounter for Culture and Education, Inc.,
a nonprofit, tax exempt corporation.
Encounter Books website address: www.encounterbooks.com

Manufactured in the United States and printed on
acid-free paper. The paper used in this publication meets
the minimum requirements of ANSI/NISO Z39.48 1992
(R 1997) (*Permanence of Paper*).

FIRST AMERICAN EDITION

LIBRARY OF CONGRESS CATALOGING-IN-PUBLICATION DATA
Totten, Michael J.
The road to Fatima Gate: the Beirut Spring, the rise of Hezbollah, and the
Iranian war against Israel/by Michael J. Totten.
p. cm.
Includes bibliographical references and index.
ISBN-13: 978-1-59403-521-0 (hardcover: alk. paper)
ISBN-10: 1-59403-521-0 (hardcover: alk. paper) 1. Lebanon—Politics and
government—1975-1990. 2. Lebanon—Politics and government—1990-
3. Hizballah (Lebanon) 4. Islam and state—Lebanon. 5. Islam and
politics—Lebanon. 6. Arab-Israeli conflict—Lebanon. 7. State-sponsored
terrorism—Iran. 8. Iran—Foreign relations—Israel. 9. Israel—Foreign
relations—Iran. 10. Totten, Michael J.—Travel—Lebanon. 11.
Journalists—Lebanon—Biography. I. Title.
DS87.5.T67 2011
956.05'3—dc22

2010038080

for
Shelly

CONTENTS

INTRODUCTION

the beirut spring

> We don't want the great Syrian prison.
> **—KAMAL JUMBLATT**

> Rafik Hariri is the person who made Lebanon into a nice place from a place that had nothing nice in it.
> **—LEBANESE SCHOOLCHILD**

On February 14, 2005, an unseen assassin in downtown Beirut activated the detonator on an improvised explosive device and turned former Lebanese Prime Minister Rafik Hariri's motorcade into a fireball. The blast ripped apart vehicles and ignited their gas tanks, shattered buildings in every direction, blew out the windows of the refurbished Phoenicia InterContinental Hotel, and left a crater in the street deep enough to swallow a house. The concussion wave shook foundations everywhere in the capital, and the sound echoed off the sides of the mountains.

Hariri's armor-plated Mercedes could shield him from sniper rounds and fragmentation grenades, but it could not protect him from this. His family could at least rest knowing that he died instantly. Bassel Fleihan, Lebanon's former minister of economy and trade, suffered burns on more than 95 percent of his body and would not succumb to his wounds until two months later. Twenty others, mostly bodyguards, also were killed, and more than 200 innocent bystanders were injured.

The scene was a horror. Not only was the former prime minister almost certainly dead, but the whole street was on fire and hundreds of burned and bleeding people were screaming. Acrid black smoke boiled from the vehicles, making rescue all but impossible.

It was an act of war and an act of political terrorism, and almost everyone suspected at once that the Syrian government did it.

Syria all but annexed the country at the end of the Lebanese civil war fifteen years earlier, and opposition to rule from Damascus had been rising at home and abroad. Hariri wasn't exactly the front man for that movement, but he was by far the most popular Lebanese leader who had tired of Pax Syriana. Syria's strongman President Bashar al-Assad rightly saw Hariri as a threat and wrongly gambled that he could shore up his own rule by dispatching the former prime minister downtown in broad daylight.

It didn't work. Lebanon exploded in revolt the likes of which the modern Middle East had never seen. About a million people[1] in a country of just more than four million descended on Martyrs Square in Beirut and demanded the immediate termination of Syria's military occupation and the banishment of its *mukhabarat* intelligence agents. Hundreds of young people set up a tent city downtown and refused to go home until the Syrian soldiers were out and free elections were formally scheduled.

The story captivated the world. It seemed the "color" revolutions that had recently toppled authoritarian regimes in the former Soviet Union—the Rose Revolution against Eduard Shevardnadze in Georgia, and the Orange Revolution against Viktor Yanukovych's electoral fraud in Ukraine—found their echo in, of all places, an Arabic-speaking country.

Bashar al-Assad and his ruthless late father, Hafez al-Assad, swore their occupation of Lebanon was a benevolent mission on the part of the forces of order. Somebody had to step in and keep the country's factions from killing each other. Most of the world accepted this for a while. Many Lebanese even accepted this at first. Lebanon had dismembered and all but destroyed itself between 1975 and 1990, and it didn't let up until Syria conquered the country, brokered the

Taif Agreement, and disarmed the combatants. If Syria left, the hot-headed Lebanese might take their M16s out of their closets again.

That's what al-Assad's people said, anyway. As if right on schedule, the uprising against Syrian rule had barely even begun when a series of car bombs exploded from East Beirut to the port city of Jounieh.

I hopped a midnight flight to Beirut from Germany just after the fourth bomb went off. Never before had I flown on so empty a plane. Even my flight to New York City two weeks after al Qaeda destroyed the World Trade Center had more people on it.

Hardly anyone wanted to fly to Beirut now that Beirut was "Beirut" again. Just about everyone in the world my age or older remembered vividly when the city epitomized urban disaster zones in the 1980s. The very name of the city had made me shudder for most of my life, conjuring images of vicious communal bloodletting; airplane hijackings; smoldering embassies; suicide bombers; and hostage-takers with their AK-47s, crazed manifestos, and ski masks.

"I am going to die here," one of my colleagues said to himself as his own flight prepared to land.

I stayed in a hotel on the west side of the city that was almost as empty as the plane I flew in on. Management discounted the rack rate so steeply that my stay was practically free. The only other guest on my floor was a big shot from some other place whose twitchy bodyguards staking out the hallway started every time they saw me coming.

Most high-end hotels hired security guards to search every car that pulled up for explosives. It didn't matter who you were, where you were from, or what you looked like—you could not park out front without first having your trunk and undercarriage searched by men wielding mirrors, flashlights, and rifles. I could forget about ordering a pizza. A sign taped to the elevator door in the lobby said, "Due to the security situation we no longer allow food deliveries from outside the hotel. Thank you for understanding."

It wasn't as nerve-wracking as it sounds. The streets were quieter than usual, but otherwise, life continued as normal. I couldn't help wondering, though, as I tried to sleep my first night, if the building was about to explode.

My hotel didn't explode, but I did tread a bit gingerly when I went downtown and met with the dissidents in their tent city. Who could say for sure that Syria wouldn't just open fire and kill hundreds of people as China's Deng Xiaoping did in Beijing's Tiananmen Square in 1989? The late father of the current Syrian president killed as many as tens of thousands in one weekend alone[2] when the Muslim Brotherhood took up arms against his government. "No one is safe," activist Jad Ghostine told me. "If they will kill the prime minister, they will kill anyone."

Thomas Friedman, the veteran journalist who cut his teeth in Beirut during the war, issued a stark warning in the *New York Times*. "There will be no velvet revolutions in this part of the world," he wrote.[3] "The walls of autocracy will not collapse with just one good push. As the head-chopping insurgents in Iraq, the suicide bombers in Saudi Arabia and the murderers of Mr. Hariri have all signaled: The old order in this part of the world will not go quietly into this good night. You put a flower in the barrel of their gun and they'll blow your hand and your head right off."

Beirut, as it turned out, actually *did* get a velvet revolution of sorts, but no one knew at the time that's what would happen. Those who knew Lebanon's history, as Friedman did better than most, had plenty of reasons to worry.

Clashes between Palestinian and Christian militias in 1975 unleashed fifteen years of sectarian warfare unprecedented in its ferocity in the Middle East since the dissolution of the Ottoman Empire. It was all the more tragic that it happened in the most liberal and democratic of the Arabic-speaking countries.

All Middle Eastern countries have religious minorities, but Lebanon is the only one without a religious majority. A little more than a third of the population is Christian, a little less than a third is Sunni Muslim, and a final third or so is Shia Muslim.[4] Druze make up roughly 5 percent.

This was Lebanon's blessing and curse. It's the most cosmopolitan place in the region when it's at peace with itself, but when it breaks down—watch out.

Its breakdown in the 1970s was just about fatal. Many in the Sunni community thrilled to Pan-Arab causes, and none so urgently as that of the Palestinians. The Sunni elite welcomed Yasser Arafat's Palestine Liberation Organization (PLO) into the country to use it as a base for its war against Israel and even helped him set up his own state within a state in West Beirut.[5]

Many, if not most, Christians were furious. When the government refused to shut Arafat down, they organized militias to do it themselves.

Sporadic clashes with small arms led to serious battles with heavier weapons, and Beirut split apart into mutually hostile cantons. The so-called Green Line ran like a burning and bleeding gash southeast from downtown and cut the city in half, the mostly Christian east side squaring off against the mostly Sunni and Palestinian west.

Soon the whole country was at war with itself. Christians fought Sunnis and Druze. Palestinians fought Shias and Christians. Syria invaded, first to save the Christians from the Palestinians and later to keep the Christians down and Israel out. The Israelis barged in to get rid of Arafat. French and American troops tried to impose some kind of order. Iranian Revolutionary Guards founded Hezbollah to fight the Israelis and hunt down every Westerner they could find. Even the Soviet Union got in on the action by helping Druze leader Kamal Jumblatt slug it out with the Christians for control of the mountains.

Some militiamen even executed civilians at checkpoints for what was printed next to "religion" on their identity cards. The war wasn't religious per se. God had little or nothing to do with it. Sects in the Middle East are communities; religion just marks the boundaries. As Jews in Israel are considered Jews whether or not they're religious, every single person in Lebanon belonged to one religiously defined group or another. Atheist "Christians" fought atheist "Sunnis," and so on. Aside from the radical Islamists of Hezbollah, hardly any of the combatants cared if their enemies went to church, prayed in a mosque, or believed God existed at all. They fought over turf, and they fought over politics.

These communities even turned on themselves. Christians battled it out with other Christians for dominance in their carved-up enclaves in East Beirut and Mount Lebanon. The Shias did the same when Hezbollah fought the secular men of Amal for control of the Israeli border and the suburbs south of Beirut.

Once considered the Switzerland of the Middle East, Lebanon became the place where the Middle East fought its wars. It was not only a battleground for its own sects and their various factions, but the principal battleground in the Arab-Israeli conflict, the first battleground in the nascent Iranian-Israeli conflict, the second-largest front after the Iran-Iraq war in the ancient conflict between Sunnis and Shias, and even a minor sort of proxy war battleground in the Cold War. It could not possibly have been any more of a mess.

It is often said that Israel is tiny, but Lebanon is only half its size. It's extraordinary that such a small place—with no natural resources to fight over—became so incredibly important, but that's what happened.

Many Lebanese said their country was cursed by geography. If it were an island, or even if it bordered countries other than Israel and Syria, its history would have had a very different trajectory. The PLO would not have used it as a base to fight Israel and therefore never would have gotten into the shooting fight with the Christians that sparked the war in the first place. The Israelis hardly would have paid it any attention, and without an Israeli invasion and occupation, Iran could not have built up Hezbollah. Syria would never have invaded or occupied it.

So yes, the country was cursed by geography as well as its internal divisions. But what could you do? Lebanon was hardly unique. Bosnia-Herzegovina, Georgia, Ukraine, Israel, Cyprus, Iraq—all these countries had similar problems.

More than 150,000 people were killed[6] in the war—a terrible number, more than 3 percent of the population. Everyone knew someone who didn't survive, and most people knew several.

The country was ravaged, no part of it more than Beirut. Journalist and author Christopher Hitchens was thunderstruck by the vast devastation when he visited after the guns finally went silent. "From the air it looked like Rotterdam at the end of the Second World War," he told me when I later met up with him there. "There wasn't a single undamaged building within a bull's roar," he added in an interview published on the website *NOW Lebanon*.[7] "There was only one functioning hotel. It looked like a moonscape." He saw a solitary old man clearing rubble away with a shovel and couldn't stop thinking about him. "I was so touched by it. I was thinking, well, lots of luck. See you in fifty years."

"You are crazy to be here right now," the young man next to me said. "Crazy." He and I sat alone yet next to each other at the bar in a fashionable establishment on Monot Street along the old Green Line that during the war was a deathly silent no-man's-land between East and West Beirut where nothing lived except weeds and wild grass.

"You really think so?" I said.

I didn't feel crazy to be there. That feeling passed after twenty-four hours. There weren't tanks in the streets. It wasn't a war zone. There were, however, far fewer people out in public than usual. Restaurants, cafés, and bars that were usually packed were more than half empty. No one had any idea what might happen next. Most thought it wise to stay home and out of the way.

Beirut had a serious case of the jitters, and I didn't have to interview anybody to know that. I heard about it constantly even while minding my own business. A taxi driver, in one of the most anguished and heartbroken voices I have ever heard in my life, told me why it was his dream to live in America. "I hate this country," he said, physically depressed and hunched over the wheel. "Christians kill each other. Muslims kill each other. Oh my God."

The young man next to me at the bar was named Claude. Obviously, then, he was a Christian. It's rude to ask a Lebanese person which sect they belong to, but names, accents, and birthplaces often give it away.

"We are getting close to the war," he said and sipped from his martini. "That's why the government is asking us all to come out and return to the nightlife. It pushes the war away."

I found it hard to believe Lebanon might be lurching toward war. It did not look—at all—like the type of place that was ready to blow. Beirut was not Baghdad, and it was not Gaza. Lebanon in 2005 was so much more technologically, culturally, socially, and politically advanced than the other hot spots in the Middle East that it looked and felt like the *Star Trek* universe by comparison.

Referring to Beirut as the Paris of the Middle East, as many have, was a bit of a stretch. Apartment complexes built during the civil war era looked only slightly better than tower blocks built at the same time in communist countries. Lebanon's premodern architecture, though, was French Mandate and Ottoman. Tiled roofs, European-style moldings, Oriental arches, and wrought-iron balconies were common. Glass skyscrapers reflecting the shimmering Mediterranean filled in space where there used to be rubble.

Beirut wasn't the cultural capital of the Arab world; Cairo was. But Beirut was vastly more sophisticated than Cairo or any other Arab city, except maybe Tunis. Hundreds of thousands of tourists visited every year for its fine dining establishments, film festivals, art galleries, outdoor concerts, and other cultural amenities too numerous to keep track of. Bookstores proliferated, and their selection was better than what you'd find in many American bookstores. Most titles for sale were published in English and French. Translation hardly seemed necessary—a huge percentage of Beirutis were fluent in both.

When wealthy Gulf Arabs needed relief from their fanatically conservative home countries, they hopped over to Beirut, where they could drink booze, gamble, and chase girls without running afoul of the law or local customs. Beirut wasn't just the Middle East's bastardized version of Paris. It was an otherwise stultifying region's freewheeling Hong Kong, its Amsterdam. And it no longer looked anything like the shattered postwar Rotterdam that Christopher Hitchens reported seeing fifteen years earlier.

Rafik Hariri did more than anyone else to clean up the place.

Few who knew him when he was young would have expected it. They certainly wouldn't have thought he'd become the richest man in the country or its prime minister. He grew up in a modest household in the Sunni city of Sidon and was not from the elite class of *zuama* who, for generations, had run parts of the country like fiefdoms. Nor was he one of the warlords from the 1980s, many of whom were now members of parliament. He didn't acquire his billions from an inheritance or from war profiteering, but from his construction company in Saudi Arabia.

In 1992, Syrian ruler Hafez al-Assad needed to replace Lebanon's incompetent Prime Minister Omar Karami with someone who better understood economics and finance. Why bother conquering Lebanon if it was nothing but a money pit and a headache? He didn't trust Hariri, exactly, but the man from Sidon seemed the best fit for the job as long as he could be kept in his place.

"Hariri would have the freedom to manage Lebanon's reconstruction and finances," historian William Harris wrote[8] in *The New Face of Lebanon*, "keeping both Lebanon and Syria afloat, as long as he left security and foreign relations to Damascus, accepted Syrian vetting of official appointments, and tolerated a financial rake-off for Syrian personalities and their Lebanese associates."

Hariri didn't seem to mind the Syrian occupation as much as he might have, at least not initially. If subservience to Damascus meant he could rebuild the country, so be it. Lebanon would be ruled from Damascus whether he took the job or not. And he was just what Lebanon needed after the long years of localized rule by militias. "While warfare was all around him," journalist Samir Atallah wrote,[9] "he came to his country loaded with rice, sugar, and light bulbs. It pained him to see how dark both city and mind were. Wherever he went, he called for reconciliation and reconstruction."

His Lebanese company Solidere did most of the reconstruction work in the city center, restoring most of the French Mandate buildings shattered by exploding rockets and mortars and gutted by fires and bombs. The rebuilt downtown was a bit antiseptic and fake looking, but it was a pleasant place all the same. Streets were closed to vehicle traffic so pedestrians could enjoy the restaurants, shops, cafés, and bars as they would in the gentrified old quarters of Europe.

"I see Beirut as a jewel lit up at night," he said to correspondent Nicholas Blanford[10] in the 1990s when asked what he expected Lebanon to look like by the year 2000. That's what he wanted. That's what he aimed for. While he couldn't say it out loud, Syria's smothering occupation and graft stifled the country's recovery and potential.

The Israeli occupation of a narrow strip of land in the south didn't help either. Jerusalem didn't suck hundreds of millions of dollars out of the economy every year like Damascus did, but the Israel Defense

Forces waged a slow-motion counterinsurgency against Hezbollah in the border area, and much of the world still thought of Lebanon as shady, unstable, and dangerous. The civil war may have been over, but lasting peace hadn't arrived everywhere in the country just yet. Without real stability, Lebanon couldn't fully rejoin the modern global economy.

Hezbollah was the one Lebanese militia that Hafez al-Assad hadn't disarmed in 1991. It was primarily an Iranian project, but Iran was Syria's closest ally, and al-Assad found Hezbollah useful.

"For Syria," William Harris wrote,[11] "Hezbollah could persist as both a check on the Lebanese regime and as a means to bother Israel when convenient." Because Hezbollah "bothered" Israel, so to speak, Israel kept occupation troops in its South Lebanon "security zone" to keep the Iranian-backed militia off its northern border.

As a Lebanese Sunni leader, it would never occur to Hariri to team up with Israel as some Lebanese Christians did during the war, but he also wasn't thrilled with the fact that the last armed non-state group in the country was a warmongering Iranian-backed Shia militia. His long-term vision depended on no war in Lebanon against anyone for any reason.

Only the Syrian army could disarm Hezbollah, just as it had disarmed the other militias, but al-Assad would have none of it. Hariri wouldn't have done it himself in any case. He wasn't a military man, and he never had been. He was a builder, a diplomat, and a compromiser. He hoped to resolve the problem with Israel and Hezbollah through patient negotiation.

The best chance came when Israel and Syria held peace talks in 2000. If al-Assad made a deal with Jerusalem, disarming Hezbollah would have to be part of the package. Lebanon might even be able to start its own peace track with Israel once Syria and Hezbollah weren't in the way.

Al-Assad, though, refused to close the deal when Israel wouldn't cede control of the northeastern shore of the Sea of Galilee.

Hariri was shocked and appalled—and not at Israel, but at al-Assad, who was jeopardizing his vision of a prosperous Lebanon at peace with itself and its neighbors. Henry Kissinger's old maxim "No war without Egypt, no peace without Syria" still applied.

The government was divided, with President Emile Lahoud and Speaker of Parliament Nabih Berri on one side and with Hariri and Druze chief Walid Jumblatt on the other.

Lahoud was a former Lebanese army commander handpicked by al-Assad for the presidency. He followed his orders, and he ran the Syrian-Lebanese security state regime like the perfect yes-man. Hariri was a well-respected Sunni leader, but Lahoud's support in his own Christian community had declined over the years almost to zero. The Christians had always felt the least affection for Syrian rule, and Lahoud was a mere instrument in the hands of al-Assad, in no way a leader of the community he supposedly led.

Berri, who was also the leader of the secular Shia Amal movement, likewise was loyal to Damascus. Unlike Lahoud, though, he did sort of represent the wishes of his community, which had always been more at ease than the others with Greater Syria.

Hariri's political party Tayyar Mustaqbal, or Future Movement in English, promoted an ideology of liberalism and capitalism, the opposite of that enforced by Syria's fascist-like Arab Socialist Baath Party regime. Hariri fell out of favor with al-Assad in the late 1990s, as one might expect under these circumstances, and Lahoud dutifully accused him of embezzlement, corruption, and conspiring with Israel against Hezbollah—the latter a serious, though spurious, charge.

No Lebanese leader felt more hostility toward Damascus than Walid Jumblatt, whose own father, Kamal Jumblatt, was assassinated by the regime in 1977. He had no more choice than to go along with the new order than anyone else, but there was never much doubt in his community or in Syria about how he felt.

He began receiving death threats in 2000 when he grumbled about Syria's refusal to redeploy troops from Beirut to the Bekaa Valley as stipulated by the Taif Agreement. It seemed like a good time to ask for a pullback, if not a withdrawal. Israel had finally withdrawn its own armed forces from the south earlier that year. Hafez al-Assad had died and was replaced by his son Bashar, who many thought might be a reformer. Jumblatt, though, was effectively declared a nonperson by the Syrian authorities, and any hope that Bashar al-Assad might liberalize his father's regime didn't last long.

Hariri and Jumblatt did well in the 2000 election, though, and the younger al-Assad had to deal with them. It wasn't long, however, before the U.S. and France grew tired of dealing with him.

In 1991, the U.S. signed off on Syria's occupation of Lebanon in return for Hafez al-Assad's "help" in ousting Saddam Hussein from Kuwait. The U.S. had enough of Syrian foreign policy, though, by the time the second Iraq war rolled around. The younger al-Assad helped terrorists and insurgents from all over the Arab world transit through Syria into Iraq to fight American soldiers and car bomb civilians. In 2003, a fed-up U.S. Congress retaliated with the Syria Accountability and Lebanese Sovereignty Restoration Act.[12]

France became disgruntled with al-Assad for its own reasons. Lebanon was like a little brother to many in the French establishment whose predecessors helped the country achieve independence in 1943. Hariri had a close, personal friendship with French President Jacques Chirac, and al-Assad knew he'd be in serious trouble if the French and Americans joined forces against him.

If he didn't want to be pushed out of Lebanon, he'd need to shore up his position. What he needed more than anything were pliable Lebanese officials who requested he stay.

Lahoud had been doing that all along and would happily keep at it, but his term in Baabda Palace was set to expire in 2004, and the law only allowed him one term. So al-Assad summoned Hariri to Damascus and ordered him to tell parliament to extend Lahoud's term by three years.

Hariri balked.

"Lahoud is me," al-Assad said.[13] "If you and Chirac want me out of Lebanon, I will break Lebanon on your head and Jumblatt's."

Hariri returned to Beirut, frightened and shaken. In his book *Killing Mr. Lebanon*, Nicholas Blanford relates a pivotal conversation between Hariri and an assistant. The two men assumed Syria could easily dispatch 100,000 Hezbollah supporters into the streets of Beirut to demonstrate in favor of Lahoud's extension.

"What," Hariri said,[14] "do you think would happen if someone fires into that crowd?"

"Hezbollah would burn the city."

Hariri did what he was told and announced to Lebanon's parliament that Lahoud's presidential term should be extended.

Despite a falling-out between the U.S. and France over the war in Iraq, the two countries did exactly what al-Assad feared most when they jointly sponsored United Nations Security Council Resolution 1559[15] ordering the withdrawal of all foreign military personnel from Lebanon, meaning but not naming the Syrians, and the disarmament of all militias, meaning but not naming Hezbollah. The resolution passed on September 2, 2004, just five days after the cabinet approved Lahoud's extension.

The following month, Lahoud's ministers threatened to quit the cabinet and bring down the government if Hariri didn't resign. So Hariri resigned and was replaced by the less competent but loyal Omar Karami.

Al-Assad, though, was still sweating. Opposition to his rule in Lebanon was becoming more brazen, and so were his actions. Member of Parliament Marwan Hamadeh, who resigned his cabinet position to protest the extension, barely survived an assassination attempt when his car exploded in front of his house.

Hamadeh survived, though, and Hariri didn't take the incident as seriously as he otherwise might have. He decided to run for office again in 2005 and figured he'd win big. Most in his Sunni community were with him, of course. Many Christians were, too. They were sick of Lahoud and his Syrian-sponsored security state. Jumblatt and his Druze community would also most likely back him, since he and they were more politically opposed to Damascus than anyone else.

Jumblatt and a number of Christian MPs mounted a public opposition movement called the Bristol Gathering, named after the plush Bristol Hotel in Beirut's Verdun district where they met to plot strategy. They hoped to overturn Lahoud and al-Assad's regime in the May 2005 election, which they wanted to be certified by international monitors.

Al-Assad and the pro-Syrian Lebanese were enraged, and they were becoming increasingly dangerous. "You will be crucified above the garbage dump of history," Assem Qanso, head of the minuscule Lebanese Baath Party, said to Jumblatt.[16]

Hariri kept a bit of artificial distance between himself and the Bristol Gathering. He didn't meet with them at the hotel, nor did he publicly attach his name to their movement. Even so, everyone knew that he was quietly with them.

With Hariri set to sweep the election, with the opposition demanding implementation of the Taif Agreement and Resolution 1559, and with increased French and American pressure, al-Assad must have felt desperate. Twelve days after the Bristol Gathering demanded the withdrawal of the Syrian military, somebody who had it in for Hariri blew him and twenty others away with a bomb so large it literally weighed tons. "They threatened him, they charged him with treason, and then they murdered him," Jumblatt said.[17]

It was the worst act of terrorism in Lebanon since the end of the civil war, and a historical hinge event that marked the end of an era.

"It was often said that the Syrians could only enter Lebanon with the support of the Christians," Nicholas Blanford noted,[18] "and would only leave if they lost the support of the Muslims."

They certainly lost the support of the Muslims, or at least the support of the Sunnis.

"The assassination instantly cemented the mass of Sunni Muslims . . . in the opposition alignment," William Harris wrote.[19] "When added to the vast majority of Christians and Druze, together at least 40% of Lebanese, simple arithmetic indicated that something close to two-thirds of Lebanon was stirring against Damascus."

Al-Assad's overlordship in Lebanon survived many things, but it would not survive this.

⌒

The Syrians and their Lebanese allies had a much easier time managing the opposition when it was small.

"There were only 200 of us at first," Nabil Abou-Charaf said when I met him downtown for coffee. He was only twenty-four years old but belonged to the original core of anti-occupation activists and became a leader of the larger youth movement almost by default.

"We held demonstrations and were arrested, beaten, and tortured," he said. "But we kept going anyway. Now we number one million. The Syrians, their Lebanese puppets, and Hezbollah can't stop us now. We are too strong and too many."

He and I sat at an outdoor table in Nejmeh Square, an area rebuilt by Hariri's Solidere company. Hariri himself drank his last coffee there just minutes before he was assassinated. I could see his table from mine covered in bouquets of flowers.

"The movement is totally led by young people," Nabil said. "Both Christians and Muslims. We stay up all night strategizing and getting to know each other. It's amazing, but it's also sad. We never really knew each other until now. Hariri's assassination broke down that wall. We are talking together—really talking and getting to know each other—for the first time."

They were children of the elite mostly, and of the middle class. The children of street sweepers and maids weren't wiling away their evening hours in bull sessions with the sons and daughters of their former enemies. Political attitudes in Lebanon, though, were often determined by the elite. They trickled down. "Lebanese people are always ready for anything," one rather parochial Christian said when he picked me up hitchhiking in the mountains. "If you lead us to peace, we are ready for peace. If you lead us to war, we are ready for war."

"It is so important," Nabil continued, "that we heal the old wounds. We cannot go back to the past, to the civil war. We want to rebuild our country." He tapped the side of his head. "And that includes rebuilding our minds. Lebanon has been so divided. We stand not only for freedom and independence, but also national unity and a new, modern, common, tolerant Lebanese identity."

Rustom Ghazaleh ran Syria's *mukhabarat* intelligence network in Lebanon from his headquarters in the ethnic Armenian town of Anjar near the Syrian border. He supposedly had 6,000 Lebanese working for him as informants in Beirut alone. They may have been useful when only Nabil and a few hundred others stood up to al-Assad and his rule, but what use were they now? Most of the country was against them.

"Every waiter," Nabil said, "every taxi driver, every shopkeeper, and every person who works in hotels is a potential informer." Just then our waiter came to the table and asked if we wanted more coffee. "We assume we are being watched constantly," Nabil continued, not caring who overheard, "because we are. We are not free, but we are no longer afraid to express ourselves. The climate of fear still exists, but it is breaking. Next time you visit Lebanon, it will be a free country."

Lebanon already looked and felt like a free country to me and would, in fact, become an actually free country before I left. Events were moving too quickly and intensely for al-Assad and his people to control the outcome or even keep up.

Tens of thousands had turned out for Hariri's funeral on February 16, 2005. Everyone but the government was invited. Strict political sectarians may have dismissed him as the leader of the Sunnis, which he was, but he was also prime minister of the whole country, and he rebuilt it for everyone. Christians, Druze, and even a smaller number of Shias made their way downtown to show their respect, cry, and even scream. They buried him between the Mohammad al-Amin mosque and Martyrs Square, where the heart of downtown used to be before it was pulverized.

A three-day strike began the following day. Demonstrations that started outside Hariri's house in West Beirut rapidly spread throughout the country. Portraits of Bashar al-Assad were ripped from the walls as though he were a dictator who had already been toppled. By the time I arrived in late March, not a single one of his posters remained outside the Hezbollah-occupied areas.

An-Nahar newspaper publisher Ghassan Tueni fulminated against Lebanon's servile government headed by Emile Lahoud and Omar Karami as well as their masters in Syria. "We warn the government of the Caliph Omar," he said,[20] "of even thinking that it can benefit from this disaster to postpone the elections to avoid there being a referendum on its incrimination."

Karami didn't have the stomach for this. He had dutifully taken Hariri's place as prime minister with Syrian backing, and now his own country hated him. His own community seemed to hate him the most. He was a Sunni, and the Sunnis were *furious*. He didn't have many real friends, only cynical allies in a corrupt and expiring system.

"May God preserve Lebanon," he said.[21] Then he quit.

Hezbollah was alarmed by all this. The only reason it still even existed as a militia instead of a neutered political party was because al-Assad found it useful and helped Iran supply it with weapons over the Syrian border. If Syria was to be thrown out of Lebanon and the pro-Syrian government replaced by a pro-Western regime, Hezbollah was in serious trouble.

On March 8, 2005, Hezbollah Secretary General Hassan Nasrallah bused 500,000 Hezbollah officials and supporters into downtown Beirut for a massive show of solidarity with al-Assad and his government.[22] They carried Hezbollah flags and portraits of the Syrian tyrant. Some were photographed brandishing pistols and knives.

Lebanon, all of a sudden, didn't look so anti-Syrian after all.

If there was any serious doubt, though, the question was settled once and for all six days later on March 14, when the opposition brought more than a fourth of the entire country downtown for the biggest demonstration in Lebanon's history. More than twice as many people went down there to demand free elections and an end to occupation than came out with Hezbollah to say thanks to al-Assad.

Unlike the Hezbollah rally, this one was genuinely multiconfessional. A token number of Christian, Sunni, and Druze citizens attended Hezbollah's event, but the overwhelming majority of people who showed up on that day were Shias. The March 14 rally brought together a huge number of people from all the other main groups.

Christian and Muslim unity was a major theme on March 14, though in practice there was really only much unity between Christians and Sunnis. The spirit of ecumenism was real, even so. A number of demonstrators carried signs with a Christian cross and a Muslim crescent placed next to each other. A vendor sold necklaces with a crescent and cross fused together into a pendant.

"They have buried their tiny differences to reveal the concept of a unified Lebanon, and that is excellent," said Maronite Christian Patriarch Nasrallah Sfeir.[23] "There was no difference between a Paul, a Pierre, a Mohammad, or a Mustafa."

Every Arab country in the world turned against Syria after this. Even Iran, al-Assad's most reliable ally, took a step back and no longer upheld Syria's occupation of Lebanon, at least not in public. The U.S. and France, of course, stepped up their campaign to get Damascus out of Beirut.

Al-Assad was particularly concerned that U.S. President George W. Bush might do something crazy, as he did in Iraq. "Please send this message," he said to Joe Klein at *Time* magazine.[24] "I am not Saddam Hussein. I want to cooperate."

⌐

Nabil took me to Freedom Camp, the city of tents around Martyrs Square built by young people who swore they wouldn't budge until their demands were met. The "permanent" population was 700, and it doubled on weekends.

"First," Nabil said, "all Syrian soldiers and intelligence agents must leave Lebanon now and forever. We need an international inquiry into the assassination of Rafik Hariri. And we demand free and fair elections—on time, without delay—in May."

They pitched their camp in Beirut's city center, the one place where all of Lebanon converged in its lush variety. From here you could sometimes hear the soft peal of church bells and the muezzin's call to Muslim prayer at the same time. Rafik Hariri was buried right across the street next to the mosque he built, which itself was adjacent to the Church of St. George. I could see the soft turquoise waters of the Mediterranean and the snow-capped peak of Mount Sannine in the Mount Lebanon range towering over the city.

In the center of camp was the Martyrs Statue, still riddled with bullet holes from the war. It portrayed two women—one a Christian, the other a Muslim—standing together over their fallen sons where the Turkish authorities hanged nationalists who clamored for independence from the Ottoman Empire in 1916.

There, Nabil introduced me to Asma Andraos, a young corporate events planner who said she had little interest in politics until after Hariri was killed and she couldn't think of much else.

"I never felt so enraged in my life," she said. "Who do they think they are?"

She may not have known much about politics, but she knew plenty about planning events, and she put everything she had into getting as many people as possible downtown on March 14.

"Ironically," she said, "Hezbollah helped. The Sunnis are usually passive and hard to stir up, but when Hezbollah brought *all those Shias* down here to support the people who murdered Hariri, they knew they had to come out in huge numbers."

That was the dirty secret everyone in Lebanon understood perfectly and few Westerners wanted to think about. Politics in Lebanon were dangerously split along a fault line more than a thousand years old. Most foreign observers, myself included, saw the upheaval as a struggle for freedom against a tyrannical system and its defenders. That wasn't wrong, but it didn't entirely explain what was happening. The rift between Sunni and Shia Muslims that erupted in the eighth century ripped right through the center of Lebanon. For all the talk of freedom, democracy, coexistence, and national unity, Hezbollah's rally on March 8 showed everyone that hundreds of thousands of people from one of the country's three largest sects had other ideas. And they had their own army.

The Middle East is sometimes derided as a region of "tribes with flags"[25] rather than authentic nation-states. Egypt has a coherent national identity, as does Tunisia, but tribalism trumps nationalism almost everywhere else. Everywhere, that is, except Lebanon.

In Lebanon, it's all about sects. And there are more than just the main three, or four if you count the Druze. The state officially recognizes eighteen different religious communities that have been cobbled together into the most unlikely of polities.

The Christians alone can be broken down into several: among them Protestants, Greek Orthodox, Greek Catholics, and Maronites. The Maronites are the largest of these and actually make up the majority of Lebanon's Christians. They're the ones who came up with the idea of an independent Lebanon in the first place, and they used their power and numbers to shape it to their advantage as much as they could.

The original Maronites were a small community of followers of Saint Maroun in the Orontes Valley of Syria who were persecuted by the Byzantine authorities ruling the area at the time. In the sixth century, they took flight to the green valleys and snow-capped peaks of the Mount Lebanon range along the shore of the Eastern Mediterranean, where they could practice their version of Christianity as they pleased. They were physically safe in their mountain fastness and, just as important, they were culturally safe.

The Arab invasion and conquest soon followed, but the Maronites refused to convert to Islam, and they were able to rejoin Christian civilization when the Crusaders arrived from Europe in the twelfth century. They forged strong cultural and political ties with France at the time that persist even today. French names like Claude, Pierre, and Michel are as common among Lebanese as Arabic names like Omar, Ali, and Mohammad.

The Maronites later forged ties with Rome and became officially Catholic, though they retained distinct traits. Their liturgy, for instance, is still in Syriac, a dialect of Aramaic, the language of Jesus. Most have never considered themselves Arabs. While they speak the everyday Lebanese version of Arabic, they trace their community's history not to Arabia but to the Byzantine Empire, the Roman Empire, and—a bit less plausibly—to the ancient Phoenicians who built Lebanon's first civilization.

When France acquired what are modern-day Syria and Lebanon at the end of World War I from the ruins of the Ottoman Empire, Maronite leaders petitioned French authorities for an independent state of their own, a free Christian homeland in the heart of the Middle East. France was not going to rule these formerly Turkish territories forever, and the Maronites shuddered at the thought of being ruled from the Sunni Arab city of Damascus. Their little piece of the Middle East had always been somewhat apart from the world of the Arabs and Muslims. Mount Lebanon had been a semiautonomous Ottoman province since the sixteenth century and a largely autonomous one since the mid-nineteenth century, as a *Mutasarrifiyah* under European protection.

A strictly Maronite homeland in Mount Lebanon, though, wouldn't be viable. They needed coastline and the port cities of Tripoli, Beirut, and Sidon, where large numbers of Sunni Muslims and Greek Orthodox Christians resided. They also needed agricultural land. Neither the mountains nor the valleys could produce very much food, and the coastal plain was narrow and yielded too little. They needed the hinterlands of the Bekaa Valley and the rolling hills to the south between Tyre and Mount Hermon. Many Shia Muslims lived in those lands.

Christians just barely made up a majority within those borders and would face a relative population decline before long. Greater Mount Lebanon may have been a Maronite idea, but it could not be a Maronite country. A cultural as well as political accommodation would have to be made with the Muslims and Arabs. The Greek Orthodox Christians weren't Muslims, of course, but they were more comfortable than the Maronites with the notion of an Arab identity and belonging. While they "Christianized" the Muslims to an extent, especially in Beirut, they were in turn partly "Arabized" by them.

The Muslims were no more a unified bloc than the Christians, and the Sunnis and Shias had some things in common with Christians that they did not have with each other. The Shias were less interested than the Sunnis in Pan-Arabism, for instance. At the same time, the coastal and worldly-wise Sunni elite felt more at ease around their Christian colleagues than with the feudal lords from the Shia hinterlands.

The Maronite and Sunni elite together forged a National Pact, where they divided up power and tried to define what it meant to be Lebanese.

It wasn't easy. Lebanon couldn't be Christian or Maronite, nor could it be Islamic. It couldn't be Arab—at least not explicitly, and certainly not exclusively. It was something else, something different, something unique in the Middle East. It was pluralist, and it was founded in a spirit of compromise as a Mediterranean country with an "Arab face," but not an Arab identity.

Christians made up slightly more than half the population, so they were awarded six seats in parliament for every five given to Muslims. The Maronites, as the dominant sect, took permanent ownership of the presidency. The prime minister's office would be reserved for the Sunnis, while the Shias were awarded the speaker of parliament. Druze and other minorities were few and therefore barred from the country's most powerful posts.

This new Lebanese republic would be guaranteed and protected by France. French was already the second language of the country, and it would be some time before it was eclipsed by English.

The Sunni rank and file didn't really buy into the National Pact that had been hammered out among the elite, and some Maronites weren't completely sold on it either. The Shias were hardly consulted and were rarely even heard from during this period. Their society was rural for the most part, and they had few champions in the capital as adept at politics as the *zuama* of the Maronites and the Sunnis.

Lebanon ended up with a weak state, and most of its people seemed to like it that way—not that they had much of a choice. Legislation couldn't clear parliament but by consensus, and consensus was difficult in a country of varied political ideas and cultural values. No community would tolerate being ruled by the others, so power was radically decentralized away from Beirut. The system was not one that could easily produce dictators or strongmen, and Lebanon became a sort of libertarian land of do-as-you-please.

The country might have been able to muddle through with its delicate sectarian and political balancing act if the region around it were sedate and at peace with itself. It's in the heart of the Middle East, though, one of the least stable places on earth. The population is so religiously and ideologically diverse that almost every political cause that arises anywhere in the Middle East has *somebody* championing it inside Lebanon. As a result, almost every regional conflict since the dissolution of the Ottoman Empire has played itself out there.

In the late 1950s, for instance, when Arab Nationalism swept through the Middle East, many Sunnis in Lebanon thrilled to its charismatic leader Gamal Abdel Nasser in Egypt and became even less interested in Lebanese nationalism, which many still thought of as Maronite, than they were before. A great many Lebanese Sunnis backed Nasser—who would soon merge Egypt and Syria into the United Arab Republic—and wished to see Lebanon dissolved into the great Arab nation. Maronite President Camille Chamoun panicked and rigged an election. The country fell into crisis, and U.S. Marines were dispatched to keep order.

The United Arab Republic wasn't long for the world. Syria seceded from it three years later. Egypt and Syria joined forces again, though, and, along with Jordan, fought the devastating (for them) Six-Day War against Israel in 1967. Egypt lost Gaza and the Sinai Peninsula; Jordan lost the West Bank; and Syria lost the Golan Heights—territories the Israelis promised to give back only after peace treaties were signed.

Lebanon managed to sit that war out, but it was swallowed nearly whole by the Arab-Israeli conflict when the Sunnis teamed up with Arafat's PLO and brought the wrath of the Israel Defense Forces down on everyone's heads.

By the mid-1980s many Maronites wished to secede, thinking the very idea of a Greater Lebanon was a terrible mistake to begin with. The radical Shia Hezbollah militia, meanwhile, hoped to replicate Iran's Islamic Revolution in Lebanon. Druze leader Kamal Jumblatt had no interest in imposing a communist dictatorship, but he merrily took arms from the Soviet Union and fought against the Maronite militias and the sectarian system that doomed him to live under a political glass ceiling forever.

It's no small wonder that Lebanon even survived. It did survive, though, and the ideas that went into its founding came roaring back stronger than ever when the era of Syrian vassalage ended.

"It is astonishing how splendidly the Syrians have made a hash of things in Lebanon," Michael Young wrote in Beirut's *Daily Star* newspaper.[26] "It's almost as if the regime were reading the lessons taught by Hafez al-Assad backward. Where al-Assad always ensured Syria's adversaries remained divided, today Damascus has unified the bitterest of old foes."

The old foes were united in more than just anger.

"March 14 was the day the Sunnis joined the Christians in the Lebanese project," political analyst Eli Khoury told me. "It was in the making before, but it finally came into being then, on that day."

The Druze had undergone serious changes, as well.

Hafez al-Assad killed their leader Kamal Jumblatt in 1977, and his son Walid was forced, when he inherited the position as the *zaim* of the Druze, to accommodate himself and his people to Syrian power. The Druze are a small minority population in Lebanon, as they are in Syria and in Israel, and they align themselves with the strong horse out of necessity. The senior Jumblatt explained it this way: "Ever alert, [Druze] gauge their surroundings and choose their words carefully, assessing what must be said and what can be said."

As with any other people, though, there are limits to how much they can take. "A man just wakes up one day and realizes he's had enough," Walid Jumblatt said to author and Middle East analyst Lee Smith.[27] "So his life changes."

Not everything changed at once, though. He was as staunchly anti-American as his father even after their Progressive Socialist Party no longer accepted arms and largesse from the Soviets. It took some time before he saw potential allies in the Americans, but he eventually did.

"It's strange for me to say it," he said shortly after the uprising in Lebanon started,[28] "but this process of change has started because of the American invasion of Iraq. I was cynical about Iraq. But when I saw the Iraqi people voting three weeks ago, eight million of them, it was the start of a new Arab world. The Syrian people, the Egyptian people, all say that something is changing. The Berlin Wall has fallen. We can see it."

He may have overstated things there, but that's how far he and his people had journeyed from the time of their alliance with Moscow.

"This is the second republic," Lebanese scholar Tony Badran wrote,[29] "the national accord of 1943 being the first. Ironically, in both instances the agreement entailed an understanding that Lebanon is not to be run like the neighboring authoritarian Arab order. That it had its own unique socio-political culture. At the time, that was mainly the Christian wish. This time around . . . it comes from the mouths of Sunnis, Druze, and not just the traditional foes of Syria." "The Syrians knew the importance of the Sunnis when they planned the hit," he added later.[30] "Unfortunately, they didn't plan on this reaction. They certainly didn't plan on the 'Lebanonization' of the Sunnis."

Some of the young people in the tent city downtown insisted their struggle was larger than themselves and their own country, that Lebanon with its sectarian divisions was more than just a microcosm of the region they lived in. It was also the place where Catholics named Pierre lived alongside Sunnis and Shias named Omar and Ali. If they could work out a formula to resolve their differences peacefully, they might save the world.

"You want to know what we're doing?" Nabil Abou-Charaf said to me seriously. "I'll tell you what we're doing. We are resolving the clash of civilizations."

Even those with more moderate ambitions thought they could set the region on fire.

"The Arab tourists might have fled Beirut after the assassination of Rafik Hariri," journalist and activist Samir Kassir wrote in the pages of *An-Nahar*,[31] "but they will return with the Beirut Spring. And this time they will not only shop and have fun, they will come seeking the red and white that today crowns the capital of the Arabs. Our Syrian brothers, from laymen to cultured businessmen, might have been startled for a second by what they mistook as hostility toward them. But it is the product of a tyranny that chokes them just as much as it does the Lebanese. They will be happy to return because they know more than others that when the Arab Spring blossoms in Beirut, the roses will bloom in Damascus."

The Middle East has an infinite capacity to smash people like him, but that's what he and his comrades were saying during the Beirut Spring in 2005.

Roses never did bloom in Damascus. Shortly after he wrote those words, Samir Kassir's car exploded around him when he turned the ignition key on his way to work in the morning. He was only the first since Hariri in a long line of journalists and officials who would be blown by the Syrian regime into martyrdom.

⁓

Shortly after the overthrow of Saddam Hussein, many hoped Iraq might become a beacon of sorts in the Middle East, a democratic country that worked and inspired Arab liberals elsewhere to press for change in their own countries. Perhaps that did happen, to an extent. Walid Jumblatt credited Iraq's first election as having an effect of that sort on him. And it's certainly possible that Bashar al-Assad would have left Lebanon a little less hastily if he didn't fear that after Saddam, he might be "next."

Most people in the Middle East, however—indeed, most people everywhere in the world—shuddered at Iraq and thought of the place as a charnel house. Baghdad looked a lot like Beirut did in the eighties. Insurgents waged a "resistance" campaign against American soldiers and local security forces, and they massacred civilians in markets with car bombs. Sunni and Shia militias brutally "cleansed" neighborhoods of the other. Al Qaeda operatives kidnapped Western civilians and executed them in front of video cameras.

Lebanon, though, as Samir Kassir said in an interview with Michael Young,[32] showed "that political liberalism can be conjugated in Arabic." Its people resisted Syrian soldiers not with improvised explosive devices but with peaceful demonstrations. What they called the Intifadat-al-Istiqlal—or Independence Uprising in English—and what Westerners dubbed the Cedar Revolution, was not at all like the Intifada in Palestine with its suicide bombers and blood-curdling threats to destroy the enemy country. The Lebanese might even work out a permanent formula for coexistence of religions and cultures. They'd be the people to do it if anyone could. Lebanon, after all, is where the East meets the West, and it always has been.

The Levant, the Middle Eastern Mediterranean, has been more advanced and cosmopolitan than the interior since the time of antiquity. It has been exposed to the West and its liberal ideas for millennia.

The ancient Phoenicians weren't exactly Westerners. The term as we use it today didn't exist then, but they were, due to proximity, influenced in many ways by the Greeks and were partially Hellenized by Alexander the Great. What is now Lebanon was part of the Roman Empire for centuries. For almost 200 years it was ruled by Crusaders from Europe, and by France from the end of World War I until independence.

Its education system, at least for the middle and upper classes, was excellent. Much of it was built by missionaries in the nineteenth century who largely failed to convert Muslims to Christianity but managed to leave behind serious English- and French-language schools modeled on those in the West. The American University of Beirut, founded in 1866 by Daniel Bliss and the American Board of Commissioners for Foreign Missions, was still considered the Harvard of the Middle East. And the American University was just one in a large network of primary and secondary institutions.

One of East Beirut's main thoroughfares was named after Charles Malik, Lebanon's ambassador to the United States in the late 1940s, who cowrote the Universal Declaration of Human Rights in 1948 with Eleanor Roosevelt.

"Everything will be different after this," University of Oklahoma Professor Joshua Landis wrote on his blog[33] from Damascus after Hariri was killed. "There is genuine sadness for Lebanon here and even a bit of envy. Watching the demonstrations and real national fervor reminds Syrians how little they have of their own."

Al-Assad could not take the pressure, and he ordered his men to withdraw. They left rapidly, in an orderly fashion, and were out of the country entirely by April 26, 2005. Not only did the soldiers leave, but the intelligence agents left, too—at least those who weren't undercover. The government then called for an election on time in May.

Hariri's young son Saad took his father's place as the head of the Future Movement, and his parliamentary list easily swept Beirut. Fouad Siniora, a more experienced politician from the same party, took Najib Mikati's place as prime minister.

I returned home a few days after the Syrians finished withdrawing and immediately made plans to return as soon as I could, to rent an apartment and live there a while. Beirut at that time looked and felt like the beginning of a new Middle East. There seemed no better place to cover the region as a foreign correspondent in 2005.

Beirut's Spring, though, didn't last.

The Cedar Revolution, the Independence Intifada, was only partially successful at best. It made little difference in the end that the Lebanese got a government that more or less reflected the will of its people. All I should have had to do was look at Iraq to see that that wasn't enough.

Iraq had elected a representative government just a few months earlier yet was in the process of violently deconstructing itself. Active remnants of Saddam Hussein's government melted away and fomented insurgency. Bashar al-Assad continued helping terrorists from all over the Middle East transit into Iraq from over his land border. Iran sponsored Shia terrorists and guerrillas who set up their own de facto statelets in the south and in parts of the capital.

Syrian soldiers were gone from Lebanon, sure, and the country's civil society had made an impressive comeback after decades of dormancy, but the occupation regime left pieces of itself behind. That's what always happened in Lebanon when foreign forces were ejected. "Each conqueror," Sandra Mackey wrote in *Lebanon: A House Divided*,[34] "has deposited something of itself with a segment of the population, creating a people fragmented into groups possessing no common identity with the whole."

Many, if not most, of the highest-ranking officers in the army had been appointed by Damascus, and they still had their jobs. Syrian intelligence offices closed, but undercover *mukhabarat* agents hadn't gone anywhere. Lebanese President Emile Lahoud, al-Assad's most loyal yes-man in the country, still had three years left in his extended term. Amal movement leader Nabih Berri had long since reconciled with Hezbollah to boost the power of the Shia community, so he was a shoo-in as speaker of parliament, no matter that the anti-Syrians won the election in May.

By far the worst legacy of the Syrian occupation, though, was Hezbollah. Syrian soldiers had withdrawn to their side of the border, but the militia al-Assad helped supply with Iranian weapons hadn't gone anywhere. Ousting the Baathists, then, produced the same result in Lebanon that it did in Iraq—a power vacuum that would soon be filled by the Islamic Republic regime in Iran.

state within a state

Pity the nation divided into
fragments, each fragment
deeming itself a nation.
—KAHLIL GIBRAN

I n 1979 a coalition of Iranian liberals, leftists, and Islamists
overthrew the tyrannical Mohammad Reza Shah Pahlavi—
and a new regime more dangerous and brutal than the last took its
place.

An alliance of liberals, leftists, and Islamists made sense at first.
The Shah oppressed them all more or less equally. But the Iranian
Revolution, like so many others before it, devoured its children.
Ayatollah Ruhollah Khomeini and his Islamists emerged the strong
horse in the post-revolutionary struggle for power, and they liqui-
dated the liberals and leftists. Drunk on power and with the wind at
its back, his new Islamic Republic regime exploded outward from
the ancient Persian heartland into the Arab world with a campaign
of imperialism and terrorism.

During the crucible of Lebanon's civil war in 1982, when Christian, Sunni, Shia, Palestinian, and Druze militias were slugging it

out with each other and with the Israelis, Iranian Revolutionary Guard Corps commanders secretly organized disaffected members of Lebanon's Shia community into militant cells of their own. They proved that their revolution wasn't only exportable to Shia Muslims who were not Persian; they proved it was durable and resilient.

And it was devastating.

On October 23, 1983, a suicide bomber rammed a Mercedes-Benz truck packed with 12,000 pounds of explosives into the U.S. Marine barracks near Lebanon's international airport, killing 241 American service members. It was the deadliest single attack against Americans since World War II and the deadliest against the Marine Corps since the Battle of Iwo Jima.

Just two minutes later, France suffered the worst single attack against its forces since the end of the Algerian War. In this attack, fifty-eight paratroopers were killed by another suicide truck bomber near the beach in West Beirut's Ramlet el Baida.

The French and Americans were neither invaders nor occupiers of Lebanon. They were guests of the government on a peacekeeping mission. Both countries soon withdrew their armed forces, and Lebanon continued to burn for seven more years.

A mysterious group calling itself the Islamic Jihad Organization claimed credit for the attacks. You may never have heard of a terrorist group in Lebanon calling itself Islamic Jihad. That's because it never really existed. Islamic Jihad was simply the nom de guerre of Hezbollah at the time.

Hezbollah's name in Arabic—*Hizb Allah*—means "Party of God." It also described itself on its logo and flag as the Islamic Revolution in Lebanon.

When the Iranian regime thrust itself into the Arab world, Hezbollah was the tip of its spear, and its leaders weren't shy about saying so. "We are," according to Hezbollah's 1985 Open Letter,[1] "the Party of God (Hizb Allah) the vanguard of which was made victorious by God in Iran. . . . We obey the orders of one leader, wise and just, that of our tutor and *faqih* (jurist) who fulfills all the necessary conditions: Ruhollah Musawi Khomeini. God save him!" "Death to Israel" and "Death to America" became its rallying cries, just as they were for the Islamic Republic in Iran.

Hezbollah's rhetoric was as brazen as its actions. "We combat abomination and we shall tear out its very roots," the manifesto said, meaning "America, its Atlantic Pact allies, and the Zionist entity." The struggle against Israel, Hezbollah said, "will end only when this entity is obliterated."

Syria conquered and occupied most of Lebanon at the end of the civil war, but an Israeli occupation force stayed behind in a narrow strip of land in the south to prevent Hezbollah attacks from the Lebanese side of the border. But in 2000, after more than a decade of grinding counterinsurgency, the worn-out Israelis withdrew their armed forces. Hezbollah had proved itself to be the most powerful guerrilla army in the whole Middle East and the only Arab army of any kind that could plausibly claim victory against Israel.

By the time I moved to Beirut in 2005, Hezbollah was better armed, better trained, and better equipped than even the Lebanese army. With its own de facto state within a state in the suburbs south of Beirut and in South Lebanon along the border with Israel, it was the first and by far the most successful outpost of Khomeinist rule outside Iran.

Its very existence as a militia was illegal under the Taif Agreement[2] that ended the civil war in 1989, and it violated United Nations Security Council Resolution 1559, passed in 2004, that mandated the disarmament of every militia in Lebanon. Hezbollah tried to skirt this by declaring itself no longer a militia but a "resistance" army struggling against Israel.

But the Party of God faced enormous pressure to surrender its weapons, as Lebanon's other militias had already done, and renounce its loyalty to a foreign power. Hezbollah Secretary General Hassan Nasrallah refused to even discuss it. He threatened[3] to "cut off any hand that reaches out to our weapons" and to "fight them like the martyrs of Karbala."

It's obvious in hindsight that when I decided to relocate to Beirut, I was moving to a country in a state of prewar. It was not, however, obvious at the time. I was a bit more seduced than I should have been by the revolution that had recently forced the withdrawal of the Syrians, but the Cedar Revolution in Lebanon had yet to contend with the Iranian Revolution in Lebanon.

I stayed in a cheap hotel on the east side of the city while looking for an apartment. While I drove around with my real estate agent in his expensive red sports car, he asked me something out of the blue that I didn't expect. "Do you think Lebanon will be okay?" His voice cracked when he said "okay."

He seemed confident, even arrogant, most of the time, but all of a sudden he sounded choked up and frightened. It was the first time since I met him that he spoke to me as though I knew more than he did about Lebanon. I didn't, of course. And he knew that. He just wanted me to make him feel better.

I moved to Lebanon partly *because* I thought his country would be okay, that it might even help the Middle East in general turn out okay in the long run. And I wanted to cover that story from the Arab world's freest country.

"I think Lebanon will be okay," I said.

He seemed to relax slightly, as though I were some sort of sage who had a better feel for the future than he did. But I was wrong.

⌒

Lebanese people are educated, talented, and industrious, and they take naturally to freewheeling capitalism. Unlike most Arab countries, Lebanon never went through a suffocating socialist phase where the state owned and controlled most major industries. Beirut's central government was so weak in 2005 it couldn't even police, let alone stifle, its people or its economy.

There were almost as many Lebanese people in America as there were in Lebanon then. There were even more in Brazil than there were in America. Like Jews and Armenians, they thrived in the Diaspora. Their homeland wasn't as wealthy as it should have been at the time because it had been strangled and looted by Syria's Soviet-style regime for so long.

Though less glamorous in the daytime, the port city of Jounieh and the suburbs north of Beirut looked a bit like Hong Kong at night. If Lebanon's international airport were north of the capital, arriving visitors might have thought they had just landed in a country as modern and prosperous as Israel.

Instead, the airport is situated south of Beirut, where land is cheap and the snow-capped mountains rise less abruptly from the shoreline. Among the first things visitors saw in 2005, then, were madness and squalor. For the airport was built right next to territory Hezbollah controlled, and everyone had to drive through it to reach the city center.

Even so, the airport road was controlled by the Lebanese government. If you squinted hard enough or paid little attention to the ramshackle housing and billboards portraying Hezbollah's grinning Secretary General Hassan Nasrallah, you wouldn't necessarily realize what kind of place you were in. There were no checkpoints or militiamen on the sides of the road waving rifles. The hard Hezbollah-controlled core was a bit to the east and mostly out of sight.

Any travelers who ventured off the airport road, however, would quickly find themselves in the middle of the capital of a de facto Iranian satellite state inside Lebanon.

Charles Chuman took me down there. He is a Lebanese American from Chicago who had lived in Beirut for years, and he knew the country better than almost anyone I ever met.

"Hezbollah is only ten minutes from here," he said one night while we walked along pleasant French-looking streets on the Christian side of the city.

I stopped in my tracks. Beirut was an attractive glittering bubble, and I had almost forgotten the stronghold of the Party of God was so close. It was hard to believe a place resembling Gaza was just ten minutes away from the Arab world's answer to the French Riviera.

But it was true, and Charles said he would show it to me.

The Hezbollah-controlled suburb of Haret Hreik south of Beirut was known as the *dahiyeh*, which simply means "suburb." There were many suburbs north, east, and south of the city, but everyone in Lebanon knew exactly which was meant by "the suburb"—it was the notorious one, the capital of Hezbollah's state within a state, where the Party of God's command and control center was located.

The U.S. State Department was right to warn American citizens to stay out of there. I had little choice, though, but to ignore the warning and go.

Charles didn't own a car, but his friend Hassane did. And Hassane said he would be happy to drive me and Charles there if his girlfriend, Rama, could come with us.

I rode in the front seat. Rama and Charles sat in the back. We drove along the civil war-era Green Line dividing predominantly Sunni West Beirut from the mostly Christian east.

Hassane and Rama were Sunnis. Like most in their West Beirut community, they attended the anti-Syrian rally on March 14.

She wore a *hijab*, an Islamic headscarf, over her hair, and she wore it because she felt like it. Feminists who said she shouldn't frustrated her as much as radical Islamists in Iran and Saudi Arabia who would use their power to force her.

As we drove farther south along the Green Line, Beirut looked less and less prosperous. Gone were the skyscraping steel and glass hotels, the gourmet restaurants where the rich and would-be rich hoped to be seen, and the fashionable clothing stores like those in Milan and Paris. Unassuming churches proliferated on the east side of the road, and the minarets of small community mosques gave the skyline some punch on the west side. Starbucks chains yielded to simpler cafés with plastic chairs. Very little architecture was recognizably French any longer. South Beirut was conservative and a bit hard-bitten, but it was still Beirut.

Then we crossed an invisible line into the *dahiyeh*, and everything changed.

Hezbollah propaganda was everywhere.

Portraits of suicide bombers and "martyrs" killed in battle with Israel hung from the sides of lampposts and electrical poles. A fresh one appeared every couple of feet. The entire urban area was blanketed with the ghostly faces of dead men.

Hassane squinted through the windshield, stuck out his jaw, and gripped the steering wheel hard. "This isn't my country," he said.

He had a point.

Lebanese army soldiers and police officers were forbidden from setting foot in the area, as though an invisible international boundary ringed the periphery. Beirut's government wasn't allowed to operate schools in the *dahiyeh*, build medical facilities there, or even collect garbage. Hezbollah ruled the roost, and that was final. If the Lebanese army and police tried to retake the area, it would mean war.

I saw hardly any evidence that we were still even in Lebanon. The national flag depicting one of the ancient cedars of Lebanon was nowhere to be seen. The green and yellow Hezbollah flag, with its upraised AK-47 assault rifle logo, had taken its place.

One poster after another portrayed Iran's Ayatollah Khomeini as though he were the ruler of Lebanon. Portraits of Syria's tyrant Bashar al-Assad also made several appearances. The *dahiyeh* looked, alternately, like a slum of Tehran or Damascus.

Laundry lines slashed across the facades of nondescript concrete apartment blocks that looked like smaller versions of Stalinist towers in communist countries. Large balcony curtains billowed in the wind like dirty ship sails. The tangled mess of electrical wires looked like cobwebs of cable between all the buildings. A few smaller structures heaved over the sidewalks toward the streets as though their fronts were slowly sinking.

Not a single international chain store or restaurant was in sight. No one would have invested foreign capital in the *dahiyeh* even if Hezbollah would have allowed it—and Hezbollah didn't. Economic globalization reeked of a sinister plot in Hezbollah circles. Those who earned substantial amounts of money independent of the Party of God would no longer need Hezbollah's social services; could form their own civil society organizations if they wanted; and might, at least in the long run, demand more freedom to operate without stifling controls as Lebanese could elsewhere.

I brought a small tourist camera with me. It easily fit in my pocket, and I could quickly take pictures through the windshield without drawing attention as long as the car wasn't stopped.

"*Don't* let them see your camera," Charles said, though his warning was hardly necessary. As we rounded a corner onto a main artery through the area, a stocky militiaman took an AK-47 from the trunk of a car and slung it over his shoulder. He didn't look like the kind of man who would be pleased to appear in my pictures.

Windows in several buildings were sandbagged. Surveillance watchtowers were erected in front of restaurants and stores.

"They've definitely ramped up the security since the last time I was down here," Charles said. "They're *extremely* paranoid now that the country has turned against Syria."

Much of the construction was illegal and had been built when waves of poor Shias fled north from the Israeli border region to the outskirts of Beirut during the war. Known at that time as the "belt of misery" by Lebanese and as Hooterville[4] by U.S. peacekeeping Marines, the area was still one of the poorest and most ramshackle urban places in the country even fifteen years later.

Most of Lebanon's Shias had always been locked out of the bustling economy and were still locked out in 2005. They had been, for most of their history, simple people who worked the land while Christians and Sunnis in the coastal cities supplied Lebanon with her merchants, traders, and professionals. For Westerners, Beirut was the economic gate to the East, and vice versa. The Shias in the south and in Bekaa Valley were neither needed nor relevant, from Beirut's point of view. Nor were the Shias, unfamiliar with the city and its ways, really welcome.

Lebanese American historian Fouad Ajami was born and raised a Shia Muslim in the south before his family moved to Beirut when he was a child. Some of his aunts and uncles of an earlier generation tried to build a life for themselves in the city and failed. "Beirut was too harsh and alien for them," he wrote[5] in *Beirut: City of Regrets*. "It was a Sunni Muslim world, and the generation that preceded mine was not prepared for the passage."

His own generation managed in the late 1940s, but it wasn't easy. "We were strangers to Beirut's polish, to her missionary schools, to her Levantine manners," he continued. "My generation among the Muslims . . . did not share the Christians' romance with France. A cultural split divided the city: in Christian East Beirut, the admired, foreign culture remained that of France, the prestigious schools taught in French. In Muslim West Beirut, among Muslim Sunnis and Shia alike and among the Palestinians, the dominant foreign language of instruction was English, and the dominant foreign culture that of America."

In 2005, the dominant foreign culture just south of Beirut was Iranian. It was a warped and distorted version of Iranian culture, however. Persia's cosmopolitanism and sophistication, its penchant for fine wine and the arts, were utterly absent. Only Iranian politics and religion were exported to the *dahiyeh*—and then only Iranian politics and religion as interpreted and mandated by Iran's current Supreme Guide Ayatollah Ali Khamenei and its bombastic President Mahmoud Ahmadinejad.

Roughly a third of Lebanon's population, but only about a seventh[6] of the Muslim population worldwide, is Shia. The community has long been haunted by an inferiority and persecution complex, and they haven't been entirely imagining things. Before Saddam Hussein was overthrown, Iraq's Sunni minority brutally suppressed the Shia majority. The Shias had been ill-treated and ill-served in Lebanon for as long as they could remember, and in Iran they were as oppressed by the Shah as everyone else, even though they made up the overwhelming majority there. And they were thoroughly repressed in many of the Arab states in the Gulf.

"At its core," Ajami wrote[7] in *The Vanished Imam*, "Shia history was a tale of dispossession." The great rift in Islamic civilization between Sunnis and Shias began just a few years after the establishment of the religion itself by the Prophet Muhammad in the seventh century. The Shias believe the Prophet chose his cousin Ali as his successor, but Ali was murdered and the Prophet's family was shunted aside by usurpers of power. Ali's partisans—the Shia—have been marginalized and oppressed almost everywhere ever since by the illegitimate, the despotic, and the corrupt.

The Shia tradition is one of quietism, according to which clerics should remain withdrawn from politics while awaiting the return of the Mahdi, or the hidden Twelfth Imam, with Jesus Christ at his side to bring peace and justice to the world. Shia theology says the Mahdi will return when the world has fallen into chaos and war, and in the meantime, the pious must wait and leave the governing of the world to the worldly.

Khomeini changed that. He believed deliberate action by the righteous might actually hasten the Mahdi's return if chaos and war were ignited by men. In the meantime, according to his innovative Velayat-e Faqih ideology—rule by Islamic jurists—the people of Iran, the Muslim world generally, and eventually the human race totally, must submit to the authority of theocratic clerical leadership. Many, if not most, Iranians eventually came to see Velayat-e Faqih as a Persian variant of fascism, but the Khomeinists were fully in charge of the state by that time.

Khomeini's revolution emboldened the ideological hard-liners among the Shias in Iran. And he emboldened some of Lebanon's Shias by giving them voices, guns, ideas, and—for the first time ever—power.

Many Lebanese Shias found Khomeini's message seductive, weary as they were from real and imagined abuses from Lebanese Sunnis and Christians, and from Israelis. His ideology, though, was not one of liberation—at least not as Westerners understand it. Individual rights didn't exist in Khomeini's world, only the rights of the community of believers against its enemies. Even many in that community suffered persecution. Inside Iran itself, clerics were more likely to be imprisoned by the Islamic Republic regime for not toeing the Khomeinist line than any other group in the country.

I saw a number of portraits in Hezbollah's *dahiyeh* of the deceased cleric Musa Sadr, a far more reasonable figure in Lebanese history and politics. He was born in Iran, but he spent many of the latter years of his life in Lebanon agitating for greater economic and political rights for disadvantaged Shias. In 1974, a short year before the outbreak of war, he founded the Movement of the Disinherited, which later established the Amal militia.

Sadr himself vanished forever when he traveled to Libya in 1978 to meet with that country's bizarre Stalinist tyrant Muammar al-Gaddafi. Libyan officials insisted Sadr disappeared in Italy, but travel records indicate that he never left Libya.

During the civil war, Amal's militia fought pitched battles with Palestinians in the refugee camps and later with Hezbollah for control of parts of Beirut. By 2005, though, Amal had scrapped its vaguely leftist ideology and devolved into a patronage system and political machine that residents of Chicago might recognize. It had also become Hezbollah's staunch ally despite efforts by Druze chief Walid Jumblatt and Sunni boss Saad Hariri to flip its leader and Speaker of Parliament Nabih Berri to their side.

The Shias were a formidable force in Lebanon now that the secular and religious halves of the community were united. Hezbollah led the coalition, of course, as it was the stronger half. Amal, though, was more than willing to accept Hezbollah's leadership for sectarian as well as political reasons. Never before did the Shias have so much might and power in Lebanon. The Christians, Sunnis, and Druze who formerly shunned them now feared them. Hezbollah, you might say, was the revenge of the Shia.

This didn't sit well with the rest of the country. "Think of it this way," one Lebanese person rather crudely explained it to me. "Imagine a bunch of poor Mexican immigrants all of a sudden becoming the most powerful armed force in America and ordering the White House around."

Posters of the slain Rafik Hariri, so ubiquitous elsewhere in the country, were entirely missing from Hezbollah's *dahiyeh*. Hariri was the *zaim*, or political patron, of the Sunnis. Hassan Nasrallah wouldn't stand for anyone in his captured community showing allegiance to the leadership of another. Nor would he give them the opportunity to even feel any loyalty to another. Hezbollah would have none of Hariri's postwar reconstruction projects in its territory, and the dreary urban blight of the *dahiyeh* was a predictable consequence.

Political crime in Lebanon was out of control, but crime of the usual sort was almost unheard of. Peter Grimsditch, managing editor of Beirut's English-language *Daily Star* newspaper, told me he thought Lebanon's system was best described as "civilized anarchy," that he hadn't been to any country in the world where he felt the power of the state bearing down on him less.

Hezbollah's stronghold was different. The Party of God ruled as a miniature one-party state. Dissenting voices were smashed. Competing political movements were absolutely verboten.

I asked a Lebanese man who used to live there what would happen if he walked into the street and shouted, "I hate Hezbollah!"

"I'd get my ass kicked," he said. "No one would do that."

With Iranian patronage, Hezbollah provided schooling and social services for people in need. The long-term effects were catastrophic. Shia children who graduated from Hezbollah schools grew up with a mindset radically different from those given a mainstream education by the state and by private English- and French-language schools. They grew up captive to Hezbollah economics, dependent on its social services for survival, while kept deliberately on the margins of Lebanon's moderately prosperous and increasingly global economy by their supposed savior.

Like Hamas in Gaza, Hezbollah wanted its people to be poor—not so poor that they lived in misery and might revolt, but poor enough that they couldn't break free of dependency. Khomeini's Velayat-e Faqih ideology, demanding total life guardianship by state-approved clerics, had been successfully exported.

"This place is creepy," I said to Charles, Hassane, and Rama, overwhelmed by the poverty and propaganda around me.

"It is," Rama said. "But don't get *too* creeped out by it. They won't wave a gun in your face or anything like that unless you do something stupid."

"This is the last place I intend to do something stupid," I said.

"Stop here," Charles said as we rounded a corner. Hassane pulled into a parking space.

"This guy," Charles said and pointed at a man selling sandwiches from a corner stand, "sells some of the best shawarma in Lebanon."

So we stepped out of the car and ordered some sandwiches. Most passers-by paid us little mind, but I picked up hostile and suspicious stares from a few young men and even a couple of women.

Some of the women surprised me. Most dressed conservatively like Rama, but a few refused to wear headscarves and opted instead for tight blouses, spray-on jeans, and knee-high boots. They looked like they belonged in Beirut's Christian Achrafieh district, not in territory ruled by an Islamist militia. The Iranian government didn't even let foreign non-Muslim women walk around Tehran dressed like that. Khomeini believed women's hair emitted dangerous sex rays that corrupted the virtue of men, and he required that every last strand be covered in public. In this way, at least, Hezbollah was more liberal than its Iranian master.

Hezbollah's captive Lebanese were freer than Iranians in other ways, too. They could drive or even walk out of Hezbollah's territory and hang out in Beirut whenever they felt like it. They weren't forced to leave the country if they wanted to drink in public or dress as they pleased, as Iranians were. Most couldn't afford the relatively high cost of a night out in the city's fashionable districts, and those who could were often made to feel unwelcome by some of the Christians and Sunnis, but some managed to enjoy the freedoms and charms of Beirut even so. Hezbollah may have wanted to stop them, but it couldn't.

Some Shias felt Beirut's proximity to the *dahiyeh* therefore was liberating. I found it disturbing and potentially oppressive. East and West Beirut were so unshackled from state power and control, they were practically libertarian, if not downright anarchist, as Peter Grimsditch had said, but Hezbollahland was a de facto sovereign police state. And when I returned to Beirut and realized how close I lived to Hezbollah, I could practically feel its breath on my neck.

No country can be ruled effectively by separate authorities— especially when one of those authorities is more or less democratic while the other pledges loyalty to a foreign dictatorship. Lebanon's post-Syrian schism was the beginning of a transition stage. Partition was neither possible nor desirable in such a small country where each sect was dispersed geographically. Eventually, the state would have to absorb Hezbollah, or Hezbollah would devour the state. And Hezbollah, in 2005, had far more dedicated fighters and firepower than the legal authorities.

The Sunni, Christian, and Druze parts of the country had mostly recovered their sovereignty and had reverted to Lebanon's democratic political norms. But Hezbollahland was still mobilized for internal and external war. Peace, democracy, and genuine national unity required not only elections but also the disarmament of the country's final well-armed militia. That wouldn't be possible unless the Lebanese could somehow wall themselves off from the region around them as the Israelis and Tunisians had done. And that wouldn't be possible while Hezbollah's base of support welcomed Iranian and Syrian power.

"They have *much* more power than the rest of us," a Christian bartender said to me late at night in a popular pub. He looked exhausted by a lifetime of severe political stress. "We can feel it."

CHAPTER TWO

hanging with hezbollah

Israel is our enemy. This is an aggressive, illegal, and illegitimate entity, which has no future in our land. Its destiny is manifested in our motto: "Death to Israel."
—HASSAN NASRALLAH

In 1984, Hezbollah kidnapped the CIA's Beirut station chief William Buckley and tortured him to death. His remains weren't returned to the United States until they were delivered in a plastic bag on the side of the airport road in 1991.[1]

Lebanon in the 1980s was ferociously dangerous for everyone, especially for Westerners. Civilians as well as officials were hunted. Hezbollah kidnapped dozens, including American University of Beirut President David Dodge and Associated Press reporter Terry Anderson, who was held for seven years.

"The hostage seizures were fully consistent with Hezbollah's declared goal of expunging America from Lebanon, its citizens as well as its diplomatic presence," historian Augustus Richard Norton wrote[2] in *Hezbollah: A Short History*. "Western hostages were held in Lebanon in despicable conditions, often alone and chained to radiators for months on end, denied even the slightest dignity."

Hezbollah's kidnapping spree made the country so dangerous for Westerners that the State Department prohibited the use of American passports for travel there until 1997.[3] Westerners outside Lebanon were also at risk.

In 1985, Hezbollah commander Imad Mughniyeh and two other gunmen hijacked TWA flight 847 from Athens to Rome and diverted it to Beirut's international airport. Seven passengers with Jewish-sounding names were taken off the plane and detained. Mughniyeh identified passenger Robert Stethem as a U.S. Navy diver on vacation, shot him in the head, and threw his body onto the tarmac. The remaining passengers—who were held now at gunpoint by nearly a dozen Hezbollah militiamen in a war zone—weren't released until two weeks later, presumably after Israel agreed to release 700 Lebanese Shias from prison.

Argentine authorities later charged Mughniyeh with wounding and killing hundreds in Buenos Aires with truck and car bombs at the Israeli Embassy and a Jewish cultural center.[4] The United States fingered him for destroying a Khobar Towers housing block in Saudi Arabia with a truck bomb, killing nineteen American military servicemen and wounding 372 others from various countries.

Hezbollah was still officially listed as a terrorist organization by the United States government in 2005, but it had been easing up on Westerners for a while. After the Israeli military withdrawal from South Lebanon in 2000, it was rightly perceived as much less immediately dangerous, if not for Israelis, then at least for Americans. Not for years had any Westerners been kidnapped or killed by Hezbollah in Lebanon or anywhere else. An official "no snatch" policy was firmly in place, and everyone in Hezbollah was forced to adhere to it. The party even opened a press office in the *dahiyeh* where reporters like me could meet its officials.

So I called Hussein Naboulsi in the media relations department to ask if I could set up an interview.

"All-oe?" he said when he picked up.

"Hello, sir," I said. "Is this Mr. Hussein Naboulsi?"

After an uncomfortable pause, he said, suspiciously, "Yes."

"Hello, sir," I said. "How are you doing?"

"Fine," he said.

"I am an American journalist," I said, "and I'd like to set up an appointment for an interview."

"I cannot talk to you," he said. "I do not have permission to talk to the press."

"I'm sorry," I said. "Someone gave me this number and told me you were the person I needed to talk to."

I waited for him to say something, but he didn't. So after another uncomfortable pause, I continued.

"Can you please direct me to the right person?" I said.

"*Who are you!*" he said, as if he suspected I was a CIA or Mossad agent. "*What do you want!*"

"I'd like to set up an appointment for an interview if that would be possible. I am interested in Hezbollah and Hezbollah's projects in South Lebanon and the suburbs south of Beirut."

"Who do you work for?" he said.

"I'm working on a story about Hezbollah for the *LA Weekly*," I said.

"What do you want?" he said.

This was the press office?

"I'd like to set up an appointment for an interview," I said.

"When do you expect to arrive in Lebanon?" he said.

"I'm in Beirut right now," I said.

Silence on the other end of the line.

"Can I make an appointment?" I said.

"I do not have permission to speak with you," he said. "I do not know who you are. Can you come down to my office?"

"Yes," I said. "Of course. I would love to."

"You have to come here *right now*," he said.

"I'm sorry, sir," I said. "I can't come down there right now. Would it be possible for me to see you tomorrow?" The next day was Friday, the Muslim day of prayer.

"Yes," he said. "Of course. Please call me tomorrow."

He sounded cartoonishly paranoid, and I wondered what on earth he would be like when I met him in person. I didn't look forward to calling him the next day, but I had to.

First, though, I casually posted a message on my website announcing that I would soon meet with someone from Hezbollah. Within a couple of hours, I received dozens of messages from concerned readers, most of whom I had never met, telling me I was a fool and about to get myself kidnapped or worse. Some warned me I'd be lucky to get out alive.

I wasn't worried. Hezbollah wasn't half as "moderate" as it liked to pretend, but journalists went down to the press office in the *dahiyeh* all the time.

I understood why Americans who weren't in Lebanon thought I was crazy to be there and even crazier to meet with Hezbollah. Beirut was violent and unstable, and from a distance it looked a little like Baghdad. Terrorism and car bombs had returned as Syrian intelligence agents waged a murder and intimidation campaign against critics of the al-Assad regime in Damascus.

Samir Kassir, the *An-Nahar* newspaper reporter and activist whom I had met earlier in the year, was killed by a bomb placed under the seat of his car. I saw his face on posters all over East and West Beirut. George Hawi, a former leader of the Lebanese Communist Party, was likewise killed by a bomb placed under the seat of his car.

The most recent act of violence at the time was the attempted hit against May Chidiac. She was a talk-show host on the Lebanese Broadcasting Corporation TV channel and, like Kassir and Hawi, was relentless in her criticism of Syria. A bomb was placed under the seat of her car, just as bombs had been placed under Kassir's and Hawi's. The explosion blew off one of her legs below the knee. Her clothing and hair caught on fire. Her left arm had to be amputated. But she survived.

Politics and journalism were extremely hazardous professions in Lebanon and had been for decades. Writers, broadcasters, and members of parliament had good reasons to fear Syria's instruments of repression, as did average citizens. Bombs continued to explode in the eastern half of the city and in other Christian areas outside Beirut, though they weren't mass-casualty terrorist attacks like those in Iraq at the time.

Most Christians believed they were being goaded into retaliating against one Muslim community or the other and sparking another civil war so the Syrians would be "invited" to return as peacekeepers. Not even the most ferociously bigoted Christians took the bait, though some may have been tempted.

Almost every Lebanese person I knew was more nervous than I was. They knew better than I did just how bad things could get in their country. Everyone over the age of twenty remembered vividly when their country was drowning in blood and fire, when the very name "Beirut" made people shudder all over the world as "Sarajevo" and "Baghdad" would later.

Once in a while, it was difficult to keep myself from thinking that one of the cars parked next to me in the street could explode at any moment and literally vaporize me. Thousands of people had been murdered by car bombs in Beirut over the years. The odds of that happening to anyone in particular weren't very high, but they were not zero.

Most foreign residents I knew in Beirut weren't terribly worried. Charles introduced me to a photojournalist named Dan who was particularly blasé about it. Dan had been to Iraq. Dan had been to Afghanistan. Dan had been to Darfur and insisted no one could comprehend how nightmarish the place was if they hadn't seen the killing fields for themselves. He had a hard time getting worked up over mere car bombs.

He and I liked each other and decided to work together on freelance assignments. I'd write the text and he'd take the pictures. We also decided to share an apartment. He wasn't getting along with his current roommate, and I couldn't afford the rent for a decent place on my meager income.

Before we moved in together, however, we had an appointment with Hezbollah's Hussein Naboulsi.

We hailed a taxi downtown. Our driver sighed and doubled the rate when I told him I wanted him to drop us off at Hezbollah's so-called Security Square in the *dahiyeh*.

"Fine," I said. I did not want to argue, and I understood perfectly well why he didn't want to go down there.

"The embassy sent you," he said after driving for a couple of minutes.

"Excuse me?" Dan said.

"The embassy sent you," the driver said again.

"Oh, for God's sake," I said. "We aren't spies."

"We're journalists," Dan said.

"I think you work for the embassy," the driver said yet again.

I had long ago lost track of how often I'd been accused of spying in the Middle East. It was actually against the law for American intelligence agents to use journalism as cover, but hardly anyone in the Middle East knew that, and hardly anyone would have believed me if I told them.

Our driver, though, had something else in mind.

"Can you get me a green card?" he said.

"We can't get you a green card," Dan said.

"We don't work for the embassy," I said.

"Maybe you can put in a word at the embassy," the driver said.

"It doesn't work like that," I said.

"I've never even *been* to the embassy," Dan said.

Our driver finally relented when he crossed the invisible boundary separating the southern edge of Beirut from the *dahiyeh*. It was obvious where Hezbollah's territory began. None of us were in the mood to talk anymore when the Hezbollah flags and posters of suicide bombers appeared.

Dan paid the fare when we reached our destination. Heads turned when we stepped out of the car in front of the building.

A man who looked like an unarmed security guard stood watch in front of a swing gate. Dan and I walked toward him.

"Salam Aleikum," I said. *Peace be upon you.* "We are here to see Hussein Naboulsi at the media relations department."

"Hussein Naboulsi?" he said.

"Yes," I said. "Hussein Naboulsi."

He pointed at my notebook and made a "give it to me" motion with his hands. I handed him my notebook and pen. He flipped to a blank page and wrote a sentence in large Arabic letters. Then he pointed toward a man up the street dressed in all black who sported

THE ROAD TO FATIMA GATE ⌒ 49

a Che Guevara-style beard and carried an assault rifle slung over his chest.

"You want us to hand this note to the guy with the gun?" Dan said.

The man nodded.

So Dan and I walked toward the Hezbollah militiaman.

"Let's hope it doesn't say 'Arrest these Americans,'" I said jokingly.

I knew, of course, that journalists met with Hussein Naboulsi on a regular basis. That's what Hezbollah's media relations department was for. He wasn't using his office as bait. Nevertheless, the *dahiyeh* had a way of making even levelheaded people like me and Dan nervous. Neither of us could forget that Hezbollah used to chain people like us to radiators.

"Salam Aleikum," I said to the Hezbollah gunman as I handed him the note written in Arabic.

He scrutinized it. Then he gently placed his large hand on my shoulder, turned me around, pointed to a building halfway down the street, and stuck his index finger into the air indicating a "one."

"You mean we should go up one flight of stairs in that building?" I said as I pantomimed what I thought were his instructions.

He nodded.

"Shukran jazeelan," I said. *Thank you very much.*

"Afwan," he said. *You're welcome.*

Dan and I crossed the street.

"I think he meant this door," he said and pointed at an entrance between two small shops.

"I guess," I said, though it was hard to be sure.

We walked up a flight of steps and passed a man who looked European on his way down. Few Westerners went to the *dahiyeh* unless they were journalists.

"This must be the place," I said.

There were two doors, though, at the top of the landing. Neither was marked.

"Which one is the press office?" I said, though of course Dan didn't know.

"Let's try this one," he said and knocked on the door on the left.

After a long pause, we heard feet shuffling up to the other side. An unshaven man in a bathrobe opened it and stared at us without saying anything. We seemed to be in the wrong place.

"Hello," I said. "We're looking for Hussein Naboulsi at the Hezbollah press office."

He still didn't say anything. He just pointed upstairs.

"Thank you," Dan said.

We ascended the stairs.

"Why can't anyone tell us where the office actually *is*?" I said.

"They seem to be keeping an eye on us," Dan said, "by having us check in with the neighborhood watchdogs."

I wasn't sure that was right. Middle Eastern people, in my experience, weren't very good at giving directions. It did seem, however, like the entire neighborhood was watching us carefully, as though we were in a surveillance state that used human eyes instead of cameras.

Once again, there were two doors at the top of the next set of stairs. Once again, neither door was marked with a sign. Once again, Dan knocked on the door on the left.

"Do you think this is the place?" I said.

"We're about to find out," Dan said.

A young woman opened the door and said "hello" in English. She wore a conservative coat that covered her arms and a headscarf over her hair.

"Hi," I said. "We're looking for Hussein Naboulsi."

"Yes," she said. "Please, come in."

Dan and I stepped inside. The press office looked and felt like a real professional press office. It was surprisingly modern. The dreary look of the place from the street and even the stairway effectively concealed what was inside.

The young woman asked us to sign in before leading us to a waiting room lined with soft chairs and couches. A large mirror took up most of the wall facing the couches—one-way glass, I supposed. Hanging on the opposite wall was a gigantic portrait of an angry-looking Ayatollah Khomeini.

I sat on a couch. Dan sat in a chair. I looked at the glass and neither of us said anything. A few minutes later, a handsome man came through the door and outstretched his hand.

"Good morning, gentlemen!" he said. "I am Hussein Naboulsi. It is a pleasure to meet you."

"Hussein!" I said as I shook his hand. "I'm Michael. It's great to meet you, finally."

He put me at ease at once. Utterly gone was his strange paranoid tone from our phone conversation.

"I'm Dan," Dan said as he shook Hussein's hand.

"Listen," Hussein said. "You are both welcome. Normally we would serve coffee, but as you know it's Ramadan." Practicing Muslims aren't supposed to eat or drink until after sunset during the month of Ramadan.

"Of course," I said. "That's fine."

He then showed us into his office and asked us to sit.

"Your English is excellent," I said. "Where did you learn it?"

"I used to live in New York," he said.

"Really?" I said. "Did you like it?"

He looked at me as though I had asked if he liked rotten cheese.

"You must have lived there in the eighties," I said. The city was famously dysfunctional and crime-ridden then.

"Yes," Hussein said. "It is better now, I know. I have heard about your Giuliani."

"What do you think about the media in the United States?" I said. Hezbollah routinely denounced the U.S. media as "Zionist," and I wanted to know what he thought of the average American journalist who stepped into his office. Did he see us as the enemy? And, if he did, would he say so?

"I don't like CNN as much as I used to," he said. "Just look at Larry King. We need someone more fresh."

Hussein was smooth.

"Have you caught an episode of *The Daily Show With Jon Stewart?*" I said.

He shook his head as if he had never heard of it.

"That's what the kids are watching these days," I said.

After a few more minutes of small talk, we got down to business.

"So," he said and clapped his hands loudly together. "What can I help you gentleman with?"

"We'd like to set up an interview with Hassan Nasrallah," Dan said.

Hussein leaned back in his chair and laughed so loud the receptionist down the hall surely heard him.

"I guess that means *no*," I said.

"Sayyed Nasrallah very rarely gives interviews," Hussein said.

"I guess most journalists don't even ask," I said.

"Everybody who comes in here asks for an interview with Hassan Nasrallah," he said.

Dan's question couldn't have been funny if it was so routine and predictable. Hussein laughed to make a point: Don't even *think* about pestering me for an interview with the boss.

"Okay," I said. "Can we get an interview with somebody else?"

"Of course," Hussein said. "I will arrange for you to speak with someone in our political bureau, somebody very high up. It will be a good interview. Don't worry about it."

"Terrific," Dan said.

"There's something else I'd like to ask you for, too," I said. "Can you give us a tour of the south?" I wanted to see what Hezbollah was up to along the border with Israel. We needed access to the south, and we needed their point of view.

"I'm sorry," Hussein said. "That won't be possible."

"Look," I said. "I'm going to write about what's going on down there. It will be best for all of us if you give me as much access as possible."

"I can't take you to the south," he said again.

"How about showing us around your summer camps, hospitals, or schools?" I said.

"All these things are closed," he said.

"Can you show us around this area?" Dan said, meaning the *dahiyeh*.

"We can't give you a guide or a tour," he said. "But you can walk around and take a look by yourself. Just don't take any pictures."

Dan winced. He couldn't do his job if he couldn't take pictures.

Hezbollah was supposed to be reaching out. Its South Lebanon Commander Sheikh Nabil Qaouk had recently said he wanted to build strong relations with American journalists and academics. So what was this business about Hezbollah being closed?

"What's the problem?" I said.

"I was given a security directive a few weeks ago," Hussein said. "I am sorry, but I have to obey it."

"If we go to the south by ourselves," I said, "can we talk to some of your people down there?"

"None of our people in the south are authorized to talk to the media," he said. I sighed. Writing about Hezbollah wouldn't be easy—or so I thought. "But I'll get you an interview with someone in our political bureau," he continued. "Just call me in a couple of days and I'll let you know when to come back."

"Okay," I said. "That would be great."

"And bring a translator with you," Hussein said.

Dan and I hailed a taxi outside and returned to Beirut. Our apartment wasn't yet ready, so I returned to my cheap hotel room, where I made a terrible mistake that would get me in serious trouble.

Before al Qaeda's attacks in New York and Washington, D.C., on September 11, 2001, Hezbollah had killed more Americans than any other terrorist group in the world. Still, I chuckled slightly at those who worried I wouldn't survive a trip to the press office. I was partly amused and partly annoyed with what I felt was excessive and even paranoid concern for my welfare. Still, I decided to post a quick note on my website saying I was okay.

"I met with Hezbollah in person today," I wrote.

I felt like gently ribbing those who didn't understand Hezbollah's own rules, but what I wrote next was reckless and foolish. I, too, had a lot to learn about Hezbollah.

"The goons picked me up at my hotel," I wrote. "They stuffed me in the back of the car, blindfolded me, drove me around in circles, then took me (I think) into the mountains to a 'safe house' to talk to the sheik."

I was joking, of course, even though that was more or less what happened to a *60 Minutes* journalist played by Al Pacino during the opening scene of Michael Mann's film *The Insider* when he arranged a preliminary meeting with Hezbollah in the 1980s.

My website was informal. It was not the front page of the *New York Times*. Still, I had to indicate that I was kidding. So I wrote, "Actually, that's not what happened at all."

Hezbollah was not amused. I should have known Hezbollah would not be amused.

⁓

I called Hussein a few days later. He said Dan and I were scheduled for an interview with Mohammad Afif, a member of Hezbollah's political bureau, back at the office.

"I know a guy who can translate for us," Dan said. "He owns a woodcrafting shop in Achrafieh and his English is perfect."

So Dan called his man Abdullah and asked him to meet us for coffee ahead of our appointment. The café he chose wouldn't have been out of place in Seattle or Portland except that it served European-style espresso instead of American. Abdullah and his wife waited for us at a table in the back.

The four of us shook hands and sat down to talk.

"Do you always work in countries at war?" Abdullah's wife asked me while squinting and nervously smoking her cigarette. Lebanon wasn't at war at that time, but the car bombs had made the country just dangerous and unstable enough that I didn't immediately catch that she was exaggerating.

"This isn't a war," Abdullah said gently. "This is a crisis."

He didn't seem to feel perfectly comfortable about going to the *dahiyeh* to meet with Hezbollah, although he was willing.

"Have you been down there before?" I said.

"Why would I have been there before?" he said. "For some *sightseeing?*"

Dan and I laughed.

He didn't say much in the taxi on the way. And he looked nervously out the window as we rolled past Hezbollah's flags and posters of "martyrs."

When we were left alone in Hezbollah's waiting room, he looked profoundly uncomfortable. His eyes turned to saucers when he saw the gigantic poster of the grim-faced Khomeini on the wall.

"This is nuts," he said. "I can't believe I'm here."

Hussein Naboulsi made a brief appearance, introduced himself to Abdullah, and chaperoned us down the hall to Mohammad Afif's spacious office.

Afif wasn't friendly and didn't pretend to be. His handshake was perfunctory, he wouldn't smile, and he had no interest in small talk.

I turned on my voice recorder and placed it between myself and Abdullah. Dan snapped pictures as I rattled off questions.

Almost everything Afif said had been scripted and packaged for Western consumption. He did not say to us what Hezbollah said on its *Al-Manar* TV station, which was banned in the United States for broadcasting terrorist propaganda.[5] He didn't refer to Israel as "the Zionist Entity," nor to the United States as "the Great Satan." He condemned the car-bomb assassinations of his Lebanese political enemies, although it sounded like he only did so because he was supposed to. He said Hezbollah wasn't interested in destroying Israel, only in justice for Palestinian refugees.

I groaned silently to myself while wishing he would say something, anything, remotely interesting and worth publishing. Almost an hour passed before he did.

He droned on and on, lecturing me and Dan about Palestinian suffering. He didn't know it, but I actually did sympathize with Palestinian suffering and did not need to be lectured.

"You should visit the Sabra and Shatila refugee camps," he said. "You need to see how Palestinians in Lebanon live."

"I *have* seen those camps," I said, which seemed to surprise him. Charles Chuman had shown them to me, and they were unspeakably squalid. What I said next surprised him much more. "And it's obvious to me that Palestinians are treated much worse in Lebanon than they are by Israelis."

He sat bolt upright in his chair. That, apparently, was the last thing he thought I would say. But he quickly recovered.

"Yes," he said. "You are right. I am sorry about that." It was my turn to be surprised. At last he didn't have a scripted response, and his answer was honest.

More interesting than anything Afif actually said were his facial expressions. I wished Dan had brought a video camera instead of a still camera so he could capture them.

"You must know," I said, "that Americans are sick to death of the Arab-Israeli conflict. Is there *any* chance we'll see peace in this region any time soon?"

Afif didn't need Abdullah to translate the word "peace." He knew exactly what it meant in English just as almost every Westerner in the Middle East knew how to say it in Arabic. And when he heard me say "peace," when he was relaxed and not thinking about the fact that I was carefully watching his face, he twisted his flat expression into a grimace. The moment was fleeting, and he composed himself almost instantly, but it's almost impossible for even the most accomplished poker players and liars to control all involuntary facial muscles that reveal their inner thoughts and emotions.

What Afif actually said—that Hezbollah sincerely hoped for peace and a mutually agreeable settlement between Israelis and Arabs—was simply not credible. Hezbollah said nothing of the sort in its own media and said nothing of the sort in its schools and its summer camps, where it indoctrinated children into a culture of martyrdom, death, and resistance.

Aside from the oft-repeated *Death to Israel* and *Death to America* slogans, those suckled on Hezbollah schooling and weaned on Hezbollah media were bombarded with hysterical bigotry, conspiracy theories, and warmongering.

"The Jews invented the legend of the Nazi atrocities," Hassan Nasrallah said[6] in a declaration on April 9, 2000. "Anyone who reads [Islamic and other monotheistic holy] texts cannot think of co-existence with them, of peace with them, or about accepting their presence, not only in Palestine of 1948 but even in a small village in Palestine, because they are a cancer which is liable to spread again at any moment."

The only terrorism and "resistance" Afif sincerely opposed was that committed by al Qaeda's fanatical Sunnis. "We *hate* them," he said, showing real emotion for the first time. "They call us cockroaches and murder our people."

Abu Musab al-Zarqawi's head-chopping and mosque-burning al Qaeda in Iraq said it was God's will that Shia Muslims be slaughtered. And al Qaeda matched its words with deeds. Thousands of Iraqi Shias had been car bombed to death by Sunni psychotics in Baghdad and elsewhere. I was hardly less offended by this than Hezbollah was. And I found myself wishing Afif and his people were moderate, reasonable, and smart enough to realize al Qaeda and other like-minded groups posed a far bigger threat to him than Americans and Israelis did. Americans, I thought, might naturally sympathize with them, with the abuse they suffered in the modern era and through the ages, if it weren't for Hezbollah and Khomeini's Islamic Republic.

A huge number of Shias in Iraq at the time were willing to fight alongside Americans, not only against Sunni death squads and terrorists but against Iranian-backed Shia militias much like Hezbollah. That was a bridge too far for most Lebanese Shias, however, who remained firmly under the thumb of Hezbollah's Khomeinists.

"People in the United States find it hard to understand how people in Hamas and Hezbollah think," veteran Middle East reporter Jeffrey Goldberg told me when I met him in Washington. "It's alien. It's alien to us. The feverish racism and conspiracy mongering, the obscurantism, the apocalyptic thinking—we can't relate to that. Every so often, there's an eruption of that in a place like Waco, Texas, but we're not talking about ninety people in a compound. We're talking about whole societies that are captive to this kind of absurdity. So it's very important—and you know this better than almost anyone—to go over there yourself and tape it, get it down on paper, and say, 'This is what they actually say.'"

I never published most of what Afif said to me, though, because it was too slickly packaged and disingenuous. I wanted to let Westerners know what the Party of God really believed, but Afif was smart enough not to tell me.

Hezbollah got itself too much bad press in the West when its members and officials were allowed to say whatever they wanted, unfiltered, to journalists. Goldberg himself published a devastating two-part exposé in the *New Yorker* in 2002 before Hezbollah figured this out and clamped down.[7]

Firas Mansour, for example, a film editor at Hezbollah's *Al-Manar* station, showed Goldberg a work in progress and said he wanted to call it "We Will Kill All the Jews." When Goldberg said he thought a title like that might encourage the recruitment of suicide bombers, Mansour answered, "Exactly."

Hezbollah eventually learned to send journalists like me and Dan to men like Mohammad Afif who were well practiced in the art of saying little that was controversial or even of interest.

On our way out, Hussein asked how the interview went.

"Great!" I said to be polite. "It was great. Thank you for everything."

"Excellent," he said and placed his hand affectionately on my back. "I am glad I could help."

"Can I ask you to set up another interview for us?" I said, hoping to meet someone a little less disciplined.

"I'm sorry," he said. "Journalists can only have one."

"*Only one?*" I said, stunned. It would have been nice if he had told me that before the interview started. Hezbollah's message, though, had to be tightly controlled, especially since the withdrawal of the Syrian military left it exposed and with an uncertain future.

"I can invite you to an *iftar* this Thursday," he said, referring to a fast-breaking meal just after sunset during the month of Ramadan. "Hassan Nasrallah will be there."

Dan smiled. "Nasrallah will be there?" he said.

"Yes," Hussein said. "You are both welcome. And you can take pictures. I will add your names to the list."

Dan and I would soon stand within feet of the boss. The event was one of the last of Nasrallah's life before he blew up the Eastern Mediterranean and found himself driven underground like an urban-dwelling Osama bin Laden.

CHAPTER THREE

we know where you live

You'd like to believe that if reporters are being physically threatened into presenting a particular message—well, you'd hope that they would find a way to push back.

—OMRI CEREN

Hezbollah's *iftar* was segregated. Only women, journalists, and VIPs were allowed in. It was held outside the *dahiyeh* across the street from the Marriott Hotel in an area controlled, if that is the word, by the Lebanese government.

Dozens of people, nearly all of them women, walked up a flight of stairs toward a double set of doors. Most wore an enveloping black *abaya* or a headscarf over their hair.

Dan snapped a photo.

A group of men abruptly stood up from a bench and walked toward us.

"Salam Aleikum," I said. *Peace be upon you*.

"You took pictures without permission," one of them said, even though we were standing in a public place.

"Who are we supposed to ask?" Dan said.

"Come with me, please."

The man led us up the steps to the front of a wide and squat concrete building. There were two separate entrances, one for women, the other for journalists and VIPs. A gaggle of Hezbollah security agents manned the doors. Several sat behind a long table. This, apparently, was where we were supposed to check in.

Dan and I showed our passports and press credentials to the man who looked like he was in charge. He stuffed them in his briefcase. Then he confiscated Dan's camera.

"Hey," Dan said. "Give me my camera back."

"Just one minute, please," he said and set the camera aside.

I sat in a chair next to the table. Dan remained standing.

"Which hotel are you staying at?" the man asked me.

I didn't like the idea of telling Hezbollah where I was staying, but I answered his question. I didn't tell him I was moving into an apartment two days later.

They kept us waiting for almost half an hour for no discernable reason while thousands of people, including at least a dozen journalists, got in ahead of us.

"What is the problem?" Dan said.

"Just five more minutes, please," the head of security said. Five more minutes for what? Our names were supposed to be on the list, and we had credentials.

A security agent stepped behind me as I scribbled in my notebook. He craned his neck and tried to read over my shoulder. I frowned at him and abruptly turned so he could not read what I was writing.

Dan paced back and forth in front of the security table.

"What is the problem?" the head of security asked him.

"I have a job to do," Dan said.

"I have a job to do, too," he said.

"You're doing a great job so far!" Dan said.

Our first two meetings with Hezbollah had gone smoothly enough. Hussein was friendly. And he invited Dan and me to the *iftar*. Yet now, just a few days later, we were prevented by security from going inside Hezbollah's one open event.

I whipped out my cell phone to dial Hussein. Perhaps he could get us in faster. The instant the head of security saw my phone, he said, "Okay, you can go in now." He did not know who I was calling and seemed to fear I had a personal connection with someone in Hezbollah who outranked him.

Another agent led me and Dan away from the security gate, through a metal detector, and to a random space past the entrance far from everything else. He wanted us to stand in this exact spot. Not three feet over there, but *right here*.

"This is a parking garage," Dan said.

No cars were inside, but he was right. Parking spaces were clearly marked out on the parts of the ground not covered by tables, chairs, security booths, or movable walls.

Thousands of conservatively dressed women sat at rows of tables in front of us. No one bothered to tell us where to go or what to do. So Dan raised his camera to take some pictures.

Three security agents descended on him.

"No photos," one of them said.

"I was invited here so I could take photos," Dan said.

"No photos right now," the man repeated.

Though we weren't allowed to photograph the women at the tables, we at least wanted to get a better look than we could from where we were standing. So we started walking.

"No!" the agent said.

It seemed we would even have to ask to use the bathroom in this place as though we were children. Or prisoners.

After standing in no place in particular like dorks for several minutes, more security guys finally led me and Dan to a small walled-off area where we could sit and eat. This was the "press room." We could not see any of the thousands of women, nor could we see the pulpit where Nasrallah was going to speak. But at least we could sit. And of course we were segregated. This was Hezbollah.

"Sit over there," an agent said and pointed to a table away from where other, mostly male, journalists sat.

I don't like control freaks, and I was done taking orders.

"*No*," I said. "We are going to sit with other people."

Dan and I sat at a set table draped with a clean white cloth. Yellow chicken, fatty beef, brown and white rice, hummus, yogurt, and vinaigrette salads were spread out in front of us. There was plenty of bottled water to go around. The food didn't look great, but it looked okay. (And it was.) I smiled when it occurred to me that my meal was paid for by the Islamic Republic of Iran. It was about time they did something for citizens of the Great Satan.

The man sitting next to me introduced himself as a Lebanese journalist named John.

"Where are you from?" he asked me.

"United States," I said.

"Ooh," he said. "Don't tell *them* that."

"They already know," I said. You couldn't just walk into a Hezbollah event without being vetted.

Suddenly a muezzin screamed in Arabic over the loudspeakers. It was a thunderous call to prayer, and it was real screaming. I had heard the call to prayer hundreds of times in Beirut, but I never heard anything like this. It was electrifying and dramatic and, strangely enough, it gave me a thrilling shot of adrenaline.

Ominous military music threatened to blow out the speakers. Then the sound system switched, briefly, to music from *Star Wars*. It switched, briefly again, to the soundtrack from *The Terminator*. Someone, perhaps the same muezzin, screamed anti-Israel incitement over the music. You didn't have to be fluent in Arabic to figure out what that was about.

After dinner, a security agent summoned all the journalists to the women's side of the wall. A small press area was roped off a hundred feet in front of the pulpit.

Secretary General Nasrallah emerged to a standing ovation. Then he droned on for an hour, so softly I could barely hear a word over the post-dinner chitchat. Perhaps these women didn't show up to hear him at all. Maybe they just wanted free food.

Dan snapped photos. I sat and passively perused the "resistance" posters on the concrete pillars and walls. Scenes of explosions, gunmen, and mayhem were plastered up everywhere. Just over my head was a photo of a child clenching a bloody rock in his fingers.

Slowly, the audience began filing out, even though Nasrallah was still speaking. He wasn't so much a blowhard as a bore. Even his "base," at least the female half of it, didn't think he was worth sticking around for.

Soon the hall was almost half empty. Maybe Nasrallah realized he had to get to the point. Perhaps it was scripted this way. Either way, he suddenly started to scream.

Israel this!

Israel that!

Oh, snore. I didn't want to be rude, but I could no longer physically stop myself from rolling my eyes.

Then a belligerent fat man grabbed Dan.

"Come with me!" he said and led Dan and his camera away.

"What's going on?" I said.

"You can stay," he said to me. "We need to speak with him," he said, referring to Dan.

"Excuse me," I said. "I need to know what the problem is here."

"Did I take a picture of something I wasn't supposed to?" Dan said and swallowed hard.

Fat man fumed with rage and refused to answer. He led us to a table at a security checkpoint near the entrance to the garage. Four security agents followed and sat us down in chairs. Two stood behind us. Two sat opposite us at the table. Fat man tried to look at the pictures on Dan's digital camera but had trouble figuring out how.

This guy would have looked like a bully even in a photograph. He had pasty white skin, a trimmed beard, small black eyes, and short cropped hair. A permafrown rippled across his forehead. He wore a thin blue button-up shirt, the kind you would find at a clearance sale at a Walmart.

"What did I do?" Dan said.

"You will not speak unless you are spoken to," fat man said. "We will conduct our investigation. When we complete our investigation, we will tell you what you need to do."

Dan and I looked at each other. "What we need to *do*?" I said.

"What you need to do," fat man said. "Give me your passport," he said to Dan. Dan reluctantly handed it over. Fat man's older bespectacled sidekick copied Dan's passport and press ID information into a notebook by hand.

I fished my cell phone out of my pocket. Once again, it was time to call Hussein Naboulsi.

"Do *not* call anybody!" fat man said. It was no use anyway. We were still in the parking garage, and my cell phone couldn't pick up a signal.

Dan and I sat in silence while the security agents darkly discussed our situation, whatever it was, among themselves in Arabic. Fat man boiled as he failed to figure out how to operate Dan's camera.

I thought about grabbing Dan and his camera and making a run for the exit. Inside was Hezbollah's mini police state. Outside was free Lebanon. But unspoken threats of violence were barely concealed beneath their swaggering postures. I knew they had guns, even though I couldn't see them. Being detained by Lebanon's Party of God was not exactly like being detained by the Republican or Democratic parties in the United States.

"Who are you!" fat man bellowed as he squinted at Dan's passport.

"Daniel _____," Dan said.

"Where do you come from!" He barked his questions the way drill sergeants give orders.

"The United States," Dan said, clearly annoyed. Obviously, he was from the United States. Fat man was looking right at Dan's passport.

"What is your first name!"

Dan sighed. "Daniel," he said.

"What is your family name! Is your family name *Isaac*?"

At last we were getting down to brass tacks. Dan hadn't taken pictures of anything sensitive. Hezbollah had fingered him as a Jew because of his name.

They knew our names before they let us in. Perhaps that explains why they almost did not let us in.

"Isaac is my middle name," Dan said. "My last name is _____."

"What is your religion!" This was not an investigation. It was an inquisition.

"Christianity," Dan said, as though it should have been obvious.

"Are you *sure*!" fat man demanded.

"Yes, I'm sure," Dan said nervously. "I'm Protestant."

"Is this your first time in Lebanon!"

"Yes," Dan said. "This is my first time in Lebanon."

"Have you ever been here *before!*"

Like when? And how? As a soldier during the Israeli occupation?

I knew Israeli journalists sometimes used second passports to travel to Lebanon and even to meet with Hezbollah. It was an open secret. And if I knew it, Hezbollah knew it.

"This is my first time here," Dan said truthfully.

"Where do you live!"

"I live in Gemmayze," Dan said, referring to a gentrified bohemian neighborhood in East Beirut.

"Where *exactly* do you live?"

"In an apartment next to Gemmayze Cafe," Dan said. I wished he hadn't.

Two Western journalists, a man and a woman, stopped by the table where we were detained. Fat man's bespectacled sidekick took the woman's video camera and rewound the tape. He sat there and reviewed every minute of footage in real time on the view screen. Lord only knows what he was looking for. The paranoia in the room was physically palpable. He caught me staring and flashed me a menacing look.

An hour or so later, Hussein Naboulsi arrived, all handshakes and smiles as usual. I never thought I would feel relieved to see a Hezbollah official, but I sure was glad to see him.

"Hussein!" Dan said. "It is so good to see you. Will you please tell us what's going on?"

"I don't know yet," he said, "but I will take care of it."

Hussein happily spoke to fat man in Arabic. Fat man glowered and growled.

I took Hussein aside. "That man is rude, hostile, and belligerent," I said. Hussein seemed surprised that I would say this. "And he won't tell us why."

"He is the security chief," Hussein said. "He is in charge of everyone here."

"We didn't do anything," Dan said.

"I know," Hussein said. "I am sorry about this. I am on your side."

Hussein, the security chief, and a handful of agents took Dan's camera and went to a room in the back. They stayed there for twenty minutes. When they finally came out and handed Dan back his camera, almost fifty pictures had been deleted from the memory card. But they said we could go.

On our way out the door, the chief said to Hussein that Dan and I were no longer welcome at any of Hezbollah's events, as if we would ever want to experience something like this again.

I thought I had an idea what Lebanon would feel like if these guys ruled it. Lebanon in 2005 was a libertarian's paradise. Under Hezbollah, though, it would be a bigoted, authoritarian, gender-segregated, micromanaging bully state.

After Dan and I reached the safety and comfort of the free Lebanese streets, I turned to him. "Do you think Hussein is genuinely a nice person?" I said. "Or are they playing a good-cop, bad-cop game with us? Maybe he's just good at his job as the artificially friendly face of Hezbollah."

"I think he's genuinely a nice person," Dan said.

"So do I," I said and nodded.

We were wrong.

⁓

Two days later, I moved from my cheap hotel in East Beirut into a two-bedroom apartment with Dan in West Beirut. I took the bedroom just off the living room. He wanted the room down the hall.

Lisa, the previous tenant, was still packing her boxes as I came in.

"Welcome home," she said and handed me the keys. "Enjoy Beirut. I'm off to Dubai."

My cell phone rang. According to the caller ID, it was Hussein Naboulsi.

"Hussein," I said as I answered. "What's up?"

"You are a liar!" he screamed.

"What?" I said, shocked to hear Hezbollah's "friendly" media liaison enraged.

"I can't believe it. You lie about Hezbollah!"

"Slow down," I said. "What are you talking about?"

Lisa paid me no mind and placed some of her books into a box. She didn't know whom I was talking to.

"I saw your website," Hussein said. "You are writing against the Party!"

I had no idea what he was talking about.

"What did I say against Hezbollah?"

Lisa glanced over at me, slightly interested in my conversation now.

"You write things that are not true!" Hussein said.

"What on earth did I write that isn't true?" I hadn't written an article about Hezbollah yet and thought he might have me confused with somebody else.

"I am looking at your website right now." He quoted my own words back at me. "You wrote, 'The goons picked me up at my hotel. They stuffed me in the back of the car, blindfolded me, drove me around in circles, then took me (I think) into the mountains to a safe house to talk to the sheik.'"

"Oh, for God's sake," I said. "That was a joke." I had forgotten I even wrote it. "I was making fun of my American readers who thought you were going to kidnap me. Did you read the next sentence? In the very next sentence I wrote,[1] '*Actually, that's not what happened at all.*'"

"I read everything!" he said.

"Then you know it was a joke. I said it was a joke. How can you accuse me of lying?"

"You are propagandizing against us!"

"Stop yelling at me," I said.

Hussein was screaming so loudly at me through the phone now that Lisa could hear him. She could see that I was annoyed and concerned, and she stopped packing her books.

"You insulted Hezbollah!" he said. "Who do you think we are?" And then he said something I won't ever forget. "We know who you are, we read everything you write, and we know where you live."

I pressed the "End Call" button on my phone as fast as I could.

Lisa just looked at me. She still wasn't sure who I was talking to.

"That was Hezbollah," I said.

"Oh, shit," she said and took a step back.

"They said they know where I live."

Her eyes slowly widened as the gravity of what I just told her sank in. She turned and looked at the door. No one was banging on it from outside in the hallway or prying it open with a crowbar.

"Well," she said and gulped. "You've been living here now for, what, ten minutes? They can't possibly know."

She was right, of course. Hezbollah thought I was still back at the hotel. No one who worked there knew where to find me, so it would be a waste of time to ask about me at the front desk.

Still, I was nervous. Terrified, actually. And I had no idea what I should do.

I called Charles and Dan, told them what happened, and said I needed a drink.

We met at a bar a few minutes later.

Dan was concerned.

Charles was furious.

"You need to threaten him back," he said.

"*What?*" I said. "Threaten Hezbollah? Are you joking?"

"No," he said. "I'm not joking."

"I can't do that," I said.

"Sure, you can," he said. "You can't imagine how paranoid Hezbollah is. You're an American. Not only do they dare not touch you; they are afraid of you."

I didn't know about that, but Charles was right that Hezbollah was paranoid. I spoke to a half-dozen Lebanese sources and friends, and they all agreed that Hezbollah was all scream and no action when it came to American journalists. No one from the Party of God would actually stalk me at my apartment. It had been years since any Western journalist had been harmed in Lebanon. I knew that already. And if Nasrallah decided to change the rules all of a sudden, Hezbollah almost certainly would not start with me.

But I couldn't get Hussein's threat out of my head. Once, on my way home from dinner, a slightly creepy individual followed me for a couple of streets and all the way into my building. We got into the elevator together. I lived on the sixth floor, but I stepped out on the fourth and walked the rest of the way up so he wouldn't know which apartment was mine. I knew I was just being paranoid, but I couldn't help it. And I couldn't keep living like this.

I needed Hussein off my case. And I was sure he wasn't accustomed to being yelled at by Americans. So I steeled myself and called him back.

"All-oe?" he said.

"Hussein!" I said in a sharp tone of voice. Then I paused for effect. "This is Michael Totten."

He instantly started screaming again. "I can't *believe* what you write about Hezbollah!"

It was as though two days hadn't passed, as if he picked up our conversation exactly where it left off when I hung up on him. This time, though, I wasn't nervous. I was angry.

"Hussein!" I said. "*You* need to shut up and listen to me."

He kept screaming about how I insulted the Islamic Resistance in Lebanon.

"Hey!" I said as loud as I could. "Shut up for a second."

He finally stopped screaming at me, surprised, I think, by the tone in my voice.

"You will *never* call me and threaten me again," I said. "Do you understand?"

"What are you talking about?" he said.

"You know what I'm talking about," I said.

"I didn't *threaten* you!" he said.

"Yes, you did," I said. "I remember exactly what you said. You said, 'We know who you are, we read everything you write, and we know where you live.'"

"I did not say we know where you live," he said.

"Don't lie to me. I know what you said."

When Hezbollah says "We know where you live," it makes an impression that is hard to forget.

"I meant we know who you are." He sounded anything but convincing.

"You said you know where I live."

"I did not say that. I did not say that. If I did say that, I was just stressed out." He didn't know what he said. "Do you think we have agents out in the streets or something?"

"Of course you have people out in the streets!" I said. "Do you think I'm stupid?"

"If I said that, yes, it would have been a threat," he added. At least he didn't try to say "We know where you live" meant he wanted to send me a Christmas card.

"It won't always be like this between us," he said. That was a lie. Someone else in Hezbollah's press office later told Dan that he and I were both blacklisted for life. "Honest to God," he continued, "it is against our principles to threaten people."

That was bullshit. He had threatened me just two days before. Hassan Nasrallah had recently said,[2] "Death to America was, is and will stay our slogan." After the U.S. invasion of Iraq, he went even further.[3] "Death to America is not a slogan. Death to America is a policy, a strategy, and a vision." What the hell was that if it wasn't a threat?

It had been years since Hezbollah hunted Western civilians in Lebanon. That much was true.

But reining in the belligerence, the authoritarianism, the intolerance, and the menacing—that was just too much to ask. Those things were too much a part of what Hezbollah was. Even the media relations office, the office that was supposed to establish contacts with Westerners who might be sympathetic, the office that hired the happy-faced, seemingly friendly Hussein Naboulsi, couldn't keep its mask on for long. Just the slightest nudge with your pinkie was enough to break their delicate public-relations propaganda system in half.

Hezbollah had made some progress since the black years of the war. Every armed faction behaved badly in Lebanon then. The men of Hezbollah, like most people in Lebanon, had mellowed out and matured a bit during peacetime. That was something.

But it wasn't enough.

Their weapons remained an affront to Lebanon's sovereignty. Their territory looked and felt like a police state, more so than even some police states I'd visited. They still threatened and bullied

Americans. Their belligerence, in my experience, seemed instinctive and unrestrainable. And they remained on a war footing with Israel.

I wasn't yet certain, but I had a very bad feeling that Hezbollah just might blow up the country. And I was right.

CHAPTER FOUR

the shatter zone

We were accepted with
perfumed rice and flowers
by the Shia in the south.
—ISRAELI PRIME MINISTER
EHUD BARAK

B eneath the snow-capped peaks of Mount Hermon in South Lebanon, Hezbollah fighters dug in for war along the violent frontier with Israel. They weren't standing army soldiers with uniforms, bases, and barracks, but guerrillas who immersed themselves in the world of civilians. Using a vast network of smuggling roads, tunnels, and bunkers, they concealed themselves and their movements from the watchful eyes of their Zionist enemies.

The national cedar tree flag didn't fly there. This was Hezbollah territory. Only Islamic Resistance flags flew from the rooftops. Lebanon's government had no writ in the area, and it hadn't since the early 1970s.

South Lebanon's border area was what foreign correspondent and policy expert Robert D. Kaplan called a shatter zone,[1] a region where government authority is either diluted or nonexistent and where conflict is therefore all the more likely, if not inevitable.

"Like rifts in the Earth's crust that produce physical instability," he wrote in *Foreign Policy*, "these shatter zones threaten to implode, explode, or maintain a fragile equilibrium. And not surprisingly, they fall within that unstable inner core of Eurasia: the greater Middle East, the vast way station between the Mediterranean world and the Indian subcontinent that registers all the primary shifts in global power politics."

The core of the former Ottoman Empire convulsed with ethnic and sectarian warfare along a necklace of shatter zones from the Balkans to the Persian Gulf long after its demise: between Turks and Kurds in Anatolia, Arabs and Kurds in Northern Iraq, Sunnis and Shias in Mesopotamia, Slavic Christians and Muslims in Bosnia-Herzegovina, Serbs and Albanians in Kosovo, Turks and Greeks on the island of Cyprus, Arabs and Israelis in the Holy Land, and between just about every ethnic and sectarian faction imaginable in Lebanon.

Even though the central government in Beirut reclaimed much of its sovereignty after the Syrians left, South Lebanon remained strictly off-limits. The new "March 14" government—named after the date when a million people showed up to demonstrate against the Syrians—surely would have adhered to the de facto armistice between Lebanon and Israel if it could have, but it couldn't. So the Hezbollah-controlled border area remained a potentially hot front line in the Arab-Israeli conflict. And because Hezbollah was nothing if not a proxy militia for the Islamic Republic regime in Iran, South Lebanon became a de facto front line in the ancient Persian-Arab conflict and the even more potentially dangerous Persian-Israeli conflict.

"Of all the shatter zones in the greater Middle East," Kaplan wrote, "the Iranian core is unique: The instability Iran will cause will not come from its implosion, but from a strong, internally coherent Iranian nation that explodes outward from a natural geographic platform to shatter the region around it. . . . Through its uncompromising ideology and nimble intelligence services, Iran runs an unconventional, postmodern empire of substate entities in the greater Middle East: Hamas in Palestine, Hezbollah in Lebanon, and the Sadrist movement in southern Iraq. If the geographic logic of Iranian expansion sounds eerily similar to that of Russian expansion . . . it is."

Now that Saddam Hussein was dethroned in Iraq and on trial for war crimes and genocide, Iranian power projection was the Middle East's main event. Few people in Lebanon understood that at the time, however, for most eyes lingered on Syria.

I could drive or even walk into the suburbs south of Beirut without being stopped. I could not, however, drive or walk into the Hezbollah-occupied south without a permit from the Lebanese army. Soldiers set up checkpoints on every road approaching the Israeli border, and they treated those checkpoints as if they marked the actual border. They couldn't help me if anything happened while I was down there, and they would not let me pass if their intelligence officers thought it too dangerous.

A Lebanese woman said she could get me through if she came with me. "I know what to say to them," she said. "Don't worry."

Her name was Leena, and she worked part time as a freelance reporter while helping foreign correspondents like me in her spare time.

She was born and raised a Shia in the south, but she didn't think much of her home region's politics. "I like to drink and dance on tables," she said. "So of course I don't agree with Hezbollah."

She wore Western-style clothes and dyed a red streak in her hair, so she didn't look like the type of person who would sympathize with an Islamist militia. Some Lebanese Shias, though, supported Hezbollah anyway for sectarian reasons. Hassan Nasrallah brought real power to their community for the first time in its history, and that was a lot.

Many secular Shias didn't fret too much about Khomeini's Velayat-e Faqih ideology that came with the Hezbollah package as long as they lived where the state wielded authority. The sovereign parts of Lebanon, ruled as they were by a multiconfessional coalition of parties, were no more theocratic than Europe.

"So you're with March 14, then?" I said to Leena.

"I'm independent," she said. "I have problems with both sides in our political system."

She seemed like the ideal person to accompany me in the south. Even before Hezbollah blacklisted me, I decided I didn't actually want to be chaperoned by one of their authoritarian minders trained in the art of dissembling. Most March 14 people, though, weren't familiar enough with the Hezbollah-controlled areas in the south to show me around, and I didn't want all my information to come from anti-Hezbollah partisans anyway.

At first I suspected that Leena declared political independence because she was a journalist who strived for objectivity. I reconsidered, though, as I came to understand Lebanon better.

Never mind the Manichean standoff between the Hariri-led March 14 and the Hezbollah-led March 8 coalitions. Lebanon had more opinions than people and almost as many parties to match. March 14 alone was more politically diverse than most countries. Opposition to Syrian and Iranian hegemony was its primary common denominator. Everyone from radical-left socialists and the strict Muslim Brotherhood to libertarian capitalists and former Christian militiamen belonged to that bloc.

There was a serious problem, however, with what was otherwise a very large tent. March 14 didn't include any significant and credible Shia political parties. The secular Shias of Amal were welcome to join, but March 14 couldn't even pry their leader and Speaker of Parliament Nabih Berri away from Hezbollah with a crowbar.

So if you were a Lebanese Shia who detested Hezbollah, you had two unpalatable options. You could join one of the predominantly Christian, Sunni, or Druze parties as a marginalized minority, or you could refuse to join any political party at all. Those who chose independence, and who therefore rejected both sectarian and partisan politics, suffered fewer symptoms of groupthink than anyone else I met in the country. Leena was one of those people.

We met for breakfast at a café on the morning we agreed to take our trip to the south. I savored my espresso and soaked up as much of the French-Mediterranean ambience as I could before we hopped in her car and drove to the shatter zone.

⁓

The Lebanese government lost control of the south in the 1970s and still hadn't recovered it. Since then, the area had been ruled by Arafat's Palestine Liberation Organization (PLO), the Israel Defense Forces (IDF), or Hezbollah. It was a battleground almost the entire time.

The Cairo Agreement[2]—brokered by Egypt's Gamal Abdel Nasser between Arafat and the Lebanese army in 1969—gave the PLO sovereignty over Palestinian refugee camps inside Lebanon and access to the Israeli border so they could fire rockets and artillery shells at their nemesis.

In 1971, Jordan's King Hussein banished Arafat and the PLO to Lebanon after they tried to topple his government. Not content to live the good life on the Mediterranean in a new land that welcomed him nor chastened by his violent expulsion during what he and his men called "Black September," Arafat continued his guerrilla and terrorist war against Israel from Lebanon. The Maronites were incensed by all this, and their anger reached the boiling point as the PLO slowly transformed West Beirut and the south into its own de facto state within a state.

The Shias of the south likewise detested the PLO and wanted it gone. Their villages suffered collateral damage from Israeli counterattacks, which they blamed, rightly, on Arafat. No one asked or even cared how they felt about being pushed around by a foreign Sunni militia or the transformation of their quiet part of the world into a war zone.

Beirut went to hell when clashes between the PLO and the Maronite Phalangist militia sparked the civil war in 1975, and the south exploded in 1978 when the Israelis invaded. The United Nations Interim Force in Lebanon[3] (UNIFIL) was established soon after as a peacekeeping force, but the PLO wouldn't quit.

The Israelis mounted a much more serious invasion in June of 1982, and this time they went all the way to Beirut. Israeli Prime Minister Menachem Begin and Defense Minister Ariel Sharon vowed not only to throw the PLO off the border but also to do what King Hussein of Jordan had done and evict Arafat and his men from the country entirely.

The IDF punched through the PLO on the border and reached Arafat's command and control center in Beirut in eight days. They struck PLO positions from sea, air, and land, and cut off food, water, and electricity, placing the whole of West Beirut under siege. Thousands were killed in the fighting.

The city's Sunni leaders summoned Arafat and his aides and said they had put up a good fight, but Lebanon had suffered enough. Lebanon, in fact, had suffered a lot. By August, French and American peacekeeping troops agreed to escort Arafat and his men out of the country.

He and his lieutenants were banished to Tunisia, another pleasant Arab country on the Mediterranean, only this time without an Israeli border to shoot at. "In Beirut, we were in exile," one of his senior aides said to reporter Thomas Friedman in Tunis.[4] "Here we are in exile from exile."

South Lebanon's Shias greeted the Israeli soldiers as liberators. It didn't matter that the Shia were Arabs and Muslims. What mattered was that they weren't Palestinians. They weren't even Sunnis. Palestinians—and the Lebanese Sunnis who embraced them and gave them license—were to blame for most of their problems. The Israelis were welcome to rid their land of that menace as long as they didn't stay.

But the Israelis stayed. Sharon and Begin had a side project going at the same time to bolster Lebanon's newly elected president Bashir Gemayel.

Gemayel, political front man for the Kataeb (Phalangist) militia, was elected in August as the PLO was evacuating the country, and he promised the Israelis a peace treaty. Before he was inaugurated, however, Habib Shartouni of the Syrian Social Nationalist Party killed him and twenty-six of his aides with a bomb hidden in an apartment above his headquarters.[5]

His older brother Amin was elected president in his place, and he stepped back from his party's alliance with Israel. Meanwhile, the Kataeb militia, under the leadership of Elie Hobeika, retaliated for Bashir's assassination by massacring hundreds, if not thousands, of Palestinian civilians in the Sabra and Shatila refugee camps in southern Beirut.

Israelis took to the streets of Tel Aviv in the largest demonstration in their country's history. Their soldiers didn't participate in the massacre, but they were allied with the Maronite militia that did. They even illuminated the camps at night with aerial flares so the Phalangists could do their dirty work in the dark. In 1983, Israel's Kahan Commission[6] found Ariel Sharon "personally responsible" and recommended that he be relieved of his post. He resigned under a storm of public pressure.

Israel drastically scaled back its objectives and left the Phalangists to fend for themselves—which suited most of Lebanon's Maronites fine. The country was not remotely prepared for a treaty or alliance with Israel, especially after Sharon's bloody siege of Beirut.

The Lebanese state was little more than a government in name only anyway. Amin Gemayel could not have enforced a peace treaty even if the government had ratified one, nor could he secure his own southern border. The IDF eventually gave up and withdrew to a "security zone" ten or so miles deep into Lebanese territory, hunkered down behind a line of defenses, and hoped to keep the war from spilling over the border again.

It didn't work. Swapping a PLO statelet for an Israeli occupation was not what the Shias of the south had in mind. Their hospitality quickly turned to frustration and, later, to hatred.

⟳

Ashura is a Shia religious holiday, and it is not joyous. It marks the anniversary of the Battle of Karbala in the year 680, where Hussein—son of Ali and grandson of the Prophet Muhammad—was slain by the forces of the Umayyad Caliph Yazid. On this day, pious Shias engage in a public demonstration of grief and lamentation. Some Shia men even flail themselves with chains or cut their heads with swords and conspicuously bleed on themselves as they make their way through the streets.

In 1983, a year after the PLO had been vanquished, IDF patrol trucks made a wrong turn and ended up in the middle of an Ashura procession in Nabatieh. The drivers fatefully tried to barge their way through a crowd. Some of the mourners threw rocks, and

Israeli soldiers shot them. The IDF looked to the faithful like a modern Yazid.

It was the last straw for many, and not only because they now had a grievance to nurture. While the Israelis proceeded to wear out their welcome, Iranian Revolutionary Guard Corps officers were busy indoctrinating the local population and organizing its disgruntled members into guerrilla and terrorist cells. According to Magnus Ranstorp at the Swedish National Defence College, Iran redeployed as many as 1,500 Revolutionary Guard members[7] to Lebanon's Bekaa Valley from battlefields in the Iran-Iraq war immediately after the Israeli invasion.

Using hit-and-run guerrilla attacks, precision sniper and mortar fire, and—what would soon become their specialty—suicide bombers, the Islamic Resistance kept the IDF bogged down in a grinding counterinsurgency even after Lebanon's civil war ended.

The Israeli public eventually grew sick to death of it all. The "security zone" in South Lebanon looked more like an insecurity zone. Israel made no claims on Lebanese territory. Most Israelis never wanted to be drawn into Lebanon in the first place and figured Hezbollah would leave them alone if they left.

The mothers of four soldiers killed in the zone galvanized public opinion[8] when they campaigned for a military withdrawal. In 1999, Israelis elected Ehud Barak prime minister in part because he promised to bring the soldiers in Lebanon home. Like everyone else swayed by the Four Mothers Movement, he figured the Lebanese army would take the IDF's place and secure its own border.

The Israelis left hastily, though, without coordinating with Beirut. Hezbollah fighters flooded the zone and set up positions along the fence. Tehran itself may as well have taken control of the border. The United Nations certified that Israel had withdrawn from 100 percent of Lebanon's territory, but to the astonishment and horror of just about everybody in Tel Aviv and Jerusalem, Hezbollah continued its war against Israel.

"From small arms to standoff weapons," Ranstorp at the Swedish National Defence College wrote,[9] "Hezbollah gradually acquired an impressive arsenal, from over a thousand 122 mm Katyusha rockets, AT-4 antitank missiles, and rocket propelled grenades

(RPGs) to mortars and antiaircraft batteries. This made it among the most sophisticated and well-armed guerrilla/terrorist groups in the world. . . . In this lethal enterprise there are few organizations as capable, precise and dangerous."

That was in 1990. By the time I arrived in South Lebanon fifteen years later, Hezbollah had boosted its arsenal by several orders of magnitude.

CHAPTER FIVE

welcome to hezbollahland

> Between Beirut and Tel Aviv there is . . . this strange dark kingdom.
> – JONATHAN SPYER

L eena and I pulled up to the last Lebanese army check-point before Hezbollah's territory began.

"Who's he?" said the soldier in charge. Leena didn't need a permit to enter the zone, but I, as a foreigner, did. And I didn't have one.

"He's a friend," she said.

"Where's he from?" the soldier said.

"I'm American," I said. There was no point in pretending I was anything else. I looked like an American, talked like an American, and carried an American passport. There wasn't a chance I could convince him I was from South Lebanon.

"Like I said, he is a friend," Leena said in Arabic with a southern accent that can't be easily faked. "I'm taking him to my family's house so I can show him where I come from."

The soldier nodded and let us pass. So much for needing a permit.

As soon as Leena and I drove away from the checkpoint, we had effectively left Lebanon and arrived somewhere else. Neither government soldiers nor police officers were allowed down there. The Shia-majority cities of Nabatieh and Tyre behind us were within the government's jurisdiction, but the only authority near the border with Israel was Hezbollah. Tehran had more sovereignty there than Beirut did.

Rapid urban migrations in developing countries are often not pretty, but the rural south appeared settled, moderately prosperous, even tranquil despite all the violence over the years. It was a relief after the impoverished and ramshackle *dahiyeh*. So many people in the suburbs south of Beirut came to the capital under extraordinary circumstances and left everything behind. Those who remained in the south had their reasons. Maybe they prospered there or couldn't bear the thought of uprooting themselves. Either way, the south was their home and had been the home of their community for hundreds of years. Though the land was rocky in places and was less suitable for agriculture than the fecund Bekaa Valley, the southerners could still work it, and they could keep the fruits of the labor.

Many single-family homes were large enough to house three generations, and every village and town had sprawling villas. The apartment buildings were simple but looked nothing like the spirit-crushing slum towers in the southern suburbs. Some of South Lebanon's money had been earned abroad in the Diaspora, and some of it came as aid from Iran's Islamic Republic, but there was real wealth all the same. None of the south's Shia villages or towns looked to my eyes like slums.

It was still Hezbollahland, though. The whole place was a gigantic outdoor museum for the Islamic Resistance in Lebanon.

Portraits of "martyrs" hung from the sides of electrical poles just as they did in the *dahiyeh*. Here, though, the portraits were cleaner and appeared to have been installed a little more recently. Posters portraying Iran's Ayatollah Khomeini and its current Supreme Guide Ayatollah Ali Khamenei were outnumbered only by those featuring Hezbollah's grinning beturbaned Hassan Nasrallah.

Billboards showed bloody and fiery depictions of mayhem and war accompanied by text in both English and Arabic. On the road beneath the crumbling Beaufort Castle, the story of suicide bomber Haitham Dbouq was told next to his portrait. "Haitham stormed into the convoy—that had 30 occupation troops in its ranks—blowing up his car amidst the vehicles that turned into fireballs and scattered bodies on the ground. Thirty Zionist casualties was the size of the material shock that hit the occupation army; the morale shock was much larger and more dangerous."

The entire area was strewn with scorched tanks, blasted trucks, and military ordnance carefully placed by Hezbollah in order to best show it off. I saw young children playing on one of the tanks, their tiny legs dangling from the turret. A gigantic cardboard figure of Khomeini smiled down on them.

Funny place, Hezbollahland. It was basically a separatist region that hadn't declared itself a separatist region. Nasrallah knew well the benefits of existing both alongside and inside the state. Beirut may as well have been the capital of a foreign country, yet he and his deputies held a few seats in its parliament.

They needed that state. Lebanon was Hezbollah's vast human shield. Israel would have to think long and hard before striking Hezbollah and damaging the country that produced the Beirut Spring and was a respectable ally of the U.S. and Europe. If Hezbollah was recognized internationally as the ruler of its own sovereign state, it would be left naked and exposed to devastating military reprisals while Beirut and Mount Lebanon went their own way and prospered.

~

Leena wanted to show me the village of Ghajar, a pinpoint on the map where three nations converged and formed the strangest of knots. The northern half of the village was in Lebanon. The southern half was controlled by Israel. All of it once belonged to Syria.

After Israel captured the Golan Heights from Syria in the 1967 war, Ghajar was stranded in a no-man's-land between Lebanon and Israeli-occupied Syria. The residents couldn't live suspended in limbo between the two countries forever, so they petitioned the State of Israel and asked to be annexed. They were Syrians—Arabs—not Jews or Israelis, but they would rather live in Syria under Israeli occupation than in Lebanon.

The Lebanese-Syrian border, though, wasn't marked. Over time, Ghajar expanded northward, without anyone even knowing it, into Lebanon.[1] And in the year 2000, when Israel withdrew from its security zone, the village was thrown into turmoil.

The United Nations wouldn't certify the Israeli withdrawal unless the northern half of the village was ceded to Lebanon—which, in the real world, meant to Hezbollah.

Ghajar's residents had been living under Israeli jurisdiction since 1967, and most took Israeli citizenship in 1981. So in 2005 the northern half of Ghajar was populated with Syrians in Lebanon with Israeli ID cards.[2]

That's where Leena intended to take me, but in hindsight I believe she mistakenly took me to a different village right next to Ghajar called Arab al-Luweiza.

Ghajar had been under Israeli control for decades, but the place Leena showed me was utterly destitute and in worse shape by far than anything else in the area, whether Christian or Shia. Some houses were crumbling boxes made out of cinder blocks. Others were shanties with tin roofs and walls. Barren ground was strewn with rubble and rocks.

A handful of barefoot children dressed in dirty clothes and playing in filthy streets ran up to us when we stepped out of the car. Somehow, they managed to smile.

"What is *wrong* with this place?" I said to Leena. The conditions were worse than in the *dahiyeh*. "Who lives here? Are these people Shias?"

Leena wasn't sure, so she asked one of the boys.

"Alawi!" he said.

The Alawi, or Alawite, sect is a peculiar religious community that makes up around 10 percent of Syria's population and a tiny percentage of Lebanon's. Most Alawites live along the Mediterranean coast in Syria and Northern Lebanon, but a few live all the way down in Ghajar. They are descendants of the followers of Muhammad ibn Nusayr, who took them out of mainstream Twelver Shia Islam in the tenth century. Their religion has as much in common with Christianity and Gnosticism as it does with Islam, and both Sunnis and Shias have long considered them "infidels."

Perhaps the strangest thing about the Alawites was that they were the rulers of Syria. The al-Assad clan was Alawite, as were most of the elites in the Baath Party, the bureaucracy, and the military.

Imam Musa Sadr, founder of Amal in Lebanon, struck a deal with Hafez al-Assad in 1974 and issued a *fatwa*, or religious ruling, somewhat implausibly declaring Alawites part of the Shia community.[3]

Yet the Alawites are not Shias. They're Alawites. The two communities needed religious cover for their budding political alliance, however, and Sadr's *fatwa* gave it to them. The relationship between Hezbollah and Damascus's Alawite regime, though, was strictly one of convenience. The two felt little or no warmth for each other.

While Hezbollah and Amal were politically aligned with the Alawite government, the Sunnis were not, and Sunnis made up around 70 percent of Syria's population. The fundamentalists among them had long detested al-Assad's Baath Party regime, not only because it was secular and oppressive but because its leaders were "heretics."

Al-Assad supported terrorist groups in his war against Israel for some of the same reasons the Khomeinists did in Iran. As minorities in the region, both were in danger without street cred from the Sunnis.

In 1982, the same year Israel invaded Lebanon and Iran founded the prototype of Hezbollah, Syria's Sunni Muslim Brotherhood took up arms against Hafez al-Assad's government in the city of Hama. Al-Assad dispatched the Alawite-dominated military and destroyed most of the old city with air strikes, tanks, and artillery. Rifaat al-Assad, the former president's younger brother, boasted that the regime killed 38,000 people in a single day. Not once since then have the Muslim Brothers tried to rise up again.

In his book *From Beirut to Jerusalem*, Thomas Friedman dubbed the senior al-Assad's rules of engagement "Hama Rules."[4] They were the Syrian stick. The carrot was al-Assad's steadfast "resistance" against Israel. No Arab government in the world was as stridently anti-Israel, in both action and rhetoric, as his. There was no better way for a detested minority regime to curry favor with Sunnis in Syria and the larger Arab world than by adopting the anti-Zionist cause as its own.

As "infidels," Syria's Alawites didn't feel they had the legitimacy to force Sunnis to make peace with Israel. That was a risky business even for Sunni leaders, as the assassination of Egypt's Anwar Sadat showed after he signed a treaty.

Because most of Syria's Alawites live along the Mediterranean coast and away from the Sunni heartland, they could, at least theoretically, be separated from Syria into their own Alawite nation. The Middle East would probably be a safer place if they had their own state. They did have their own semiautonomous government under the French Mandate between 1923 and 1937.

"The Alawites refuse to be annexed to Muslim Syria," Suleiman al-Assad, grandfather of President Bashar al-Assad, wrote in a petition to France.[5] "In Syria, the official religion of the state is Islam, and according to Islam, the Alawites are considered infidels. . . . The spirit of hatred and fanaticism imbedded in the hearts of the Arab Muslims against everything that is non-Muslim has been perpetually nurtured by the Islamic religion. There is no hope that the situation will ever change. Therefore, the abolition of the mandate will expose the minorities in Syria to the dangers of death and annihilation."

The Alawite State was dissolved back into French Mandate Syria,[6] however, and has been an integral part of the country ever since. Had the Alawites declared and received independence, they might even have been natural allies of Israel for the same reasons the Middle East's Christians and Kurds are. After all, when the Alawites of Ghajar were given a choice to live under a Lebanese or Israeli government, they chose Israel's. And they made that choice when Lebanon was considered the Switzerland of the Middle East, years before it descended into chaos and horror and war. Israel's occupation of the Golan Heights freed them from tyrannical Syrian rule, and it freed them from the Sunni demand to resist the Zionists.

The Alawites on the north side of Ghajar, however, were severed from their adopted country and abandoned to Hezbollahland, even though they were Israeli citizens and had no connection to Lebanon.

They were cut off from Jerusalem, and they were cut off from Damascus. They were even cut off from Beirut. In 1967 they found themselves in a no-man's-land between Israel and Syria, and in 2000 they found themselves mired in Hezbollahland between Israel and Lebanon proper. Meanwhile, the village was Nasrallah's flash point of choice. Hezbollah fighters liked to pick fights with the Israelis by firing from the northern side of the village into the southern half and bringing reprisals down on everyone's head.

The people of Ghajar weren't the only ones who lived right on the border. The Lebanese village of Kfar Kila and the small Israeli town of Metula were nearly built on top of each other. The first time I saw Metula from the Lebanese side, I couldn't even grasp what I was looking at.

"That village is in Israel," Leena said and stopped the car next to a field.

I scanned the tops of the hills for a settlement somewhere off in the distance, but I couldn't see what she was talking about. "What village?" I said.

"That village right there," she said and pointed at a row of houses in front of us.

"*Those* houses right there?" I said. They were only a few hundred feet from where we were parked. "Aren't they in Lebanon?"

"Look closer," she said. "See the fence?"

There it was. The fence along the border ran just a few dozen feet behind the houses as though it demarcated a property line, not an international boundary. I could have stepped out of the car, walked right up to it, and had a conversation in a normal tone of voice with an Israeli family hanging out in the yard.

Hezbollah guerrillas were dug into the hills and holed up behind us in Kfar Kila's houses.

I tried to imagine how I would feel as an American if the Taliban controlled territory thirty or forty feet from my house.

"This is nuts," I said and stepped out of the car to snap pictures. "The border is not even guarded."

"The fence is electric," Leena said. "It won't shock you, but it will alert the Israelis, and they'll come out to investigate. So don't touch it."

"Why on earth would any Israelis want to live so close to Hezbollah?" I wondered out loud.

Unlike in Ghajar, the residents of Metula and Kfar Kila weren't divided artificially or by accident. They were divided by ethnicity, by religion, by nationality, and by war. They lived just a few minutes' walking distance apart, but most of the time they managed to do so without killing each other.

Americans at the time were fighting counterinsurgencies on the other side of the world in Iraq and Afghanistan. When Israelis fought counterinsurgencies against the PLO and Hezbollah in Lebanon, they did so literally in their backyard. I could have walked up to the fence and thrown a hand grenade into an Israeli's kitchen window. No one would have been able to stop me. If Hezbollah fighters decided to shoot Jews in Metula, they wouldn't miss.

Yet the border was quiet.

"This is not what I expected," I said.

"Everyone who sees this is surprised," Leena said. "That's why I like bringing foreign journalists down here."

I wasn't sure what I was supposed to make of it, though.

Hezbollah had launched attacks against Israel several times since the IDF left, often in and around Ghajar. Yet most of the time, the border was strangely and eerily quiet. Otherwise, Metula would have been destroyed or abandoned.

It was impossible to mistake calm for peace, though, which is what made the border unsettling.

"I want to wave hello to someone in Israel," I said, though I knew it was illegal.

"*Don't*," Leena said. "I'm responsible for you, and I could get in serious trouble."

Israel still had friends in South Lebanon who passed on information, including actionable intelligence, about Hezbollah. Hezbollah knew it, too, which is why it would not even tolerate hand signals to Israelis. I knew better than to wave and bring down the wrath of a militia on my head and Leena's, but I wished I could defuse the tension on the border by an iota, and I wanted Leena to know it.

She and I arrived during a lull in a storm that had been raging for decades. The border may have been calm at that moment, but the calm was so tense I could feel it. The Lebanese side was saturated with so much violent Hezbollah propaganda that I doubted very seriously that the calm was sustainable.

The rest of what Leena showed me that day seemed to confirm that.

She drove us into Kfar Kila and parked next to the fence, where we could see some of Hezbollah's outdoor museum pieces—an Israeli truck up on blocks that Hezbollah destroyed with an antitank mine, a rocket launcher pointing at Israel beneath camouflage netting, and two stone monuments representing the American "Great Satan" and the Israeli "Little Satan." I also saw two kinds of donation boxes where people could give money to Hezbollah for either charity or "resistance" operations.

Just beyond the edge of the village was one of the world's strangest tourist attractions.

Fatima Gate had been the crossing point between Israel and Lebanon before 2000, when the border was open. The gate itself was mere feet on the Israeli side. It was wrapped in cyclone fencing two stories high, the kind you see behind home plate on a baseball diamond.

Visitors from all over the Arab world drove down there from Beirut to throw rocks at Israel. Dozens of fist-sized stones were stuck in the fencing.

Thousands of Lebanese people had passed through that gate when the border was open. Those with security clearance were allowed into Israel to work and play. At that time, the border might have appeared almost normal, but only because Israel controlled both sides. If I had felt like being provocative, I might have asked residents of Kfar Kila what they thought the border region would have been like had Hezbollah, rather than Israel, controlled both sides. South Lebanon might have been sort of okay, but Metula, I thought, would not have fared very well.

At least the Israeli homes on the other side of Fatima Gate were out of rock-throwing range. They were not, however, outside rifle, mortar, and rocket range. Living in a house so close to South Lebanon in 2005 was like living on a seasonal floodplain or atop a tectonic fault. The false peace couldn't hold. How could it hold?

Hezbollah's hatred of Jews and Israelis was white-hot and total. It was difficult, if not impossible, for Westerners like me to wrap our minds around it.

It must have felt the same way to some of the South Lebanese. Once in a while, those who lived at the edge of Kfar Kila could look out their front windows and see the same soldiers who had patrolled their own streets driving around in armored trucks. Israeli soldiers didn't pick fights by randomly firing across the border as Hezbollah sometimes did, but they could shoot back when provoked, and they could shoot back with much greater firepower. The place was a powder keg no matter which side you lived on.

"A guy from Hezbollah TV came down here to Fatima Gate once," Leena said, "and some Israelis having a picnic on the other side recognized him. 'Hey!' they said. 'You're that guy from Hezbollah! What's up?' He was furious. He wanted to say something, but no one here is allowed to talk to Israelis. So he growled at them." She smiled. "He just clenched his teeth and went, *Grr*."

I laughed.

"It's absurd, isn't it?" she said.

Even more absurd was the tomb of the disputed dead man on top of a nearby hill.

The Lebanese said Sheik Abbad was buried there. The Israelis said, No, the tomb belongs to Rabbi Ashi. I didn't know who was right, nor did I care. Neither did anyone else who wasn't Lebanese or Israeli. The dead man, whoever he was, was buried exactly—precisely—on the border between the two countries. The United Nations arm-twisted Israel and Lebanon into painting a blue line lengthwise down the tomb's center. One side of the man's body lay in Israel, and the other side lay in Lebanon.

Hezbollah erected a billboard next to him that faced south and taunted Israelis with horrific images of violence and war—dead bodies gunned down in a street, a soldier with skin missing on one side of his face holding a rocket launcher, and a Hezbollah militiamen holding up the severed head of an Israeli man by his hair. Underneath these gruesome photographs was text written in Hebrew referring to Israelis who had been captured and never returned: "Sharon don't forget, your soldiers are still in Lebanon."

CHAPTER SIX

something
dark
is coming

Levanon is the most
mournful word in the
mouth of a Hebrew-
speaking mother.
—LEE SMITH

O n November 22, 2005, Hezbollah fighters fired rockets
and mortars at the Israeli side of Ghajar, stormed over
the border, and engaged IDF ground forces in battle.

Israel retaliated with air strikes against Hezbollah targets in the
villages of Shebaa and Kfar Shouba, in the Al-Mari Valley, outside
Khiam, and southeast of Tyre.

Beirut's *Daily Star* reported more than 250 explosions.[1] Israel
said it was the largest counterattack inside Lebanon since the withdrawal of their occupation forces five years before. One Israeli and
three Hezbollah gunmen were killed.

Hardly anyone in Lebanon or Israel was surprised. The only way
Hezbollah could justify its existence as an autonomous militia was by
getting into a shooting war with the "Zionist Entity" once in a while.
Israel had to be seen as a threat. If it looked like a peaceful lamb of a
country, the Islamic Resistance would have to close up its shop.

Hezbollah especially needed a conflict with Israel in late 2005. United Nations investigator Detlev Mehlis had just fingered top Syrian officials in the assassination of Rafik Hariri, and the international community was gearing up to punish al-Assad and his government. Hezbollah leaders hoped to channel the ire of their countrymen onto Israel instead of their besieged patron regime in Damascus.

Israeli planes dropped leaflets along the southern border and over Beirut. "Hezbollah brings a strong prejudice to Lebanon," the text said.[2] "It is an instrument in the hands of its Syrian and Iranian masters. The state of Israel is watching over the protection of its citizens and sovereignty. . . . Who is protecting Lebanon, who lies to you? Who throws your sons into a battle for which they are not prepared? Who wants the return of destruction?"

Public opinion in Beirut hardly budged. Border clashes with Israel were ho-hum at this point. Almost every Lebanese person I knew thought the al-Assad regime was a more pressing problem—an unacceptable state of affairs for Syria, Iran, and Hezbollah. Hezbollah needed Israel to be seen as the greater of threats, whether it was or not.

Hezbollah didn't have much of an excuse for starting a shooting war. The only territory left to "liberate" in 2005 was the microscopic Shebaa Farms.

Hezbollah claimed the land as Lebanese, but it was taken from Syria in the 1967 war.

Israel wished to be rid of it. Why give Hezbollah an excuse to keep fighting?

"Shebaa is two fields and a cow," activist Nabil Abou-Charaf told me. "Nobody lives there."

The United Nations wouldn't let Israel hand Shebaa Farms over to Lebanon since the tiny area supposedly belonged to Syria.[3] Syria, though, wouldn't claim or renounce it. Al-Assad wanted the acreage to remain in a nationless limbo. Hezbollah was still useful to him, and Hezbollah needed something to fume about.

Temporary flare-ups had been erupting on the Lebanese-Israeli border in and near the Shebaa Farms ever since the IDF withdrawal, and the pattern was always the same. Hezbollah started a fight, Israel responded for a few hours with more deadly and accurate firepower, and Hezbollah stood down. Few people were hurt or killed on either side, and neither the Lebanese nor Israeli public even seemed to mind very much. The skirmishes looked and felt to most like after-shocks from the previous war that was supposed to end in 2000.

A few days later, an Israeli paraglider crossed the border, either intentionally or by accident, and landed in Lebanon. Hezbollah fighters opened fire. Israeli soldiers cut a hole in the border fence, pulled the man through to safety, and placed him under arrest. Hez-bollah claimed he was a soldier. Israel insisted he was a civilian.

Hezbollah fighters shot at everyone they saw crossing the border for any reason. One of my American friends in Beirut lived in Israel the previous year, and he told me he once foolishly tried to cross from there into Lebanon with some friends. He had visited Lebanon before and knew a place where a gate in the fence was sometimes left open, most likely for cross-border smuggling. He thought he could just drive a rental car through since the border didn't look guarded.

Unseen Hezbollah fighters put bullet holes in the hood of his car the instant he nosed into Lebanon. He slammed the car into reverse, ducked his head under the dash, and drove backward as fast he could. Hezbollah stopped firing as soon as he was back on the Israeli side and had crashed the car into a tree.

That border was no place to screw around or act like an idiot. Soon it would be no place for Americans like me or him to visit at all. Hardly anyone on either side of the border had any idea, but the latest eruption was just a prologue for something much larger.

⁓

Abu Musab al-Zarqawi, a Jordanian from the city of Zarqa, founded al Qaeda in Iraq in 2004. He had four principal goals: destroy the government, eject the Americans, subjugate the Shias, and impose a fanatically rigid Sunni Islamist dictatorship.

After Saddam Hussein's Sunni Baath Party regime was demol-ished by the United States in 2003, Iraqi Shias—who made up about 60 percent of the population—were placed in the saddle through democratic elections. Most Iraqi Sunnis found this intolerable, but they weren't in the mood to do much about it. History was not on their side any longer.

Al-Zarqawi wanted to change that. Al-Zarqawi wanted to fire them up. An insurgency was rising against the American occupiers; perhaps the Shia government could be swept away along with the superpower. He wanted his civil war. And he got it in early 2006 after a half-dozen of his men sneaked into the al-Askari Mosque in Samarra, tied up the guards, and planted explosives that destroyed the golden dome later that morning.

The al-Askari Mosque, also known as the Golden Mosque, contained one of the holiest shrines in all of Shia Islam. The tenth and eleventh imams—direct descendents of the Prophet Muhammad—were buried there in the year 944. Shia militias responded exactly as al-Zarqawi expected they would—by fighting back, death-squad style.

Iraq's civil war was officially on, and it reverberated powerfully in South Lebanon.

I drove down there from Beirut with British historian Andrew Apostolou in the spring of 2006, just a few weeks after al-Zarqawi's atrocity.

There was no chance I could talk our way past the checkpoints on our way into Hezbollahland as Leena had, so we stopped at the Lebanese army base just east of Sidon and asked for a permit.

"What is your nationality?" the ranking military officer said.

"He's British," I said, referring to Andrew. "And I'm American."

The officer clasped his hands loudly together. "You are *not* going down there today," he said.

"Why not?" I said.

He made an *I-don't-know* face that was terrifically, intentionally, and even comically insincere.

"Is it for security reasons?" I said.

"Of course," he said. "You can go," he said to Andrew. A British passport apparently wasn't a problem. "But you," he said, meaning me, "can't go anywhere near the border right now."

"Why not?" I said. "What's going on?"

He laughed.

"Oh, come on," I said. "You can tell me. Who am I going to tell?" He didn't know I was a journalist.

"No," he said firmly and shook his head.

"Are you worried I will do something?" I said. "Or are you worried something will happen to me?"

"Something might happen to you," he said.

"Is it Hezbollah? The Israelis? What?"

He made his goofy *what-do-I-know* face once again. "I am sorry," he said. "It's too dangerous. You aren't going."

Andrew was given a permit in a matter of minutes.

"I can drive you as far as Nabatieh," I said to him as we walked back to the car. "You can take a taxi from there to the border."

"Thanks, mate," he said.

So we drove together as far as Nabatieh, a small Shia city just outside the Hezbollah zone. When we reached the city center, I thought for a moment that we had driven into an anguished Ashura procession, just as an Israeli convoy had in 1982 when Hezbollah's insurgency took off.

Thousands of wailing mourners paraded through the streets carrying black Shia flags. Banners bearing the face of Ali streamed from the lampposts. Loudspeakers broadcast a furious sermon.

But this wasn't Ashura—the annual commemoration of the slaying of Hussein at the Battle of Karbala. That had taken place a few weeks before. This was a funeral, if that's the right word, for the al-Askari Mosque and its golden dome that al-Zarqawi and his vicious sectarians had blown apart in Iraq.

My heart ached for these people and their justified rage. There was a problem, however. Hezbollah, like the Khomeinist regime in Iran, accused American soldiers of destroying the mosque.

"They invade the shrine and bomb there because they oppose God and justice," Iranian President Mahmoud Ahmadinejad said.[4] "Such actions are the acts of a group of defeated Zionists and occupiers."

"This probably isn't where we should be right about now," I said to Andrew.

He nodded. "Let's head to the outskirts of town," he said, "and I'll hop in a taxi to the border from there."

I found three parked taxis in front of a café and helped him secure a reasonable fare with the driver. He wasn't particularly worried about heading into Hezbollahland without me, despite what the

Lebanese army officer had told us earlier and despite the seething and misplaced anger in Lebanon's Shia community over the terrorism committed against their brothers and sisters in Samarra.

His driver took him to the ruins of the Beaufort crusader castle—now with a Hezbollah flag snapping defiantly from the rampart—overlooking the border area. "The mosque in the valley below was blaring out Nasrallah," he later told me. "And the looks in some of the villages were not friendly. It was a beautiful place, but perhaps time to head back to Beirut."

I felt slightly nervous myself while driving north out of Nabatieh and back toward Beirut. Even though most people who lived there were Shias, the city was not controlled by Hezbollah. The mood on the street, though, was so tense I could practically feel it on my skin.

I got lost on my way back to the main road and found myself in a poor part of town where portraits of Bashar al-Assad were bolted to the lampposts. Every third or fourth person scrutinized me and my car. I was obviously not from around there. The colored license plate that marked every rental car in Lebanon gave me away, as did my European complexion. From the point of view of the more paranoid residents, I was likely a spy.

South Lebanon wasn't Iraq, but it looked, felt, and was much more volatile than it had been when I went down there with Leena.

If I wanted to know what had changed on the border, I would need to swing around and talk to officials on the other side. It was time to visit the Zionist Entity.

⌒

The hatred for Israel among Lebanon's Shia cannot be explained simply by the fact that they were Muslims and Arabs and were therefore supposed to hate Jews—not when they initially hailed the Israelis as liberators from Arafat and the PLO. Nor can a bloody dustup during Ashura explain it. Not even the fomenting of a "resistance" culture by Iranian Revolutionary Guard Corps units was enough by itself.

THE ROAD TO FATIMA GATE ⌒ 101

The Shias of Lebanon adopted the view of the strangers from
Persia for complex cultural and historical reasons that had little to
do with Jews or with Israel. Khomeini promised to lead them out of
the wilderness once and for all. He gave them dignity. He gave them
respect. And he gave them fire. Musa Sadr—also a stranger from
Persia, yet emphatically not a Khomeinist—had already stirred them
with his call to political action. Their day in history had, at long last,
arrived.

Many welcomed Iranian power in Lebanon as long as it boosted
their own. Why shouldn't they? The Iranians may have been Persians, but they also were Shias. Besides, everyone else in Lebanon
had foreign support. The Christians had the French and the Americans, and the Sunnis had the Saudis and the rest of the Arabs aside
from Syria. Until Khomeini came along, the Shias didn't have anybody. Even their own feudal leaders could hardly be bothered about
their material and political needs.

If militant anti-Zionism was part of the bargain, so be it. Why
shouldn't they fight off the Zionists anyway? The Zionists, from
their point of view, acted just like the Caliph Yazid's men in Karbala
when they occupied land that didn't belong to them and shot people
dead in the streets during Ashura.

Shia hatred of Israel, in both its Persian and Arabic forms, may
never have matured had the Sunni Arabs reached a settlement with
the Israelis before the Iranian Revolution in 1979.

Virulent hatred of Jews was never a strong force in Persian culture. Before Khomeini overthrew him, the Shah had excellent relations with Jerusalem. And why shouldn't he? Most Persians, just
like most Kurds, were reluctant to side with their ancient Arab foes
against Israel or anyone else. The Arab-Israeli conflict, after all, was
between *Arabs* and Israelis, not Muslims and Israelis. It was also,
more specifically, a conflict between *Sunni* Arabs and Israelis.

The Islamic Republic leaders did their damnedest to change
this, no doubt for sincere reasons, but also because it served them
strategically. They wished to be hegemons of the whole Muslim
world, and they couldn't achieve that without first dominating the

Arab world of the Middle East. *That* wouldn't be possible if they were allies with Israel. Iran's alliance with Israel was a serious liability and had to be scrapped. And that raised the question: If points were deducted for an alliance with Israel, shouldn't points be gained for resistance?

Khomeini made his pitch to the Arabs. They feared and loathed him as a Shia and a Persian, but they had to admit that what he and his successors said was compelling.

The Iranian message to the Arabs, Amir Taheri explained in his book *The Persian Night*, was straightforward.[5] "Forget that Iran is Shia, and remember that today it is the only power capable of realizing your most cherished dream, the destruction of Israel. The Sunni Muslim Brotherhood promised you it would throw the Jews into the sea in 1948, but failed. Pan-Arab nationalists, led by Nasser, ushered you into one of your biggest defeats in history, enabling Israel to capture Jerusalem. The Baathists under Saddam Hussein promised to 'burn Israel,' but ended up bringing the American infidels to Baghdad. Yasser Arafat and the Palestinian 'patriots' promised to crush the Jewish state, but turned into collaborators on its payroll. Osama bin Laden and al Qaeda never gave two hoots about Palestine, focusing only on spectacular operations in the West to win publicity for themselves. Sheikh Ahmad Yassin and Hamas did all they could to destroy Israel but lacked the power, like flies attacking an elephant. The only force now willing and able to help realize your dream of a burned Israel and drowning the Jews is the Islamic Republic as created by Khomeini."

The Iranians needed credibility with Sunni Arabs if they wished to lead the Middle East. Lebanon's Shias needed credibility, too, if they ever hoped to acquire real power for themselves in a Lebanese political system that, from their point of view, had always been leveraged against them.

And they got it by taking up sword against Israel just as Khomeini did.

Most Lebanese Sunnis hated Israel, but few were willing to die over it. Lebanon barely participated in the 1948 war against Israel and sat out the 1967 war altogether. The Sunnis wouldn't even put up much of a fight when the Israelis invaded in 1982. Sure, they gave Arafat room for his own war, but then they let the French and the Americans take him away.

The Shias disliked and distrusted the Sunnis as ever, but at the same time they suffered from a terrible inferiority complex that was nearly as old as their religion itself and that had been exacerbated by recent events.

"The Shia of the southern hinterland," wrote Fouad Ajami,[6] who was himself from that part of Lebanon, "had endured Palestinian power, the rise in their midst of a Palestinian state within a state. The Palestinian gunmen and pamphleteers had had the run of that part of the country. Arab nationalists in distant lands had hailed that Palestinian sanctuary; Arab oil wealth had paid for it. The Shia relief in 1982, when Israel swept into Lebanon and shattered that dominion, was to the Arab nationalists proof that the Shia stepchildren were treasonous. Then a Shia militant movement, Hezbollah, rose to challenge Israel. Its homicide bombers, its policies of 'virtue and terror,' acquitted the Lebanese Shia in Arab eyes."

The Islamic Resistance was genuinely popular in Lebanon while Israel occupied part of the south. Even some Christians considered Hezbollah fighters heroic. But when the Israelis left, Hezbollah refused to disarm—a suspicious turn of events. The *other* militias had disarmed at the end of the war. Something about Hezbollah wasn't right. Hassan Nasrallah seemed to want something else, something more, if he was holding onto his arsenal after his stated objectives were met.

Hezbollah's political base became more supportive of the Khomeinist political program than Iranians themselves, especially after the hard-line Iranian President Mahmoud Ahmadinejad turned an enormous percentage of the Iranian public against the government. It's strange that a community outside Iran backed the Iranian president more than Iran's people did, but that's what happened.

And it might have happened even without an anti-Ahmadinejad backlash. At the end of the day, Khomeinism, as Taheri makes clear, was designed to appeal more to Arabs than Persians. Khomeini only cared about Iran as a step to his leadership of the Muslim *umma*. There was nothing particularly Iranian or even Persian about his ideology or his political aspiration. He even claimed to be an Arab himself, and he renamed major streets in the capital after historic Arab figures.

Ahmadinejad and Khomeini's successor Ali Khamenei were as radical as they had ever been, but much of the Islamic Republic establishment mellowed out after a while. Revolutionaries almost everywhere tend toward conservatism after they win in order to consolidate their gains and protect their new system. Very few people have the energy to maintain radical fervor for decades.

Meanwhile, their Shia comrades in Lebanon hadn't won anything, and they were outnumbered in their own country. If they eased up, they'd lose, especially now that the Syrians were no longer around. Many feared they'd be marginalized all over again if the Cedar Revolution meant a de facto new republic was born.

The Cedar Revolution was agonizing for most of Lebanon's Shias. Despite their vast religious and ideological differences, the Sunnis and Christians were united again, and they were united at the Shias' expense. The main thing the Sunnis and Christians agreed on was the eviction of Syrian and Iranian power from Lebanon—which could only hurt the Shias who depended on Syrian and Iranian power in Lebanon.

Hezbollah and its junior partner Amal could have joined the political mainstream, but Nasrallah and his people didn't take naturally to compromise and the give-and-take of pluralist politics. Hezbollah had grievances to avenge—against the Sunnis, the Christians, the Druze, the Israelis, the Americans, the Saudis, just about everyone. Nasrallah needed to plan something radical, something extreme, to overturn Lebanon's new anti-Syrian and anti-Iranian politics. So he did.

⁓

Israel startled me from the air.

Whoa, I thought, as I looked out the window of the plane over the suburbs of Tel Aviv. If the border had been open, I could have driven down there in just a few hours from my apartment, but this place looked like the other side of the world. Trim houses sprawled in Western-style suburban rows. Their red-tiled roofs looked somehow more Southern Californian than Mediterranean. Swimming pools sparkled in the sunlight.

My Lebanese friend Hassan called Israel "Disneyland." I thought about that and laughed while watching it roll by from above.

The airport shocked me, as well, although it probably wouldn't shock most Westerners. I had just spent six consecutive months in an Arab country and suddenly saw more straight lines and right angles than I was used to. There were more women, children, and families around than I had seen for some time. Obvious tourists from places like suburban Kansas City were everywhere.

Arab countries have a certain feel. They're masculine, languid, worn around the edges, and slightly shady. Israel felt brisk, modern, shiny, and confident. With its clean and orderly streets, its glass skyscrapers, and its booming technology sector, Israel looked richer and more powerful—and it was.

Lisa Goldman kindly welcomed me to the country and met me for drinks in a smoke-filled bohemian bar. We talked, as almost everyone did, about The Conflict.

She was a journalist who had moved from Vancouver, British Columbia, to Israel years before when Ehud Barak was still the prime minister. Peace between Israelis and Palestinians looked imminent then. Israel was on the threshold—finally—of becoming an accepted and normal country in the Middle East. It was the perfect time to relocate, a time of optimism and hope. A cruel three weeks later, that dream was violently put to its death. The Second Intifada exploded. Israel was at war.

"2002 was Israel's *annus horribilis*," she wrote on her website.[7] "The economy had bottomed out; suicide bombers were detonating themselves in Israel's cities nearly every day; and Israeli soldiers and Palestinian gunmen were killing each other in the occupied—and re-occupied—territories. Each day brought a stupefying new tragedy, for Jews and Arabs alike. Confined by the IDF to his headquarters, the Muqata, in Ramallah, Yasser Arafat had become an international media darling—'cause everyone loves the perceived underdog. Many international airlines had suspended their flights to Israel, having deemed it too dangerous. The hotels were empty of tourists; Israel had become a pariah nation."

"It was so traumatizing," she added in person when we met. "And everybody blamed us. I don't think I will ever get over it."

She kept going to restaurants, cafés, and bars even while bombs exploded almost daily. She even chose to sit in front of the windows, the least safe place in any establishment.

"The staff kept asking me if I was sure I wanted to sit there," she said. "I did. Even when the Intifada was at its peak, you were far more likely to be killed in a traffic accident than by the bombers."

She was right about that. Most dangerous countries in the Middle East were safer than they appeared from a distance. The region was not one never-ending explosion. Even so, suicide bombs are far more terrifying and traumatizing than car crashes. They're murderous. They're malevolent. They're on purpose.

My American friend in Beirut, the one Hezbollah shot at when he tried to drive into South Lebanon, also lived through the Intifada. He thought he had grown used to the threat of random violence and that it hardly fazed him anymore. One morning, while sipping a latte at a Starbucks in Beirut, he realized he had been kidding himself.

"I was just sitting there reading the newspaper," he said, "when somebody walked in and shouted. I dove under the table and sent my chair flying. Nobody *else* hit the floor. Everyone stared, wondering what on earth had got into me."

Palestinian suicide bombers often yelled "Allahu Akbar," *God is great*, just before depressing the detonator and exploding themselves. Few things in Israel terrified like a man stepping into a public establishment and screaming all of a sudden, and my friend carried that fear with him into Lebanon.

"It's especially disturbing when you know what those bombs do to the human body," Lisa said.

"Do I want to know?" I said. I was not sure I did.

She shrugged.

"Okay," I said. "Just tell me."

"Arms and legs go flying in every direction," she said. "Heads pop off like champagne corks. You just can't believe anyone hates you that much."

CHAPTER SEVEN

everything could explode at any moment

This country is like a cake.
On the top it is cream.
Underneath it is fire.
—HEZBOLLAH SPOKESMAN

In late 2005, the Palestinian front in the Arab-Israeli conflict was unusually quiet. The Lebanese-Israeli border, though, was getting ready to blow. No one I knew had heard the first thing about it. The only reason I had any idea something was wrong was because a Lebanese army officer wouldn't give me a permit for the checkpoints.

Lisa and I drove up there from Tel Aviv to see if Israeli military officers were more willing to talk about what was happening than their Lebanese counterparts were.

We met Israel Defense Forces Spokesman Zvika Golan at a base in the north. He told us to follow him in his jeep as he drove to an elevated lookout point next to an IDF watchtower that opened up over Lebanon.

I stood next to the fence and looked onto a Shia village a quarter mile or so down the hill. Groves of olive trees had been planted halfway up another hill on the other side of the village. Lisa, Zvika, and I stood at a forty-five-degree angle from the roofline, and we stood in the open without protection. People below in Lebanon could easily see us.

"You aren't safe here right now," Zvika said.

"I know," I said. "The Lebanese army wouldn't let me anywhere near the border a few weeks ago. What's going on?"

"Hezbollah is planning an operation," he said.

"How do you know?" I said.

"We know," he said and nodded.

The Lebanese military officer told me more or less the same thing a few weeks before when he wouldn't let me cross into Hezbollah's territory. He didn't say the threat was from Hezbollah, but he didn't have to.

"We really want the Lebanese army on this border," Zvika said.

Lebanon and Israel technically had been at war for many decades, but the two countries' armed forces had never actually fought one another. Israel had fought *in* Lebanon, but not against the Lebanese army or government. Israel's Lebanon wars were only waged against the PLO, the Syrian army, and Hezbollah.

"Are you in contact with the Lebanese government?" I said.

"We pass messages to the Lebanese army through the U.N.," he said.

"How well are they received?" I said.

"Oh, they're received *very* well," he said. "The only problem is the Lebanese army can't act against Hezbollah."

He introduced me to a young bearded lieutenant on border patrol duty.

"I have worked on the Jordanian and Egyptian borders," he said. "This is the worst. The strangest feeling here is that the other side is a no-man's-land. There is no authority that you're working against. It is extremely out of the ordinary to see any Lebanese police or army. Only Hezbollah is armed."

"What do you see when you look at Lebanon?" I asked him.

"I see poverty and difficult circumstances," he said. "I see poor farmers who work hard. After so many years of war, the last thing they probably want is more war."

"Do you know what you're looking at when you look into the towns?" I said.

"We track movement on the other side," he said. "I can tell you exactly what each of those buildings are for."

The buildings weren't far. If the border were open and the fence not in place, we could have walked there in just a few minutes.

"What about people?" I said. "Can you tell who belongs to Hezbollah and who just happens to live there?"

"Ninety-nine percent of the time, I know who I'm looking at by their face," he said. I smiled when I imagined Hussein Naboulsi in Hezbollah's media relations department reading *that* if he still kept a file on what I wrote.

The lieutenant was easily ten years younger than me, but he was so ground down from world-weariness he sounded like a man thirty years older who had not slept for days.

"Any minute now something huge could break out," he said. "I am afraid to go home and leave my soldiers. When Hezbollah decides to do something, they do it. And they're pretty good at it."

"What do you think they'll do next?" I said.

"I have no idea," he said. "They could do anything. Kidnapping. Sniper."

"How do you feel about that?" I said.

"Well," he said. "You get pretty cynical about it after a while."

"Do you think they're watching us?" Lisa said.

"They are watching you right at this second," the lieutenant said. "You are definitely being photographed. It's possible you're being watched through a sniper rifle."

To say I felt naked and exposed at that moment would be a real understatement. I felt like my skin was invisible, that psychopaths were boring holes with their eyes straight to the core of my being. At the same time, I knew they did not see me as a person. They saw me as a potential target.

Hezbollah wouldn't hurt me in Lebanon, even after Hussein Naboulsi called up and threatened me. All bets were off while standing next to IDF soldiers in Israel, though.

I wouldn't say I felt scared, but I certainly didn't feel comfortable. The earth seemed slightly tilted. Lebanon looked unhinged and psychotic from the Israeli side of the line. I kept having to remind myself that there was a lot more to the land of the cedars than nutcases with guns in the hills who liked to pick off Jews on the border.

"How dangerous is it here, really?" I asked the lieutenant.

"I say this to my guys every morning: *Everything could explode at any moment*. Just after I said it this morning, a busload of pensioners showed up on a field trip. An old woman brought us some food. It's crazy. They shouldn't be here. You shouldn't be here."

"What's happening here is very unusual," Zvika, the IDF spokesman, said.

Iranian Revolutionary Guard Corps officers had moved into South Lebanon again to help Hezbollah construct watchtowers fitted with one-way bulletproof windows right across from Israeli army positions.

"This is now Iran's front line with Israel," an IDF officer told a reporter at London's *Daily Telegraph*.[1] "The Iranians are using Hezbollah to spy on us so that they can collect information for future attacks. And there is very little we can do about it. More powerful weapons, including missiles with a range of thirty miles, are also being brought in."

I asked Zvika about the last time Hezbollah and Israel got into a hot war, when the divided village of Ghajar came under attack.

"It was last November," he said. "Hezbollah invaded Ghajar in white jeeps that looked like they belonged to the U.N. We bombed their positions with air strikes. After a while, the Lebanese army asked us to stop. So we stopped right away."

"You stopped just because the Lebanese army asked you to stop?" I said.

He looked surprised by my question.

"Of course we stopped because they asked," he said. "We have very good relations with them. We're working with them and trying to help make them relevant."

The Lebanese government never even hinted at anything like that in public.

The rhetoric that came out of Beirut in Arabic rarely had much to do with reality. The government regularly affirmed its "brotherhood" with Syria, its former murderous master that knocked off elected officials and journalists. Undying loyalty to the Palestinian cause was constantly trumpeted, even as Lebanon treated its hundreds of thousands of Palestinian refugees like zoo animals. Arab Nationalism was another regular theme in its pronouncements, even though Arab Nationalism was more dead in Lebanon than in any other country around.

"The U.N. says Hezbollah started the last fight," I said to the lieutenant. "Do you ever start any fights?"

"They always initiate," he said. "We never do. I want to go home. I want to read the newspaper and get more than three hours of sleep every night. We have no business here."

"Are you scared?" I said.

"I am scared," he said. "As an officer, I want my men to be scared."

"Are they?" I said.

"Not enough," he said. "Not enough."

⌒

Lisa and I followed Zvika as he led us in his jeep to the kibbutz of Malkiya right on the border, within immediate striking distance of Hezbollah's rockets and mortars.

He pulled off to the side of the road, pointed out a U.N. base just over the fence on the Lebanese side, and yelled something at the U.N. soldiers in Hindi. They waved and hollered back, also in Hindi. By happy coincidence, both Zvika and the peacekeepers were from India. Theirs was, perhaps, the only verbal communication that ever crossed that fence.

At Malkiya we met Eitan Oren, an Israeli Kurd from Eastern Turkey. He gave Lisa and me a quick tour of the place, which was unremarkable in almost every way. It looked, to my eyes anyway, like just another small Israeli town, only with fewer roads and more footpaths connecting the buildings.

"It's dying here," Eitan said. "Socialism is out. Capitalism is in. The ideology collapsed. I was never a socialist. I don't belong in the concrete jungle of Tel Aviv. I'm a nature boy. I belong here."

Here, though, was right on the rim of a volcano. Hezbollahland was *right there*. And, as Zvika kept telling Lisa and me, the border was gearing up to explode.

The four of us got into Eitan's pickup so he could take us on a brief driving tour.

"Since our withdrawal, the enemy—*Hizb Allah*—is on the fence," he said. "See that post on the mountain?" A rocky hill loomed above us just over the border with a small square building on top of it. I could just barely make out a Hezbollah flag when I squinted. "They are watching us right now. You are safe, though."

"Don't believe what he says," Zvika said and laughed darkly. "You are not particularly safe right now."

I later met a young Israeli woman who had also moved from Turkey to Israel. She toured the border with some university classmates, and they found themselves face-to-face with Hezbollah militiamen patrolling their side of the fence.

"It was terrifying," she said. "They bared their teeth at us like wolves. One of them slashed his throat with his finger."

Zvika took off the top half of his uniform and stripped down to a T-shirt so he would look like a civilian. He did that, I think, to protect Eitan, Lisa, and me more than himself.

Eitan pulled off the main road and into his peach orchard next to the fence.

"Lots of drug fields right across the border right here," he said. "Across the border are mostly Shias. We used to have a *great* relationship with them."

That was sort of true, up to a point. Israelis once had a great relationship with *some* of the Lebanese Shias who served in the South Lebanon Army, worked day jobs in Israel, or even went down there as tourists through Fatima Gate.

"Nasrallah is a bright guy," Eitan said. "I wish his energy were directed toward something good, but Hezbollah has been infected by Iran."

"What do you think of ordinary people on the other side?" I said.

"Every day I wave at Lebanese people," he said.

"Do they ever wave back?" I said.

"Not usually, no," he said. "They are cold. A few are friendly, though."

"Do you know why most of them are cold?" I said.

I wasn't sure how much Israelis knew about why things were the way they were inside Lebanon. He already knew I had been living in Beirut, and he could tell by the tone of my voice that I knew the answer.

"I don't know," he said. "Why?"

"Because waving hello to an Israeli is treason," I said.

He looked startled and more than a little disturbed.

"I didn't know that," he said. "Some wave hello to me anyway. Do you know why?" I didn't. "Because they are my friends. They *know* me." He sounded more cheerful now. "We used to work together when the border was open. Come with me, my friends. I want to show you something."

Lisa, Zvika, and I got into his pickup and drove for another few minutes along the fence.

We got out at an elevated clearing.

"Look at this," Eitan said and pointed to what was left of a small stone structure just off the road. "It's the old British customs building."

The walls were mostly intact, but the roof was gone. It appeared to have been damaged in war, as though a rocket or mortar had landed on top of it.

"Look over there," he said and pointed into Lebanon. "You see that destroyed building just on the other side of the fence? That's the old French customshouse."

The French building obviously had been destroyed by charges placed at the base. The roof was almost at ground level; the building had pancaked onto itself.

"It, too, was used when the Lebanese-Israeli border was open," Eitan said. "Hezbollah blew it away. Nasrallah wanted to make sure there was no contact at all between our two peoples."

It's a lot easier to hate people when you don't know them personally, when you can't hang out and talk, when you don't work together, and when you can't wave hello. An open border and a free exchange of thoughts and ideas was Hezbollah's worst nightmare. The vitriolic and eliminationist propaganda from Iran and Hezbollah was instantly proven ridiculous upon contact with average Israelis.

"What do you want to see happen here, Eitan?" I said.

"I wish we could have peace and an open border," he said. "Like a normal country. Like it is between Oregon and California. Right now we call the Lebanese enemies. But they are not really enemies. I know them. Some are my friends. The only enemy is Hezbollah."

Eitan and Zvika leaned against the front of the truck. Eitan thought Israel's withdrawal from South Lebanon was a mistake.

"Hezbollah is the only Arab army to ever defeat us," he said.

Zvika patiently shook his head. "They didn't defeat us," he said.

They got into a minor civil argument about it. The officer thought it was wise to withdraw the armed forces. The civilian did not. The officer insisted Hezbollah did not defeat Israel. The civilian insisted Hezbollah did. The officer feared Hezbollah. The civilian did not and even seemed to respect Hassan Nasrallah as well as Lebanon's Shia civilians. The officer's point of view made sense. Eitan's was a bundle of unworked-out contradictions.

Israelis couldn't reach out in friendship and park tanks on Lebanese streets at the same time, especially not after all that bloody history. There was something else, too, something Eitan had not seemed to consider. The only reason Hezbollah lost its popularity in Lebanon was because Israel had withdrawn to its side of the border. Lebanese didn't like Israelis occupying their land any more than they liked Syrians occupying their land. The Cedar Revolution may not even have happened if Israel still occupied part of Lebanon in 2005. Syria may well have seemed like the lesser of enemies.

Eitan took us back to Malkiya and showed us the community day care and nursery. He told me the residents built their nursery in the center of the kibbutz, where the children are surrounded by protective adults, "just as a baby in the womb is protected by the body of its mother."

Stairs led down a passageway under the children's playground to an entombed concrete bomb shelter. I wondered how on earth the adults could raise infants mere feet from murderous enemies, but I didn't ask. The question was too implicitly critical. I liked Eitan, and I wasn't about to tell him how he should raise his children.

He seemed to sense my unease, though, and said it would be a catastrophe if the northern part of his country were left abandoned and darkened.

The Lebanese on the other side of the fence felt the same way. Most didn't realize Israel had no intention of reoccupying South Lebanon. They also felt like they were on the rim of a volcano. Most Shias in the south felt safer thanks to Hezbollah. Hezbollah did an excellent job of convincing its support base that it was a defender of Lebanon rather than a potential magnet for an invasion.

Lisa and I stopped at the grocery store on our way out and bought snacks for the road. We had two more stops to make before returning to Tel Aviv. Eitan came with us into the store. When I pulled cash out of my pocket, he told me to put it away.

"We don't use money here," he said. "This is a community!" Zionist socialism suddenly seemed a little less dead than he had let on.

Lisa and I said our good-byes to Eitan and Zvika, got back in the rental car, and headed up the road toward Metula and Ghajar.

Metula was the place Leena had shown me, the one I first thought was in Lebanon. It was so close to the fence that a Lebanese kid could hit somebody's house with a rock. Lisa and I wanted to see the Israeli side of nearby Fatima Gate, which Israelis called The Good Fence.

She told me that several groups of Israelis had driven up there and peacefully confronted the rock throwers. "We don't hate you," they said.

It never did any good. People who went out of their way to throw rocks at others couldn't be easily dissuaded by niceness. Besides, being friendly with Israelis was treason.

The road to Fatima Gate was closed that day. IDF soldiers told us we weren't allowed beyond a barricade that shuttered the road. So we drove on toward Ghajar, the Alawite village that had been split down the middle between Israel and Lebanon and that one day might be returned to Syria.

This was where Hezbollah launched its most recent invasion the previous November.[2] Lisa told me she saw local Arab residents screaming on the television news, demanding that Israel ramp up

116 EVERYTHING COULD EXPLODE AT ANY MOMENT

the security in their town and better protect them from Iran's proxy killers.

She and I both wanted to interview some of these people. I wanted to explore the prosperous Israeli side and compare it with the destitute Alawite Village I had seen in Lebanon. It didn't look promising, though. Everyone driving into Ghajar had to navigate a slalom-like obstacle course of concrete blocks just to get to a checkpoint.

The soldiers at the checkpoint turned us back for our protection. They were braced for an attack. Everything could explode at any moment.

CHAPTER EIGHT
the july war

Israel's final departure
from Lebanon is a prelude
to its final obliteration
from existence.
—HEZBOLLAH

Early in the morning on July 12, 2006, Ehud Goldwasser and Eldad Regev were on patrol near the Northern Israeli town of Zar'it, just south of the border with Lebanon, when unseen guerrillas ambushed their Humvee. Three of their fellow soldiers were killed in the attack, but Goldwasser and Regev fared even worse: they were captured by Hezbollah and dragged over the border fence into the wilds of South Lebanon.[1]

The Israeli response was formidable. Another Israel Defense Forces soldier, Gilad Shalit, had been snatched just two weeks before by Palestinians and smuggled through a tunnel into Gaza. Israelis were in no mood to tolerate cross-border attacks on two fronts at once. Prime Minister Ehud Olmert promised[2] "a very painful and far-reaching response." He launched artillery and air strikes at Hezbollah's positions in South Lebanon, at the command and control centers in the suburbs south of Beirut, and at infrastructure throughout the country, including roads, bridges, and Beirut's international airport.

Hezbollah's response was likewise ferocious. Its fighters fired thousands of World War II-era Katyusha rockets at Israeli civilian-population areas in the cities of Haifa, Kiryat Shmona, Nazareth, and Tiberias. The entire northern sixth of the country—including Arab-majority areas—was blanketed with constant daily rocket attacks. Hezbollah wanted a brief border skirmish and an exchange of prisoners but instead found itself in a full-scale war that produced millions of refugees and devastated parts of both countries.

I was in Iraq when it started and could not get back to Lebanon—the Israeli Air Force had put holes in the runway at the airport to prevent Hezbollah from flying the captured soldiers out to Iran. So I teamed up with my friend and colleague Noah Pollak, then-assistant editor at *Azure* magazine in Jerusalem, and took a rental car from Tel Aviv to the Israeli side of the front.

By then the war had been blazing for weeks. The Israeli government was proposing a cease-fire to end it even though Israel had so far gained practically nothing. It wasn't yet over, but it was already widely seen as a debacle. There was talk in the local newspapers about removing Olmert from the prime minister's office immediately. But the farther north we drove, the less relevant any talk of cease-fires and parliaments seemed. The fighting raged on, and we were approaching Hezbollah's shooting gallery.

Haifa, Israel's third-largest city, was empty and burning, as was every other city in the country near the Lebanese border.

Traffic thinned as we drove, but we hadn't yet seen overt signs of war. At some point we would cross an invisible boundary between the "safe" part of Israel, supposedly beyond the range of Hezbollah's rockets, and the kill zone. Neither Noah nor I knew exactly where that boundary was, but every mile we traveled brought us closer.

When we arrived at the resort town of Tiberias on the shore of the Sea of Galilee, it looked like a city at the end of the world. The streets were entirely empty of people and cars. More than a million civilians had packed up their valuables and fled south in their vehicles. Only a handful of brave, elderly, sick, poor, stubborn, and possibly suicidal people remained. It would have made a terrific set for a zombie movie.

"Stop the car," I said to Noah. "I want to get out."

Noah stopped the car in the middle of a major intersection. There was no need to pull over or park because there was no traffic.

I stepped out of the car. It was the middle of summer, and we were well below sea level. The air was unbearably hot, humid, heavy, and still. Nothing moved. Nothing seemed real. I heard no sound at all, except the chirping of birds, in the middle of a major city at noon. *We shouldn't be here*, I thought. I expected an explosion at any moment, but I couldn't see any damage and wasn't sure whether we were actually inside, or just near, Hezbollah's rocket range.

I got back in the car and we continued to drive. Just past the city and beyond the shores of the sea, we saw hillsides scorched from Katyusha fire. We were inside the zone now and could be killed at any time without warning.

As we approached the city of Kiryat Shmona, I braced for hell. It seemed to be Hezbollah's target of choice. It was so close to the border—less than two miles away—that there was no time to warn civilians to head to the bomb shelters when incoming rockets were detected on radar. They often exploded at the same instant the air-raid sirens turned on, and sometimes even before.

Storms of incoming rockets moved through the north like malevolent weather. Lisa Goldman had been up there just a few days earlier with a colleague, and she described the scene as a horror.

"The nearly abandoned city reminded us of scenes in Hollywood movies set in Grozny," she wrote,[3] "or Sarajevo, circa 1992. Brush fires set off by Hezbollah rockets blazed everywhere, creating a thick pall of smoke that dimmed the usually bright Levantine sunlight. Bits of ash floated about like snowflakes, the smell of smoke permeated the air and was absorbed in my clothes and hair. And the constant booms, explosions and sirens provided loud background music—a live, postmodern version of Albinoni's *Adagio in G Minor* for this long shot of *Apocalypse Now: The Middle Eastern Version*." Lisa and her journalist colleague drove as fast as physically possible through burning streets, walls of fire just feet from each side of the car.

Noah and I heard air-raid sirens wailing even out in the countryside as we closed in on the city. Israeli civil defense instructed everyone to pull over and get out of and away from their cars when they heard the sirens. A nearby explosion could startle drivers and cause them to crash. That wasn't all. Katyusha shrapnel punctured vehicles as though they were made of paper, and direct hits to gas tanks instantly turned cars and trucks into fireballs.

When we finally reached the city, it looked surprisingly okay from the main road. Although we drove fast through the streets and the nonfunctioning traffic signals, I saw no fires, no smoke, and no serious damage. It was a good day to drive through.

I unfolded our map and looked for the turnoff to Kibbutz Misgav Am. Military historian Michael Oren, author of *Six Days of War*[4] and spokesman for the IDF Northern Command, waited for us there. It wasn't clear which road we should take, so after we passed Kiryat Shmona, we pulled off to the side of the road and asked directions from two officers in an idle police car.

I stepped out into the road and nearly jumped out of my skin as I heard and felt a loud *BOOM* from just on the other side of a nearby hill.

"Outgoing," Noah said to put me at ease. I laughed and said "Of course," although to me at the time there was no such thing as *of course*. Noah had visited the border just a few days before and was much more comfortable in that environment. I hadn't yet learned to distinguish the sounds of incoming and outgoing.

The officers told us how to get to Kibbutz Misgav Am, which was was near a military base on the border. They didn't ask us who we were, what we were doing, or why on earth we wanted to go there. War creates a crazily "libertarian" environment where, as was said in the time of the Roman Empire, the law falls silent.

Once we knew where we were going, Noah and I drove through an increasingly dodgy-looking environment where tents, tanks, and heavy artillery pieces were set up in fields burned away by incoming fire.

We turned left past Kiryat Shmona and drove up the steep hill toward the base. Thick smoke boiled off the top of a ridge. Israel was on fire. I did not want to be there.

Concrete bomb-blast walls lined the road. In a few short minutes, we reached Misgav Am overlooking the snaking fence on the Lebanese border. Noah parked next to the remains of a car that had taken a direct hit and was utterly blown apart. The largest piece remaining was a hubcap. A thick black oil spot pooled in the center of the former car's wreckage.

I stepped out of our car and braced for an explosion. The Israelis fired artillery shells over our heads every couple of moments toward points unknown on the other side of the horizon. I jumped every time and tried in vain to get used to it.

Noah approached a reservist sitting next to a bomb-blast wall and asked if he knew where we could find IDF Spokesman Michael Oren. The reservist had never heard of him. Oren would later become Israel's ambassador to the United States.

"It's quiet today compared with yesterday," the reservist said. "A rocket fell thirty meters from me yesterday. But I just kept reading the newspaper."

"How can you *do* that?" I said. I felt raw and exposed, horribly vulnerable to Hezbollah's random destruction. Even the thunderous sound of outgoing ordnance made me want to dive into the dirt.

"I have to keep myself normal and clear," he said. "I have been here for three weeks. There have been lots of rockets in Haifa today. But none here."

Earsplitting outgoing artillery shells exploded from cannons just a few dozen yards from where I stood. Car alarms went off everywhere. Ten thousand volts of adrenaline instantly kicked into my system. I instinctively ducked my head and wondered, for a split second, whether I should take cover behind the wall. For the uninitiated, even the sounds of nonthreatening outgoing fire trigger every urgent survival mechanism in the human body.

Three Katyusha rockets slammed into the side of the Golan Heights on the other side of the valley. Rockets often landed in clusters. Hezbollah usually fired several rockets at once in the same direction. If one hit anywhere even vaguely near you, watch out. More were probably coming.

I didn't know what the Israeli army was shooting at when they fired their shells into Lebanon. Those who fired the shells didn't know either. Unlike Hezbollah, though, they were shooting at actual targets. They were not just firing at random toward Lebanese farmland and towns. IDF soldiers on the other side of the border marked specific targets and called in coordinates.

Michael Oren still hadn't arrived. Where was he? Noah and I got back in the car and drove down the hill toward Kiryat Shmona. Noah punched Oren's number into his cell phone.

"Where are you guys?" he said and paused. "Okay, we'll wait for you at the bottom of the hill."

So we drove to the bottom of the hill and got out of the car next to an open field arrayed with tanks and gigantic guns.

Bang, followed by an arcing tear in the atmosphere.

Bang, followed by the sound of ripping sky.

A mile or so in front of us, a series of glowing surface-to-surface missiles hurtled toward Lebanon at impossible speeds and somehow got faster as they flew farther.

Jets screamed overhead on their way into Lebanon. The Israeli Air Force scrambled their fighters to take out Katyusha launchers and rain down hell from the sky onto Hezbollah's critical infrastructure—especially in the town of Bint Jbail and in the *dahiyeh*.

The air-raid sirens wailed. Rockets were detected crossing the border, which was less than a mile from where we were standing. Noah and I moved into a bus stop fitted with bomb-blast walls and hoped the rockets would hit the fortified side, not the open side, if they landed anywhere near us.

Bang. Bang. More outgoing artillery. Shells tore menacingly across the sky in an arc over my head.

The air-raid siren kept wailing. It sounded like World War II outside.

Hurry up and get here, Michael Oren, I thought. *I can't take much more of this.*

Whump. An incoming Katyusha landed somewhere off in the distance. The air-raid siren winded down.

"Man, this is intense," I said to Noah. "Are we crazy to be here?"

"Probably," he said.

～

We finally found Michael Oren back up top where we had looked for him before, standing on a ridge next to some bushes and squinting through binoculars at Lebanon in the distance.

Noah knew Oren from the Shalem Center in Jerusalem and introduced me to him. Oren greeted both of us warmly.

The Israeli government was proposing a cease-fire. I wanted to know what Oren thought of it, although I suspected already that he wasn't thrilled. Israel had accomplished very few of its objectives in Lebanon.

"It's probably the best we could get under the circumstances," he said. "We don't have a lot of leverage right now."

Israel's Second Lebanon War looked, to me anyway, like a disaster in the making almost from the very beginning. Successful foreign interventions are nearly impossible to pull off in Lebanon without either massive public support from the Lebanese—something the Israelis were extremely unlikely to ever receive—or a massive deployment of ruthless brute force of the sort only the Syrians had recently been comfortable using.

The war almost looked as though it might have gone differently during the first couple of hours. Many Lebanese initially shrugged at Israel's opening counterstrike. Everyone knew Hezbollah started it, and the Party of God wasn't well liked by the majority of Lebanese anyway. Some even welcomed and cheered Israel's bloody-minded reaction. The Lebanese army wasn't strong or cohesive enough to give Iran's private militia a thrashing, so if the Israelis didn't fight Hezbollah, nobody would fight Hezbollah.

That sentiment didn't last long. Olmert blamed the Lebanese government, not just Hezbollah, for the attack. It didn't matter to most Israelis that the Lebanese government had nothing to do with the killing and kidnapping of their soldiers—the attack came from inside Lebanese territory. So the Israeli Air Force destroyed targets even in areas outside Hezbollah's control. Even some Christian and Sunni regions where the overwhelming majority despised Hezbollah were hit by Israeli air strikes.[5]

Sympathy inside Lebanon for the Israeli "enemy of my enemy" plunged after that happened. Hezbollah briefly managed to rebrand itself as a national fighting force. Israel's air strikes overwhelmingly landed in Hezbollah-controlled areas, but not all of them did, so almost everyone in Lebanon felt like they could be killed. The Lebanese army—as usual during Israel's wars—sat out the fighting. If Hezbollah didn't fight the Israelis, nobody would fight the Israelis.

Temporarily lost in all this was the fact that Israelis wouldn't be shooting at Lebanon in the first place if it weren't for Hezbollah.

On July 30, 2006, Lebanese rage against Israel reached its apogee when history eerily repeated itself. The Israeli Air Force destroyed a three-story building in the village of al-Khuraybah near the larger town of Qana. Twenty-eight people, many of them children, were killed.[6] IDF Chief of Staff Dan Halutz apologized for the deaths of civilians and blamed Hezbollah for using them as human shields. Lebanese Prime Minister Fouad Siniora accused Israel of committing a war crime.

Killing civilians near Qana—and it didn't matter whether or not the Israelis did it on purpose—was bound to send the Lebanese over the edge. Qana was where a nearly identical incident took place ten years earlier. On April 18, 1996, the IDF shelled a United Nations compound while Hezbollah fired Katyusha rockets into Northern Israel from a few hundred yards away.[7] One hundred and six people were killed. The incident is known inside Lebanon as the Qana Massacre, and it is infamous.

Whatever remaining scrap of sympathy or understanding some Lebanese had for Israel's point of view vaporized after "Qana" was repeated. The Israelis knew they screwed up, and they knew they screwed up badly. Air strikes were halted for forty-eight hours even as the Katyusha rockets kept flying.

I told Michael Oren that I'm not normally pessimistic about the performance of Western armies in wars but that this one didn't look good. Cities, towns, villages, roads, bridges, and houses in Lebanon had been bombed. Hundreds of civilians had been killed. Hezbollah fighters had also been killed, but the Katyushas were still flying just as fast and as often as they were at the beginning. It didn't look like much had been accomplished. Hezbollah, astonishingly, was popular in Lebanon all over again, yet another civil war could easily ignite once the inevitable postwar backlash kicked in.

"Talk me out of it," I said. "Tell me if I'm wrong."

He didn't want to say much. I could tell from the look on his face that he was not happy either, but he was an official spokesman and had to be careful with what he said on the record.

"Has anything been permanently accomplished up there?" I said.

"Some things, yes," he said. "We destroyed a lot of their infrastructure. They had more weapons and more underground bunkers and tunnels than we had any idea. People coming out of there say it's vast."

"What do you think about the proposal for an international force on the border?" I said. The United Nations would, in fact, soon put more troops on the Lebanese side of the border ostensibly to prevent Hezbollah from controlling that part of the country again.

"The problem with that," he said, "is that the force could act as a shield for Hezbollah. Hezbollah could fire missiles right over the tops of their heads and make it very difficult for us to go in there and stop them. It needs to be a combat force in Lebanon, not a peacekeeping force."

"Hassan Nasrallah declared victory today," I said.

Oren laughed. Of course he would laugh. It was obvious well in advance that Hezbollah's secretary general would declare victory no matter what happened as long as he wasn't captured or killed. The Arab bar for military victory had been set low for decades. All their side had to do was survive. They "won" even if their country was torn to pieces. The very idea of a Pyrrhic victory, where losses exceed paltry gains, seemed not to occur to leaders incapable of defeating the State of Israel in battle.

"Look at Nasrallah today," Oren said. "In 2000 he did his victory dance in Bint Jbail. He can't do that this time. His command and control south of Beirut is completely gone. We killed 550 Hezbollah fighters south of the Litani River out of an active force of 1,250. Nasrallah claimed South Lebanon would be the graveyard of the IDF, but we only lost one tenth of 1 percent of our soldiers in South Lebanon. The only thing that went according to his plan was their ability to keep firing rockets. If he has enough victories like this one, he's dead."

"Have Hezbollah's fighting techniques evolved or degraded since 2000?" I said.

"They're the same," he said. "They're good. These guys are very experienced. They have been fighting for a long time. But we've killed more than 25 percent of their fighting force. I think they'll break. All armies break. Killing even 1 percent of a Western army is a disaster. It's prohibitive."

Another IDF spokesman stood at Oren's side. I was surprised to see this guy. He was the famous Hollywood screenwriter Dan Gordon, and he volunteered for the job. Credits to his name include *The Hurricane* with Denzel Washington and 1994's *Wyatt Earp*. I thought it was crazy that an American civilian would volunteer to work in a Middle Eastern war zone until I remembered that I was doing exactly the same thing myself.

Gordon walked me to another lookout point just at the top of another ridge over Lebanon. A village with apparently intact buildings lay just below. We had no cover. The windows of the buildings looked threatening. The last time I stood on that border just a few months earlier, Zvika Golan warned me that Hezbollah might be watching us through a sniper scope.

"Have you had any sniper attacks?" I asked Gordon.

"Yes, actually we have," he said and stepped back. "This is probably not a good place for us to be standing."

I thought it strange that I was more sensitive to the danger than he was. That, I suppose, was an advantage of being unaccustomed to war zones. My extreme discomfort kept me from feeling like I was invincible. That would come later after I adapted.

"Hardly any journalists have mentioned this," he said, "but at the very beginning of this thing, when Hezbollah captured our soldiers, they also tried to invade, conquer, and hold the town of Metula along with two other towns. And they were repulsed."

Of course Hezbollah was repulsed. It was a guerrilla army. It didn't have standard infantry troops.

"We do have one serious asset from this war," he said. "Hassan Nasrallah got his ass kicked. And he knows it."

"Did he really get his ass kicked?" I said. "The IDF fought Hezbollah for years to a standstill before. What made you think it would be easy to get rid of them this time?"

"This time it's different," he said. "This time we're going in there to kill them. We are not trying to hold on to territory. This is actually working. We are not stuck in the mud. Oh, and here's another tangible: Hezbollah-occupied Lebanon no longer exists."

Later I received a phone call from my friend and colleague Allison Kaplan Sommer in Tel Aviv. "Have you heard the news?" she said.

I hadn't.

Neither had Dan Gordon. Neither had Michael Oren.

"The cease-fire is dead," she said. "The ground invasion is starting."

Individual ground units had been making brief jaunts into Lebanon from the beginning, but Olmert had just decided to launch the real thing.

Noah and I lost access to our spokesmen. The war was ramping up and they were summoned to meetings. So we drove to the border town of Metula, the one Hezbollah had tried to invade, and watched Israel's invasion of Lebanon from the roof of the Alaska Inn.

⌒

War does strange things to the mind. The first time you hear the loud *boom*, *bang*, and *crash* of incoming and outgoing artillery, you will jump. You will twitch. You will want to take cover. You will want to hide. You will feel like you could die at any second, like the air around you is drenched with gasoline, like the universe is gearing up to smash you to pieces.

It's amazing how fast you get used to it, even if you have no military training and grew up in tranquil suburban America.

It took me four hours.

Any given location in Northern Israel and South Lebanon would almost certainly never be hit with a missile, bullet, bomb, or artillery shell. Lebanon was hit more frequently, and Israel was hit more randomly, but the vast majority of people in both places weren't even scratched, let alone killed.

Explosions jack your survival instinct up to eleven, but after a while, straight math kicks in. You run numbers in your head, even subconsciously. Most places aren't ever hit, so what were the odds, really, that you would be standing in one of the few places that were hit at the precise moment it happened?

Being under fire in Northern Israel was not like, say, walking around loose by myself in Baghdad. No one was out to get *me*. Only Hezbollah fighters and its leaders in Lebanon were targeted as individuals. All of Northern Israel was a collective target, but a very large one that I vanished into almost completely.

The odds that any given place in Northern Israel would be hit were the same as the odds that any other given place in Northern Israel would be hit. Hezbollah's rockets landed almost at random. They were pathetic military weapons, but perfect terrorist weapons.

There were a few exceptions. Kiryat Shmona was hit quite a lot. Metula was hit hardly at all, although Hezbollah did fire a mortar round into the side of the Alaska Inn two hours before Noah and I arrived. Still, anywhere out in the open was just as dangerous as anywhere else out in the open.

This is logical, but the mind doesn't always work like that when sensing danger from the environment.

Driving on an empty road and looking at an impact site up ahead was unsettling. Kibbutz HaGoshrim put me at ease because it was idyllic and sheltered by shade trees. Yet neither location was safer or more dangerous than the other.

The trees at the kibbutz blocked out the sky and made me feel protected. Obviously, the branches of trees could do nothing to stop or slow a Katyusha rocket, but when you're under fire from above, the sky feels like a gigantic malevolent eyeball. When you're underneath trees, the gigantic malevolent eyeball can't see you. Therefore a rocket won't hit you. That's not how it was, but that's what it felt like.

During my first several hours in the war zone, I constantly tried to figure out what I could do to make myself safer. Should I stand here instead of there? How about if I crouch down a little bit? Maybe if I sit on the ground, a rocket will miss my head? I figured it was better to stand near things than away from things, as long as those things were not cars.

All this thinking was useless. I would either be hit or I wouldn't. Walking or driving faster could get me away from an incoming rocket, or it could get me closer. It was all totally random.

Fear has a purpose. It forces you to think hard and fast about what you can or must do to protect yourself. As soon as you realize there is nothing more you can do, fear loses its purpose and vanishes. It really does.

New York City immediately after September 11, 2001, was a much scarier place than Northern Israel during the war once I got used to it. It wasn't *safer*, not even remotely, but there is only so much adrenaline in the human body.

This is the fatal weakness of terrorism. What's a terrorist to do once the terror wears off?

While Noah and I sat on the roof of Metula's Alaska Inn watching Israel gear up for the ground invasion, a voice below blared something in Hebrew over a loudspeaker.

"What was that?" Noah asked an Israeli woman standing next to us.

"He said, 'Go to the shelters because a rocket is about to hit the roof of the hotel,'" she said.

"Seriously?" I said.

"No," she said and laughed. "But a rocket really is coming. It really is time to go to the shelters."

We waited for the elevator. It seemed to take forever.

"Where is the shelter, anyway?" I said.

"I don't know," the Israeli woman said.

The elevator doors opened. We all got in. It took ages to get down to the lobby.

When the doors opened on the main floor, none of the people in the lobby or restaurant were moving. They were all perfectly calm as though nothing out of the ordinary was happening. All of us, though, heard the sirens.

Everyone knows fear is contagious. What I think is less understood is that calm is also contagious.

I walked up to the front desk and asked the young man standing next to the register whether they had a bomb shelter.

"Of course," he said.

"Should we go down there or does nobody care?" I said.

"Nobody cares," he said.

"Let's get a Coke," Noah said.

So we grabbed two seats in the restaurant and asked the waiter for two Cokes.

I heard a faint *whump* somewhere off in the distance. The rocket had landed. Nobody moved. Nobody cared.

~

The Israel Defense Forces wanted to snap up as much territory as possible between the border fence and the Litani River before agreeing to the cease-fire that ended the war. And it didn't take long to reach the Litani.

From our perch on the roof, Noah and I watched as much as we could. All day long, outgoing artillery shells tore through the sky on their way to Hezbollah targets. As soon as the ground invasion was set to start, all fell eerily quiet.

For a brief period, the only visible evidence of war was a fire burning in a Lebanese field off to our right.

Just south of Metula, the war was a little more obvious, even though it was quiet there, too. Tanks and heavy artillery were set up in an idyllic field. It was a jarring sight. The scenery was lovely in Northern Israel. Lots of Israelis and foreigners liked to visit on holiday because it was so picturesque and serene, yet war machinery was scattered all over the place. War, in my mind, was supposed to occur in ugly places.

The Israeli invasion of Lebanon didn't look like an American invasion of anyplace. When Americans go to war, they fly to the other side of the world and spend weeks or even months preparing, then push hundreds of miles through enemy territory on the way to their targets. Israeli soldiers just took out some wire cutters, snipped holes in the fence, and *walked* into Lebanon.

Tanks rolled into Lebanon, too. From the top of the Alaska, Noah and I saw a whole line of them getting ready to blast through Fatima Gate into Hezbollah's territory.

The scene was ominous, but it felt perfectly calm. Birds chirped. You could have put the sunset on a postcard. The streets of Metula were clean and well ordered. A man in sweatpants, a T-shirt, and running shoes jogged down the sidewalk with his dog alongside him, its tongue lolling out the side of its mouth. I waved hello to an elderly grandmother in her gardening hat drinking from a tall slender glass on her front porch. Why on earth hadn't these people left with everyone else?

Noah ordered ravioli in a restaurant and I ordered pizza. I asked a woman behind the counter whether she was being paid extra wages for serving food in a war zone. "No," she said and shrugged, as if to say, Why should they pay me more money?

Shepard Smith from Fox News broadcast live from the roof of the Alaska, although I doubt he had much to report. Little was going on at the time. Metula was a nice little town with restaurants and bed-and-breakfasts. And that's what it looked and felt like, at least while the war lulled for a few hours.

Shortly after the sunset, Noah and I walked down the street to the line of tanks just outside town so we could interview some of the soldiers.

A young soldier with sunglasses and a pierced eyebrow asked me to take his picture. "Put me in your magazine," he said, "next to the hot models in swimsuits and lingerie."

"I'll see what I can do," I said and laughed.

I raised my camera to take another soldier's picture.

"No, no, no!" he said and held up his hand. "Last time I went into Lebanon, every guy with me who had his picture taken earlier that day was injured. None of us who didn't have our pictures taken were injured. I know it's superstitious and stupid, but I need to feel good before I go in there."

"What's it like fighting Hezbollah?" I said.

"It depends," he said.

"On what?" I said.

"On the place and on the day," he said. "Sometimes when we go into Lebanon, nothing happens. We can't find the Hezbollah. Other times they are everywhere and it's hard."

"Do you ever see civilians?" I said.

"No," he said. "Not in the towns. Only in the villages."

"What do they do when they see you?" I said.

"They go inside," he said.

"Do they say anything to you?" I said.

"No," he said. "They don't say anything, they don't wave, they don't throw rocks. They just go in their houses."

Noah chatted with two young men who were getting ready to push into Lebanon ahead of the tanks to clear mines. They didn't seem nervous at all, although their work must have been extraordinarily stressful.

That was about all we could get out of the soldiers. They seemed happy to see us, not at all suspicious that we might be hostile journalists or even anything *other* than journalists. No one asked us to show credentials, but they didn't want to say much specific. I got the impression they enjoyed having us around as a distraction from the grim work ahead.

"Can we go with you guys into Lebanon?" Noah asked one of the soldiers.

"Do you *want* to?" the soldier said.

"Yeah," Noah said.

The soldier didn't know if it was possible. Maybe it was, and maybe it wasn't.

I didn't want to. I would later embed with American soldiers and Marines in Iraq, but I felt queasy about hitching a ride with an army on its way into Lebanon. I wasn't Lebanese, and I didn't like Hezbollah any more than the Israelis did, but Lebanon was the closest thing I had in the world to a second home.

One Israeli soldier I spoke to whom I'll call Eli spent the entire war in and out of South Lebanon. He and his unit worked in some villages nine or so miles in from Metula. His job was to go in and mark artillery targets.

"These whole villages," he said, "they were empty, just filled with Hezbollah terrorists. No civilians were walking around South Lebanon. I know. I was in their villages. In their houses. Anyone who was there was definitely working for the Hezbollah or working as a Hezbollah fighter."

"You didn't see any women?" I said. "It was mostly men and no children?"

"I never saw one woman or any children in Lebanon," he said. "I was going in and out for the whole time since the day the soldiers were kidnapped. We flew from my unit straight to the north in helicopters."

Houses all over South Lebanon were destroyed, sometimes by Hezbollah, mostly by Israelis. It's not clear, though, that Israelis deserved most of the blame. Not only did Hezbollah build houses explicitly for use during a war but they also used civilians and their strictly residential houses as shields. They hid behind private homes and fired rockets from inside populated areas. The Israeli Air Force took out every rocket launcher it could, thus destroying much of the civilian infrastructure next to the launchers.

"Did they use populated areas to fire?" Eli said. "It was clear that they did. Except Israel also dispersed fliers ordering all the civilian population of South Lebanon to leave. Anyone who was in those villages was probably helping Hezbollah fighters. Hezbollah could take any house they wanted because the whole place was empty. Everyone left. When we were fighting, we were fighting from house to house. They would just skip houses and go to a different house. We would detonate one house; they would fire a few from another house and skip to yet another one. They would go wherever they wanted. It was their area in South Lebanon. It's not like *they* thought about them as civilian houses."

Australian reporter Chris Link published revealing photographs in the *Herald Sun* newspaper on July 30, 2006, that showed Hezbollah fighters wearing civilian clothes and operating an antiaircraft gun in a suburban neighborhood.[8] Perhaps Hezbollah neither knew nor cared, but installing military targets like antiaircraft guns in residential neighborhoods is against the laws of war. It recklessly endangers the civilians who live there. Meanwhile, destroying an antiaircraft gun in a residential neighborhood with an air strike *isn't* a war crime. The laws and conventions of war are absolutely clear about this,[9] and they squarely said Hezbollah was at fault for turning those areas into targets.

"If there was a full-out war," Eli said, "you know, tanks against tanks, combat units against combat units, and everything done out in the open—Israel would definitely, *totally* defeat and win. Guerrilla warfare is extremely hard. It's stressful because it's not a real army; it's not an army. It's like cells. You're fighting against cells that are operated by bigger cells."

The Americans were fighting the same kind of war at the same time just a few hundred miles away in Iraq. It wasn't going much better for the U.S. than it was for Israel. The Americans were just as bewildered in Iraq as the Israelis were in Lebanon. Both fought invisible enemies in the alleyways of an alien society where they had little leverage. American soldiers and Marines weren't strictly limited to one- or two-day little jaunts into Iraq followed by hasty withdrawals, and at least they weren't trying to fight a counterinsurgency primarily with the Air Force, but the wars in both Lebanon and Iraq were going badly for similar reasons. Guerrilla fighters and terrorists were humbling two of the most powerful and sophisticated armed forces in history. Whatever institutional knowledge about effective counterinsurgency strategies that once existed within the ranks of Western military officers seemed, in the middle of 2006, to have been lost.

"There are people walking around towns," Eli said, "with weapons, who aren't wearing uniforms. They look like civilians. I mean, in every civilian house in Lebanon, there is a shotgun. And that's not because they're against the IDF or because they're against Israel; it's that most people in the small villages, they're hunters. They hunt for food. But we also saw people walking around with AK-47s and handguns. Those are definitely Hezbollah people in civilian clothes."

Arabs were once among the most militarily powerful people on earth. Shortly after the founding of Islam in what today is Saudi Arabia, they surged north into Mesopotamia and the Levant and west across North Africa in a massive and rapid expansion of power. It had been a long time, though, since the Arab world fielded competent armies capable of conquering territory. Some Israelis thought that was the only reason they could even survive in the Middle East while surrounded and greatly outnumbered by enemies. When legendary war hero Moshe Dayan was asked about Israel's secret to success in modern warfare after defeating three armies in six days in 1967, he said, if you have to go to war, it helps to fight Arabs.[10]

Hezbollah fighters, though, were the most formidable enemies Israelis had ever faced. "We think of Hezbollah as the Iranian army," IDF Spokesman Jonathan Davis told me, and they were not entirely wrong in doing so.

"The chief of the military in Israel did not come from the army," Eli said. He came from the Air Force. "He did not use the ground troops as well as he should have. He would send ground troops one kilometer in, they would stay for a few days and walk out. And every time we went in and went out, people got killed."

Night fell. The Israeli soldiers were gearing up for a real ground invasion this time instead of just a quick hop over the border, and they were getting twitchy. There's something about darkness in war, even during the quiet times. All were less talkative than before, and there was clearly no way Noah and I could get any useful or interesting information out of them at that point.

So we walked the line of tanks.

"Don't be here," a soldier said.

"We're journalists," I said.

"I know," he said. "But this is a war zone. Don't be here."

So we went back to the hotel in the dark and sat on the roof.

The view north into Lebanon was an ominous sight.

The Lebanese town of Kfar Kila directly faced Metula across a small patch of farmland. There wasn't any no-man's-land in between. The two towns were in different countries, but they were almost in the exact same location. If it weren't for the border, I could have walked from one to the other in less than ten minutes.

But that night all of Lebanon was black. It was as if Lebanon did not exist. The lights of emptied Israeli ghost cities twinkled behind me, but Lebanon was enveloped in a vast darkness.

A fire burning in a Lebanese field off to my right grew bigger and brighter. No fire department existed on the other side that could douse it. South Lebanon, always lawless and beyond the control of the state, was a truly anarchic and perilous place on the night of August 11.

Distant flashes lit up the horizon. A low rumble of war in the distance sounded like thunder. It sounded like the physical breaking of Lebanon.

⌒

The next morning Noah and I heard loud automatic weapons fire coming from the other side of the fence in Kfar Kila. No one seemed to be guarding either side of the border. No one could have stopped us from walking to our doom had we been dumb enough to cross over.

We did not dare. Most of the violence was on Lebanon's side. We were near enough to hear it and could walk to it in just minutes, but we were just out of range as long as we stayed in Israel.

Far more dangerous were the Hezbollah fighters themselves. If we were caught and questioned, and if they found no recent Lebanese entry stamps in our passports, they would know we had crossed illegally from the Israeli side. We had no good reason to think we would be released unharmed under such circumstances. It's possible, and perhaps even likely, that Hezbollah would assume, if they found us, that we were Israeli intelligence agents. Risking *that* would not have been brave; it would have been stupid.

The most surprising thing about looking into Kfar Kila from Metula was how little damage was visible. I had expected to see serious destruction in the Lebanese border towns, but the towns I could see didn't appear damaged at all.

Noah scanned the buildings from the roof of the Alaska with a pair of binoculars borrowed from another reporter. He couldn't locate a single damaged building or house, not even among those that were right on the border and easiest for Israelis to hit.

Obviously, there was damage in South Lebanon. Those thousands of outgoing artillery shells weren't landing on nothing. For all I knew at the time, Hezbollah's de facto southern capital Bint Jbail was a pile of rubble. I would soon visit Bint Jbail and find that much of it really *was* a pile of rubble, but Lebanon's towns in the vicinity of Metula seemed to be more or less intact.

The war was just about over. IDF spokesmen were given gag orders and couldn't say anything to me, Noah, or anyone else. Military police shooed us away from the soldiers and told us to stay in the hotel or get out of the area. We decided it was time to head back to Tel Aviv.

Our fuel was running low, so we stopped to fill up the gas tank just south of Kiryat Shmona.

Israeli gas stations could be incredibly frustrating for foreigners. After Noah swiped his credit card at the pump, the computer asked for his Israeli national ID number. Noah lived in Israel at the time, but he's American. He didn't have a national ID number to enter. Obviously, I didn't either. So we asked an IDF soldier who happened to pull up in a truck if he would use his credit card and ID number to get us some gas if we gave him cash.

"Of course," he said and swiped his card into the machine. "Where are you guys from?" he said as he punched in his number.

"We're both Americans," Noah said.

"Are you tourists?" he said.

I laughed. "*Here?*" I said. "No, we're not tourists. We're journalists."

"There are adrenaline tourists up here," he said. "There are agents in Tel Aviv and Jerusalem who set up the tours."

It couldn't be *too* dangerous in Northern Israel if this sort of thing was going on, I thought. Surely there were no "adrenaline tours" in South Lebanon at the time.

Just then a Katyusha rocket exploded inside a residential neighborhood in Kiryat Shmona a few hundred yards from where we were standing.

"Wow," Noah said. "Let's go take pictures of that."

"No," said the soldier. "Don't go there."

More rockets often followed the first. They arrived in pairs and in threes. So we didn't go. We went kinda sorta near it, but we kept a prudent distance. We drove to a place where we could take pictures without actually standing where another rocket was likely to explode at any moment.

On the way back to Tel Aviv, we passed once again through entire towns eerily emptied of people. Very few houses or stores had been looted. It would have been easy to steal just about anything in cities depopulated of even police officers, but hardly anyone did. War brings people together with a shared sense of purpose. While the laws fell silent in the north of the country, common human decency didn't.

Common human decency held up on the Lebanese side, too, for the most part. Despite the fact that large numbers of Christians and Sunnis feared and loathed Lebanon's Shias and blamed them for starting the war, many provided shelter in their own homes for refugees fleeing the south.

Hezbollah didn't behave nearly as well.

On July 16, 2008, Hezbollah agreed to return the bodies of captured soldiers Ehud Goldwasser and Eldad Regev in exchange for Israel releasing captured Hezbollah fighters and the infamous child murderer Samir Kuntar. On April 22, 1979, in the northern Israeli town of Nahariya, Kuntar killed policeman Eliyahu Shahar, civilian Danny Haran, and Haran's four-year-old daughter, Einat, by placing her head on a rock and smashing her skull with the butt of his rifle.

When the bodies of Goldwasser and Regev were returned to Israel, former Chief Rabbi of the IDF Yisrael Weiss said, "If we thought the enemy was cruel to the living and the dead, we were surprised, when we opened the caskets, to discover just how cruel. And I'll leave it at that."[11]

⮑

What Israelis call the Second Lebanon War, and what Lebanese call the July War, created hundreds of thousands of refugees on each side of the border. That's where proportion ended. Israel had a real army and a real air force and was able to inflict severe damage on its enemies. Hezbollah, meanwhile, was only strong enough to inflict light damage and a relatively small number of casualties.

The so-called Party of God could sabotage Lebanon and terrorize Israel, but Hassan Nasrallah's "martyrs" could not repel or even slow an invading army. They could only harass that army and kill a minuscule percentage of its soldiers.

While most foreign journalists packed up and left Israel as soon as each side stopped shooting, I drove back to Kiryat Shmona to do a little postwar inspection of what had just happened.

Israel's most targeted city looked intact from a distance, and even up close, the damage wasn't all that severe. Rockets landed all day in the city for weeks, so I expected to see destroyed homes. There may well have been some, but I drove all over town and couldn't find any.

The worst damage I saw was relatively minor under the circumstances. A Katyusha had hit the roof of a carport. A parked van was torched. The nearby kitchen window was blown in by shrapnel. A portion of the side of the house was damaged. Anyone standing at the kitchen sink when the window blew in certainly would have been killed, but the house itself could be fixed without too much difficulty.

Katyusha rockets are pip-squeaks. They don't feel like pip-squeaks when they're flying in your direction, but they are. They can't be aimed worth a damn, and they'll only do serious damage if they ignite something else after impact, such as a fuel station or the gas tank of a car. Forget trying to use Katyushas against a properly outfitted and trained Western army. They have little military value unless they're fired in barrages at close range. From a distance, they can be counted on only to break a few things at random in the general direction they're aimed.

They did break a few things in Kiryat Shmona, especially because Hezbollah was clever enough to pack them with ball bearings. Buildings and houses all over the city were riddled with pockmarks from shrapnel that looked, when I squinted, like bullet holes from automatic weapons fire. Broken glass crunched under my feet when I walked. Kiryat Shmona looked like a city that had suffered massive firefights in almost every neighborhood.

Anyone who spent any significant amount of time walking those streets during the war would have been in extreme danger. The city itself, while scarred on the surface, may have been otherwise almost intact, but it was an extraordinarily lethal environment for humans while the rockets were falling.

Katyusha shrapnel kills people who aren't wearing body armor and wounds those who are. Believe me: You don't want to be hit with this stuff. The rockets may be nearly useless against an army or infrastructure, but they're devastatingly effective as terrorist weapons against civilian population centers. Shrapnel may not hurt an apartment building too badly or even slow down a tank, but it will tear *you* to pieces if you're in the way.

There was a lot of talk in the media about Hezbollah's targets in Israel. Some insisted Hezbollah aimed its Katyushas at the Israeli military. The fact that twelve soldiers were killed by a rocket just before I arrived on the border was used as evidence for that claim.

But Hezbollah hit a little of everything in Northern Israel: houses, trees, streams, grass, apartments, roads, vineyards, and cows. Thousands of rockets exploded in that part of the country. The odds that none of the rockets would hit a *single* IDF soldier were minuscule.

The truth is, I was far safer on military bases, in open fields, and on tiny kibbutzim than in cities during Hezbollah's rocket war. A disproportionate number of their rockets landed in urban areas.

Rockets rained down on Kiryat Shmona almost constantly even though there were no soldiers, no tanks, no artillery pieces, no bases, nothing of military value in the city at all. None of the journalists I met were willing to risk their lives by lingering there, but we were all relatively relaxed on IDF bases. The odds of us being hit there by a rocket were merely random, the same as if we were out among cows in the fields. The city of Haifa, which was almost twenty miles from the border, was hit more often than bases that were right on the border and which were therefore easier targets. The odds of being hit in Kiryat Shmona were fantastically higher than the odds of being hit anywhere else. Our lives depended on correctly computing the odds.

If Hezbollah really did the best they could to avoid killing civilians with their inaccurate rockets, as they and their apologists claimed, I would have set up shop in Kiryat Shmona and stayed away from Israeli soldiers for my own protection. But the situation was exactly reversed.

What happened in Israel and Lebanon in July and August of 2006 was a radical break from the past. Arab armies couldn't invade Israel without being quickly repelled or demolished. Even terrifying waves of suicide bombers could be beaten back with separation barriers and human intelligence. But Hezbollah was able to fire barrages of rockets throughout the conflict all the way up to the cease-fire. The IDF defeated three armies in six days in 1967 but couldn't even slow the rocket war down in a month.

Israeli intelligence agents at the Ministry of Defense told me they feared missile war was replacing terrorist war. It seems they were right. Hamas later replicated Hezbollah's strategy and ramped up its own relatively low-key rocket war out of Gaza against the Israeli cities of Sderot and Ashkelon. Only missile war could force hundreds of thousands of Israelis to flee their homes, and both Hamas and Hezbollah threatened to one day blanket the entire country with barrages of missiles and make Israel uninhabitable once and for all.

Feelings of existential dread increased markedly after the Second Lebanon War. Israel is a small country, haunted by horrors past. "Daytime Israel makes a tremendous effort to create the impression of the determined, tough, simple, uncomplicated society ready to fight back, ready to hit back twice as hard, courageous, and so on," Israeli novelist Amos Oz once said.[12] "Nocturnal Israel is a refugee camp with more nightmares per square mile I guess than any other place in the world. Almost everyone has seen the devil."

This war was a transition, the testing of a new doctrine. It was a potential disaster for Israel but in the end an even bigger disaster for those who thought it was a terrific idea. I wouldn't want to be anywhere near Lebanon or the Palestinian territories of the West Bank and Gaza if sophisticated Iranian-made Zelzal missiles were crashing into the sides of Tel Aviv apartment towers and skyscrapers.

When I left Israel and made plans to return to Lebanon, I could feel it: War was coming again, and it was coming like Christmas.

CHAPTER NINE

hezbollah's
putsch

Lebanon no longer wishes to
make battle on your behalf
or on behalf of your half-
baked medieval ideas.
–LOUIS-NOEL HARFOUCHE

All those against the
revolution must disappear
and quickly be executed.
–AYATOLLAH RUHOLLAH KHOMEINI

The July War briefly united most Lebanese against Israel.
Nobody ran off to join Hezbollah, but tensions were
largely smoothed over while most felt as though they were under
attack by the same enemy.

It didn't last. Few thought it would.

Lebanon at the best of times felt like it might explode at any
moment. The country barely held together, like unstable chemicals
in a nitroglycerin vat. Even before the war, the slightest ripple of
sectarian or political tension sent people scattering from the streets
and into their homes. They were far more twitchy than I was, in
part, I think, because they understood better than I did just how
precarious their civilized anarchy was.

Friends in Beirut sent messages to me while I was in Israel during
the war. Most Lebanese were going easy on Hezbollah while the

bombs were still falling, they said, but a terrible reckoning awaited as soon as the war ended.

Some people couldn't even wait that long.

Clashes broke out in south Beirut's flash-point neighborhoods where Sunni areas abutted the *dahiyeh*. Farther north, Christian mobs smashed cars displaying Hezbollah logos. A friend said the atmosphere reeked of impending sectarian conflict like never before. One radical Christian militiaman from the bad old days said the civil war would resume a month after Israel cooled its guns. "Christians, Sunnis and Druze will fight the fucker Shia," he told reporter Emily Dische-Becker,[1] "with arms from the U.S. and France."

Some Israelis thought that would be great. *The Lebanese might take care of Hezbollah at last!* But the March 14 government couldn't win a war against Hezbollah, not even after the Party of God was weakened by more than a month of Israeli air strikes. Hezbollah was the most effective Arab fighting force in the world, and the Lebanese army was the weakest and most divided. The Israelis beat three Arab armies in six days in 1967, but even they couldn't take down Hezbollah after almost two decades of bloody counterinsurgency. I could never understand why Israelis thought the drastically weaker Lebanese army could disarm Hezbollah if they couldn't.

The majority of Lebanon's people were wise enough to take the gun out of politics at the end of the civil war. Lebanon was the only Arab country that chose dialogue, elections, compromise, and debate over the rule of the boot and the rifle. Hezbollah, though, remained outside that mainstream consensus and did everything it could, with backing from the Syrian and Iranian governments, to strangle Lebanese liberalism in its cradle.

Seizing Hezbollah's weapons by force wasn't possible, so the March 14 coalition hoped to disarm Hezbollah through persuasion and consensus. There was never a chance they could have succeeded only a year after Lebanon achieved independence, not with the al-Assads and the Khomeinists in power in Damascus and Tehran.

Democracies don't hold up well in seas of autocracy. It looked like Beirut's Spring might die the same death as the Prague Spring in the late 1960s, crushed under the treads of Soviet tanks and smothered until the day the world around it had changed.

Israel and Lebanon—especially Lebanon—were both doomed to burn as long as Hezbollah existed as a foreign-sponsored militia freed from the leash of the state. The punishment for taking on Hezbollah was war. The punishment for not taking on Hezbollah was war. War, as it turned out, was inevitable even if the actual shape of it wasn't.

No one could know what would happen in Lebanon in the aftermath of July. But I was almost certain the country would fly apart into pieces. The only question was how far the pieces would fly and how hard they'd land.

～

I no longer lived in Beirut, but I returned during the coolness of late November, three and a half months after the end of the hot summer war, and found that the city was little changed, at least on the surface. My old neighborhood of Hamra in West Beirut was intact. Reconstruction of civil war-era damage had continued downtown. More restaurants and pubs had opened on the east side. Beirut looked and felt more hip than it used to. The city didn't appear to be reeling from or slouching toward war at all.

On second glance, though, all was not well. I was the only guest in my eight-story hotel, and I startled the staff when I stepped into the lobby first thing in the morning. "Why are you still here?" one bartender asked me. He didn't know I was a reporter, and he thought it strange I hadn't bolted for the exits as the next political crisis was gearing up to punish the country.

Most of my friends and many of my acquaintances left during the last crisis and hadn't returned. Milk was still hard to come by in grocery stores and even some restaurants because the Israeli Air Force destroyed Lebanon's milk factory. Party and sectarian flags were flown on the streets in abundance, a telltale sign that post-Syrian patriotism and unity were coming apart even on the March 14 side.

Just nine days earlier, on November 21, 2006, four gunmen assassinated MP Pierre Gemayel, the minister of industry and the son of former President Amin Gemayel, by ramming his car with their own and brazenly firing 9mm rounds into him through the front windshield.[2]

And to top it all off, Iran's private army threatened to topple Lebanon's government.

The March 14 coalition commanded a majority of votes in the parliament and the cabinet, and Hezbollah was disgruntled. It had its own state within a state, but not enough clout inside the legitimate state to block what it didn't like.

The Party of God wasn't particularly concerned the government would attempt to disarm it by force. March 14 may have had enough votes, but it did not have enough bullets. Nor did it have the will. No one in Lebanon's political elite wanted to fire the first shot in a new civil war. Hezbollah was, however, all worked up about the United Nations Special Tribunal for Lebanon set up to investigate and indict the assassins of Rafik Hariri.

Nasrallah had the power to more or less do what he pleased, but the veto-proof March 14 majority also had the power to do what *it* pleased short of defanging Hezbollah. The party could not, and did not, sit idly by while the Lebanese government and the international community geared up to punish Hariri's assassins.

Hezbollah felt under siege—by the Israelis, by the Americans, by Arab heads of state, by the United Nations, and even by the Lebanese government. Nasrallah wanted—he needed—more power than he had in Beirut. So he sent thousands of his supporters downtown to demand the resignation of Prime Minister Fouad Siniora, and he told them to stay there until his March 8 bloc was given veto power in Lebanon's cabinet. If the government wouldn't voluntarily submit to a Hezbollah veto, Nasrallah's people would occupy and shut down the city center until the March 14 bloc surrendered.

Aside from Hezbollah, the Syrian Baath Party, and a few irrelevant crackpots on the margins, hardly anyone in the world thought anti-Syrian demonstrations and sit-ins constituted a crisis during the Beirut Spring in 2005. But nearly everyone—including the Arab League and every Arab government in the world except Syria's—recognized, for one set of reasons or another, that it's a problem if a terrorist army loyal to another state topples or neutralizes a legitimate government.

I had barely recovered from jet lag before Hezbollah took over the streets. I asked Carine, one of my few remaining friends who had not left the country, if she wanted to join me downtown, but she refused to be seen anywhere near the made-for-TV event. She didn't want to artificially inflate Hezbollah's headcount by one. So I went down there alone with my camera and notepad.

The city looked like a besieged wartime capital bracing for an invasion. The Lebanese army had deployed in full force. Soldiers stood watch on most central-area streets. Armored personnel carriers were parked in the middle of intersections. Guns with enough firepower to shoot through buildings were mounted on corners.

Hezbollah also dispatched its "discipline" men to prevent and break up fights. It was oddly comforting that Hezbollah's pragmatic higher-ups would be protecting me and everyone else from their fans.

Rally organizers blasted earsplitting military music through gigantic speaker towers. Some of it sounded more or less like the patriotic pop I heard at March 14 rallies the previous year. Other pieces of music, however, sounded like the soundtrack to a fascist revolution or putsch.

Most people behaved well, but the city felt creepy.

Squads of rowdy militant teenagers shouted "Nasrallah! Nasrallah! Nasrallah!" and violently pumped their fists into the air.

A loutish gang of young Shia men from the *dahiyeh* walked along the line of separation between downtown and middle-class Christian East Beirut. They loudly booed and jeered as they looked east, all but daring the Christian residents to come out and "get some." Beirut felt a bit like Belfast, Northern Ireland, during the time of the "troubles."

A small angry-looking child wearing military fatigues wandered around loose on his own. He was dressed like a guerrilla fighter, but he could not have been older than four.

A twelve-year-old kid with a Hezbollah flag saw me and sneered.

Hezbollah's own security guards with their walkie-talkies and earpieces stared at me and closely watched every move I made.

Nasrallah ordered his people to fly only Lebanese flags. A swarming mass of menacing green and yellow "resistance" banners featuring an upraised AK-47 assault rifle wouldn't look good in front of the cameras. So Hezbollah waved Lebanon's benign national cedar tree flag instead.

Since I had visited Hezbollahland, the sheer cynicism of flying the Lenanese flag was obvious. Lebanese flags were ubiquitous in the Christian, Sunni, and Druze parts of the country. Lebanon was one of the most beflagged countries I had ever seen. But national flags scarcely existed in the areas under control by Hezbollah. The Party of God had a state within a state, after all, with parallel institutions, schools, military, police, and even its own foreign policy. So why shouldn't Hezbollahland have its own flag? The cedar tree banners downtown were mere props in a media battle. Hezbollah wanted to look mainstream and patriotic.

Michel Aoun's predominantly Christian Free Patriotic Movement did fly its orange flags downtown, though. The Aounists were Hezbollah's Christian fig leaf, the only non-Shia party of any significance that dared form an alliance with a party so implacably hostile to the Lebanese project. What good would a fig leaf be if it were invisible? So the Aounists burnished their orange. The Aounists had to be seen.

I felt better with them around. The Hezbollah demonstrators who came downtown early were the true believers, the ones who would have come down even if Hezbollah had not paid them to do so. (Each person was paid thirty dollars to attend the rally, and everyone who camped downtown during the long occupation was paid another thirty dollars for each day they stayed.) Hardly any women were down there at 1:00 p.m., and some of the men were pumped full of macho swagger like coked-up frat boys looking for fights.

The Aounists in orange may have been fools for forming an alliance with a bullying Islamist militia, but they were civilized people who had no interest in war or jihad. If anyone in the crowd were to give me any trouble, the nearest group of Aounists could provide a friendly refuge.

A handful of other microparties showed up—Marada, the Communists, and a few that were so insignificant I did not even know they existed until I ran into them. Most damning was the presence of the swastika-looking flag of the Syrian Social Nationalist Party, founded by Antun Saadeh in 1932 and modeled after the Nazi and Fascist parties of Germany and Italy.

At 2:45 p.m., the March 8 crowd had become genuinely enormous.

A car roared past bristling with Aoun's Free Patriotic Movement and Marada flags. Marada was a tiny pro-Syrian Maronite party in North Lebanon headed by Suleiman Franjieh. Seeing Aounists and people from Marada in the same car was bizarre. During most of Syria's postwar occupation of Lebanon, the Aounists were at times the fiercest critics of the Syrian occupation. Much of the Christian community was enraged by Aoun's new alliance of sorts with the erstwhile enemy, and he lost a great deal of his popularity as a result.

The Aounists had the distinction of having been present at both major rallies—at the massive anti-Syrian demonstration on March 14, 2005, and at the Hezbollah-led push against the March 14 government. I doubted they understood how strange they looked to distant observers who wondered why on earth a supposedly democratic Christian political party was aligned with Islamists.

So when I found two Aounists sitting at an outdoor table at an East Beirut café adjacent to downtown, I asked if I could join them and if they would be willing to explain themselves to a primarily American audience.

"Of course," said one and gestured for me to sit.

"Pull up a seat," said the other. "Can I buy you a coffee?"

The first wore an orange hat. The second wore an orange scarf. Both smoked cigars and calmly watched the crowd. A man at the next table scowled at them both.

Everyone else ate their lunch as though it were a normal day in Beirut, as though a huge mass of Hezbollah supporters chanting slogans weren't just a few dozen feet from the tables. The dreadful feeling of a renewed civil war hung over Lebanon like a pall, but if these people weren't nervous, how could I be? Then again, we were a self-selecting lunch crowd. Thousands of Beirutis turned on the news, braced for the worst, and stayed home.

The first man introduced himself as Jack and said he worked as a pilot for a major airline. The second said his name was Antonios. He worked as a tour guide at the Roman ruins at Baalbek.

"So why are you with Aoun and Hezbollah?" I said.

"Aoun is honest and correct," Antonios said. "Hezbollah in America is seen as terrorists, I know. I understand. But they are a large party in Lebanon and we have to live here with them. So we have to convince them to come back, to put down their arms and join the rest of us. We cannot do it by fighting."

At least they didn't want to do it by fighting on that day. Another Aounist I knew explained their strategy to me the previous year: "We'll extend our hand and ask them to join us," he said. "But we can't wait forever. If they refuse to disarm, we'll crack the shit out of them."

"On the other side," Jack said, "is the Hariri family, which has governed since 1990 with and without help from the Syrians. They're only interested in keeping the Ministry of Finance so they can pay no taxes and steal from us. Hariri spent ten million dollars in the north on his election campaign. But he stole that money from the government, from us."

"Siniora should accept this and resign," Antonios said. "We are voting with Aoun because he is honest and not corrupt. March 14 doesn't want a man like that in charge of finance."

I doubted most Aounists were aware that after Khomeini took power in Iran, he smashed his liberal and leftist former allies. Aoun's people, by cozying up to Khomeini's militia in Lebanon, were playing with fire.

"I understand why you don't want a war with Hezbollah," I said. "But why does that mean you have to form an alliance with them? Do you really believe Hassan Nasrallah is your friend?"

"No," Jack said. "He isn't our friend. But if Hezbollah is truly a part of the government, they will give up their arms."

"Hezbollah no longer uses arms against Lebanese," Antonios said.

This was almost true, but not quite. I would soon meet Lebanese in the south whom Hezbollah had shot at with machine guns during the July War. I hadn't met those people at the time, though. Jack and Antonios may have had a hard time accepting it even if I had told them about it.

"Hariri accepted Hezbollah's arms back in 1990," Jack said, which was true.

The situation was different then. South Lebanon was still under Israeli occupation.

Hardly anyone who wasn't a Shia supported Hezbollah keeping its weapons after Ehud Barak ordered the IDF out of South Lebanon. Nasrallah's guns warped Lebanon's delicate power-sharing arrangement. The Shia had their own foreign-backed army while no one else did. Not even Hezbollah's allies in the March 8 bloc, like these Aounists, thought that was acceptable.

The Aounists had legitimate grievances against the March 14 government, but they paid little attention to the broad picture.

"Aoun's calculations fail to take in some dangerous regional realities," wrote Tony Badran at the Foundation for Defense of Democracies.[3] "Syria is more than pleased to see Aoun attacking the anti-Syrian government. So is Iran, whose supreme guide, Ayatollah Ali Khamenei, recently predicted the defeat of U.S. and allied interests in Lebanon. Wittingly or not, Aoun is serving these foreign masters for free."

The strangest thing about Aoun's alliance with Hezbollah and Syria was that Aoun was Lebanon's most militant enemy of Syria when he was commander of the army in the latter part of the civil war.

"Why is it," I said to Jack and Antonios, "that Michel Aoun is now pro-Syrian when for years he was the staunchest anti-Syrian leader in Lebanon?"

"Aoun is not pro-Syrian," Antonios said. "He just wants normal relations with Syria. We can't fight Syria."

Of course Lebanon couldn't fight Syria. Not militarily, at least, any more than tiny Kuwait could free itself from Iraq's invasion and annexation in 1990. Aoun, you could say, had surrendered to Syrian power, or at least acquiesced to it.

"What do you two think of U.S. foreign policy here?" I said.

"We love America, but have doubts," Jack said. "They let Syria come in here in 1991 for help in Iraq." Jack was referring to former Secretary of State James Baker, who green-lighted Syria's overlordship in Lebanon in exchange for "help" during the first Persian Gulf War in 1991. How Hafez al-Assad lent any meaningful assistance in ousting Saddam Hussein from Kuwait wasn't clear.

"The U.S. will hand us over to the Syrians again for help in Iraq," Antonios said. "That is what Washington is speaking of doing right now."

Actually, the U.S. government's Iraq Study Group (headed by none other than James Baker himself) explicitly said handing Lebanon back to Syria was off the table, that Bashar al-Assad could not expect any American support for his Levantine adventures.[4] But this detail had been lost in the wash, and I could hardly blame Jack and Antonios for suspecting the worst now that Baker was back.

This wasn't the first time Michel Aoun made a tactical alliance with those who had little or nothing in common with him instead of forging ties with more natural allies.

He formed an alliance with Saddam Hussein, Hafez al-Assad's old Baathist rival, when he declared war against Syria in the 1980s. The Aounists were the last militant anti-Syrians in Lebanon before the country succumbed to Syrian domination. Aoun and his men fought hard, but they couldn't hold off the Syrians forever. He was exiled to France after he surrendered.

The U.S. used diplomatic pressure to help get Aoun out of exile in 2005, but he never forgave the American government for greenlighting his defeat. He still harped on that point even in late 2006, as did his partisans. They seemed to believe Syria would have been unable to rule Lebanon if it hadn't been for James Baker—a dubious assumption at best.

Even so, the U.S. did have a bad habit of being fickle with its friends in the Middle East. Many people in the March 14 bloc likewise were worried the U.S. might abandon them to Hezbollah, the Iranians, and the Syrians. Some anti-Americans in March 14 told me the reason they didn't trust America wasn't because they hated the U.S. but because Americans were unreliable allies who cared only about themselves and not about Lebanon.

In any case, Aoun's alliance or détente with Syria, like his alliance with Hezbollah, was strictly tactical. He wanted to be president more than anything else, the March 14 coalition told him to get stuffed. Perhaps he figured that once he was in office, he could do whatever he wanted, that he wouldn't owe a thing to the Syrians or to Hezbollah. Unlike the al-Assad-appointed Syrian stooge-of-a-president Emile Lahoud, Aoun was hard to control. The man was a loose cannon and always had been.

Michael Young at Beirut's *Daily Star* thought Aoun would almost certainly fail.[5]

"The general knows he and his own are the weakest link in the campaign against Prime Minister Fouad Siniora. The Aounists cannot long endure an open-ended sit-in, both because they are not earning salaries to do so and probably because the looming holiday season threatens to melt their momentum. And there is something else: Aoun realizes that as package deals are unwrapped left and right to resolve the ongoing crisis, his chances of seeing the presidency diminish. Indeed, the latest basket of ideas from Arab League Secretary General Amr Moussa includes a proposal for the March 14 coalition and the opposition to consent to a compromise president. If that process goes through, Aoun will not be the chosen one . . . can the general then convince Hezbollah and the Syrians that he's their man? If the Syrians are back in town by then, their preference will be for someone more controllable; and if they are not, this will mean that all sides must accept a compromise candidate. In neither case does Aoun fit the bill."

Jack and Antonios didn't seem particularly interested in foreign policy or the presidency. They kept steering the conversation back to corruption.

"According to the people ruling Lebanon," Jack said, "money is the only thing that matters."

"Nasrallah is honest," Antonios said. "He takes care of his people. Sure, he gets money from Iran, but everyone gets money from outside."

"Does Mr. Bush pay taxes?" Jack asked me.

"Of course," I said.

"Hariri doesn't," he said. "This is justice?"

"No," I said. "Of course it isn't justice."

"Siniora has been in government for fifteen years," Antonios said. "We have no medical scheme, no national education, fifty-five billion dollars in debt, and no retirement system. Why? Two hundred dollars a month is the minimum wage. We try to increase it, but they say they have no money. Then they spend 800 million dollars on a new company. This is why we are with Aoun. Our government is not a government. It is like we are ruled by a private corporation for the benefit of the boss."

I liked these guys, and I sympathized with some of their complaints. They weren't fascists or terrorists. They were liberals, basically, although most of the March 14 bloc parties were more or less liberal by Middle East standards, too.

"Foreigners should stop sending money to Lebanon," Jack said. "The government will just steal it. They should send someone like you here to watch exactly what happens to that money."

"Thanks, guys," I said and laughed. "But accounting isn't really my specialty."

The waiter came by our table.

"Do you want another coffee?" Antonios said.

"Get another coffee!" Jack said.

"I'll have another coffee," I said to the waiter.

Jack puffed on his cigar.

The main reason Hezbollah wanted veto power was so it could sabotage the United Nations tribunal that would indict and punish the assassins of Rafik Hariri. Why on earth, though, would the Aounists want to block that when they were originally part of the March 14 movement that ousted the Syrian occupiers from Lebanon in the first place?

"So, what about the tribunal?" I said to Jack and Antonios. "Do you really want to block the investigation?"

"We are worried," Antonios said, "that [Saad] Hariri wants to use the tribunal to go after people whose faces in Lebanon he doesn't like."

I think I must have audibly sighed when he said that. Saad Hariri had no control over whom the U.N. would indict. But these two lived in a part of the world where politics had always been a ruthless and murderous business. Political enemies really did disappear into dungeons. Voicing the "wrong" opinion in a newspaper column could get you car bombed on your way to work in the morning. Foreign powers really did manipulate local governments for their own craven gain. Paranoia naturally thrived in environments like Lebanon's, and I was surprised it wasn't a bigger problem than it already was.

"We are not against anybody," Antonios earnestly said. "We just support our country. We are normal people and we work every day."

"Do you think there will be more war in Lebanon?" I said.

"No!" Jack said. "Not with ourselves, and not with Israel. I think there is a deal under the table between the Israelis and Hezbollah. Both sides lost and don't want to do it again. The situation in the south is finished. If it happens again, Nasrallah will lose his case."

I hoped Jack was right, but I feared he was not. Hezbollah had restocked its Iranian arsenal in a matter of months. If Nasrallah wanted peace or at least an armistice, he kept his intentions very much to himself.

If Hezbollah were to increase its share of government power, more war with Israel would only be that much more likely. And the more official state power Hezbollah had, the more incentive the Israelis would have to attack central Beirut and the state's institutions during the next round.

Jack and Antonios were in a bad spot. At some point, Hezbollah would have to be mainstreamed. But if Hezbollah became mainstream because Lebanon joined the "resistance," rather than because Hezbollah was disarmed and reformed, nowhere in Lebanon would be safe from Israeli reprisals.

The alternative, though, was also quite grim.

"If Israel can't defeat Hezbollah, how can Siniora and Jumblatt?" Antonios said. "We have to negotiate with them. If we don't, then we will divide on sectarian lines and we will no longer have a country. Look at that mosque next to the church."

He gestured toward the Mohammad al-Amin Mosque, where Hariri was buried, and the Maronite Cathedral of St. George right next door.

"We need this," he said. "Christians need Muslims. And Muslims need Christians. That is what Lebanon is."

~

Hezbollah's rally downtown lasted only a couple of hours, but thousands of hard-core supporters stayed behind after the others went home. They built a tent city, set up camp with blankets and sleeping bags on the sidewalks in front of businesses, and settled in for a long occupation that would last almost a year and a half.

The so-called Freedom Camp built by young anti-Syrian activists after Hariri was killed wasn't disruptive, but Hezbollah shut down the city center entirely. These people weren't just college kids. Though the guns were out of sight, Hezbollah was the most powerful armed force in the country.

Militant Party of God supporters also tried to seize and occupy Prime Minister Siniora's office. Siniora warned Hezbollah that if the building was taken, he would no longer have control of his "street." Translation: *If you seize the state's institutions, Lebanon's Sunnis will declare war.*

Hezbollah knew this was true. Many rank-and-file Sunnis, Christians, and Druze *did* want to declare war and were only held in check by their more temperate leaders.

So Hezbollah backed off, but the occupation and shutdown of the city center looked as though it might drag on indefinitely. The government, business owners, and the majority of Beirut's citizens braced themselves for a long and bitter siege of the capital.

I ventured downtown again the day after the media-friendly protest was over. Hezbollah didn't want any more attention from journalists by that point. Ubiquitous Hezbollah security agents with the telltale sunglasses and earpieces stared at me coldly and tracked my movements as I walked past.

Hundreds of tents were set up all over the place. Most were made of white canvas. I snapped a few pictures, and nobody stepped in to stop me.

One group of tents in a parking lot across from the Mohammad al-Amin Mosque were all made of black canvas. *What's up with the black tents?* I wondered. I walked over and raised my camera to take a picture.

Five earpieced Hezbollah agents with sunglasses descended on me at once. They surrounded me and screamed "No!" Then they pushed me away from the tents and got in my face so I could not see behind them.

Nothing like that ever happened to me at the March 14 Freedom Camp.

I had been accused of spying many times while in Lebanon, though often only half jokingly, so it wouldn't surprise me in the least if that's what the men of Hezbollah thought I was doing. Many Lebanese were paranoid—sometimes with good reason—but no one was as paranoid as Hezbollah.

"Sahafi!" I yelled back at them. *Journalist!*

"No, no, no!" they yelled and pushed me again. I lowered my camera, threw up my hands, and turned to walk away. Then they left me alone.

Hezbollah, by this point, was developing a seriously bad reputation among Western journalists. A reporter friend was harassed by the media relations department over an entirely innocuous article he wrote about the party for a mainstream left-wing American magazine. *Time* magazine's Christopher Allbritton wrote the following on his blog during the July War:[6] "Hezbollah is launching Katyushas, but I'm loath to say too much about them. The Party of God has a copy of every journalist's passport, and they've already hassled a number of us and threatened one." *USA Today* reporter Charles Levinson would have his own troubles later. "My experience with Hezbollah this week has left an unpleasant taste in my mouth," he wrote on his blog *Conflict Blotter*.[7] "I had heard this from other journalist friends who have recently returned from Lebanon, but discovered it for myself this week: their interaction with the press borders on fascist."

That's how Hezbollah rolled. There were a couple of reasons more journalists didn't mention this sort of thing in their articles. Allbritton touched on one—they were intimidated. A simpler reason, though, was because most journalists didn't write first-person narratives. Industry rules generally didn't allow reporters to describe these kinds of incidents. Most editors required journalists to write themselves out of their stories. Others didn't want to be blacklisted like I was. They needed, or thought they needed, quotes from and access to Hezbollah.

I walked across the street deliberately in full view of Hezbollah's security agents, sat down on the sidewalk in front of heavily armed Lebanese soldiers, and furiously began taking notes. I wasn't actually angry, and I chuckled inside as I did this because I knew they could see what I was doing.

They wouldn't do anything to me. I wanted to let them know their obnoxious behavior had just earned them bad press. They violated my first rule of media relations: *Be nice to people who write about you for a living.*

I scribbled my furious notes, looked them in the eye, scribbled more furious notes, looked them in the eye again, and scribbled more furious notes.

Hezbollah wasn't half as media savvy as its officials liked to believe. Harassing foreign journalists may have kept some of them in line, so to speak, but it backfired with the rest of us. Bullying writers who were free of the old-school media constraints of third-person "objectivity" was the media war equivalent of dropping a hand grenade down your pants.

One of the security agents was smart enough to figure this out. He slowly walked up to me.

"*What?*" I said in as pissed-off a tone as I could muster as I looked up at him. I was not really angry. It was just theater, and I was having fun.

He pointed at my camera, said something unintelligible, then pointed at the black tents.

"Yeah, yeah," I said. "I know, I know." I went back to writing furious notes.

"No, no, no!" he said.

"*What?*" I said, genuinely annoyed now.

A group of six teenagers saw the commotion and came over to see what was happening. One offered to translate.

"He said it is okay to take pictures," he said.

"It's okay?" I said, and completely dropped my affected hostility. I could not help but smile. I had just taught Hezbollah security agents that there were consequences when they weren't nice to journalists.

"Yes, yes," another kid said. "Come on." He offered his hand and helped me up.

"Thanks, guys," I said.

"Don't worry about them," a third teenager said. "They are handicaps."

"Come on!" another said. "Come with us! We'll show you around!"

They led me back across the street to the black tents. I lifted my camera and snapped a quick photo. The picture was not particularly interesting. It had no real value. But I almost lost it. Another Hezbollah security agent saw me take the picture and ran up to me.

"No!" he screamed and waved his arms. He menacingly put his face four inches from mine. "How many pictures did you take!" he yelled.

"Just one," I said.

"Delete it right now!" he screamed. "You were told not to take pictures!"

Who were these guys to tell me what to do, anyway? Lebanon was, at least theoretically, a free country. Hezbollah wasn't the government, and I was taking pictures in a public parking lot.

"No," I said, "I was just told that I could take pictures." I looked at my new teenage friends, waiting for them to back me up.

"Yes, yes, it's okay," one of the kids told the security man.

"No!" the agent said. "You delete it right now!"

"Fine," I said. "I'll delete it on one condition—if you tell me *why* I can't take a picture. What are you doing here that you want to hide?"

The truth is I would have deleted it without any conditions. I didn't actually care about having that picture, and the last thing I needed was to get in a fight with these people. I just wanted to know what he would say when I asked him why he was paranoid. I doubted very much that he would know how to answer.

"Never mind!" he said as he threw his hands in the air, turned around, and stormed back into the tents.

"What on earth is their problem?" I said to the kids who stuck up for me and offered to show me around.

"Don't worry," said the one who had taken my hand. "They are handicaps."

They were, indeed, "handicaps," at least mentally. If they actually thought I was a spy—but I don't know, maybe they didn't—their behavior would have told me all I needed to know. It was obvious which part of the tent city housed the leadership. It was the one place, the black-tented section, where security completely freaked out when I showed up with my camera. If I were to call up the CIA or the Mossad and give them air-strike coordinates—or whatever it was Hezbollah was afraid of—all I'd have to say was "aim for the black tents."

The teenagers who had volunteered as my guides, translators, and advocates led me to the much larger section of the camp where everyone else lived and slept in white tents.

"Which party are you with?" I asked them.

"Hezbollaaaaaaaah," said the lead kid and grinned. "Here, here, take a picture of this car!"

I took a picture of a car with a Nasrallah poster taped to the back window.

The kids talked and moved fast with the boundless energy of young people on an adventure.

"That's Hassan Nasrallah," he said and pointed at the poster in the car window I had just photographed. "Do you know Hassan Nasrallah? He is a big hero."

"Why is he a hero?" I said.

"He resists the Israelis!"

"Are all of you guys with Hezbollah?" I said.

"Yes!" one of them said. "We are all with Hassan Nasrallah!" They seemed to expect me to agree with them that Hassan Nasrallah was a big hero, even though they knew I was American. At least they didn't seem to think I'd mind that they supported Hassan Nasrallah. I doubted they felt any hostility toward me personally.

"So, what is it you hope to accomplish downtown?" I said.

"We want Siniora to leave," one of them said.

"We want to fuck Siniora," said another.

"I know," I said. "Why do you want to get rid of him, though? What do you want from the government that you can't get with Siniora?"

"War!" said one of the kids.

"We want war!" said another.

A third kid slapped the second on the side of his head. The slapped kid laughed and pushed his hand in his friend's face.

I couldn't tell if this playful spat broke out because they didn't agree with each other about wanting more war or because they weren't supposed to admit it in front of a foreign reporter. Some

Hezbollah supporters truly didn't want more war with Israel. Some sincerely believed Israel would attack again no matter what, that Hezbollah was Lebanon's only defense.

"We want to unite Lebanon and have a democracy," said the kid who seemed to be their leader. He was the most mature and collected, and the others deferred to him with their body language.

"You have a democracy, though," I said. "You didn't win as many seats in the parliament as you would like, but that doesn't mean you don't have a democracy. You can't always get what you want in a democracy."

"The American government rules Siniora," said another. "They interfere in my business."

"In what ways?" I said.

"America helps Israel against Lebanon and sells them weapons."

None of these kids wanted to give me their names. I took notes of our conversation, but I can't tell you who exactly said what.

"What about Syria?" I said. "America helps Lebanon against Syria."

"Bush killed all those politicians because he doesn't want peace in Lebanon."

"Why wouldn't Bush want peace in Lebanon?" I said.

"I don't know!"

"Americans don't want war in Lebanon," I said. "It would not serve our interests or yours. Do you think Americans want chaos in Lebanon just for the heck of it?"

"We don't hate the American people, only the government."

"Okay," I said. "So why then does Hassan Nasrallah repeatedly say 'Death to America'?" I asked these questions in the most friendly and casual tone of voice I could muster.

"He only means death to the American government."

"Why doesn't he make that clear then?" I said.

"He does!"

"No, he doesn't," I said. "He says 'Death to America.' What would you think if George W. Bush gave speeches where he screamed 'Death to Lebanon'? Come on, guys. Be honest with me. I want to know what you really think."

"I want to go to America," the leader kid said. "I love America and I want to live in America. America is rich and free. I want to be rich and free, too."

I think he was sincere. His politics were a product of Hezbollah's schools, his community, and his peer group. But politics in the Middle East were less personal than in the West, in part because Middle Easterners were accustomed to having their politics dictated to them from above. Politicians were usually above accountability and beyond control of the people. These kids assumed that's how it was in the Western countries, as well.

Street-level anti-Americanism was sometimes more moderate, complicated, and contradictory than it appeared from far away. There often was a vast gulf separating those in the Arab world who incited anti-Americanism and those who more passively went along with it. The difference in temperament between Hezbollah's grim security guards and the kids who showed me around was just one example.

"So," I said. "Who do you think won the war in July? Israel or Hezbollah?"

"Nasrallah!"

"We beat Israel!"

"Does that mean you want to do it again?" I said.

"Yes!" half of them said.

"No!" the other half said simultaneously.

One of the kids who said "no" slapped one of the kids who said "yes." Again, I couldn't tell if that was because they didn't agree with each other or because they weren't supposed to sound like warmongers in front of Americans.

Most Lebanese gave me their honest opinions. Even those with completely crazy opinions told me straight up what they thought without showing even a hint of embarrassment. Sometimes, though, I wasn't convinced people were straight with me. This was one of those times.

The gang took me around the tent city and introduced me to their friends. Some were a bit wary. I could read it on their faces. *Who's this American, and why am I meeting him?* Most, though, were perfectly friendly. They shook my hand, smiled, and said "Welcome."

For some now-forgotten reason, I thought one of the people I was introduced to was Druze, and I was surprised. Only a minuscule handful of Druze supported Hezbollah. The overwhelming majority were with Walid Jumblatt and the March 14 government. So I was happy to meet one of the tiny fraction who were outside the community's mainstream.

"You're Druze?" I said to him.

He shook his head in confusion, clearly because he didn't understand English. I switched to Arabic.

"Inta Durzi?" I said. *Are you Druze?*

A look of horror and disgust washed over his face.

"*La*," he said. *No.* "Ana Shia." *I am Shia.*

I didn't mean to insult him, but apparently I did. So much of what passed for politics in Lebanon was really just sectarianism.

"Jumblatt is a handicap," the leader said.

"Can I take a picture of you guys?" I said.

Most said no. So many people in Lebanon were paranoid about somebody or other. Most feared the Syrians. Hezbollah feared the Americans and the Israelis. These kids might have even feared their own government.

Two did let me take their picture, however.

I said my good-byes, genuinely thanked them for their time and hospitality, and walked toward downtown Beirut's restaurants and shops.

Every business was closed, even those away from the camp. The military had blockaded all streets leading to the center of town with checkpoints and coils of razor wire. The government didn't want Hezbollah to seize the portion of Beirut rebuilt and refurbished by Hariri's people.

I approached a Lebanese army soldier standing watch.

"Is it okay if I take a picture?" I said.

He put his hand on his heart. "No, please, not today," he said. "I am sorry."

"No problem," I said. "Thank you, though."

He must have had no idea why I thanked him. I did so because I appreciated that he spoke to me like a normal human being and like a typical Lebanese—friendly, welcoming, and polite. The contrast between average Lebanese people—and I'm including Hezbollah's casual supporters in that group when I say this—and Hezbollah's official party members and elite was extraordinary.

Hezbollah's top men were temperamentally identical to inflexible communist dogmatists. If they ever made themselves rulers of Lebanon—and it would surely mean war if they tried—the country would no longer be recognizable.

CHAPTER TEN

from jerusalem to beirut

There is a Lebanon that
exists in the distance,
too far away to see from
Israel's northern border.
—NOAH POLLAK

"**B**efore departing for Lebanon," Noah Pollak wrote in *Azure* magazine,[1] "the traveler who has been in Israel should purge himself of any evidence of having stepped foot in the Jewish state, from bus tickets and loose change to the notepad with Hebrew writing on the spine. The voyage from Jerusalem to Beirut could take, under different circumstances, four hours by car or forty-five minutes by air—the two cities are about 150 miles apart—but today it involves a daylong travail of buses, taxies, aircraft, the duplicitous use of two passports, and the making of false statements to Lebanese customs officials."

Noah did all these things because he joined me in Beirut from Jerusalem to cover Hezbollah's putsch and to survey the destruction in the south of the country. Anyone who had ever set foot in Israel, even as a tourist, was barred from entering Lebanon. The government wasn't particularly strict about enforcing the ban, but an Israeli stamp in your passport would likely get you deported and possibly even arrested.

This was Noah's first trip to Lebanon. I was happy to show him around and introduce him to the "party" that fired missiles in our direction when we covered the July War together from the Israeli side of the border.

His plane landed at two o'clock in the morning, and his taxi driver took him alongside the edge of Hezbollah's downtown encampment. Even in the middle of the night, demonstrators were out the streets screaming slogans.

"What are they saying?" Noah said.

The driver rolled down his window and told the demonstrators an American was in the car and wanted to know what they were saying. One of the men in the street came up to the taxi.

"We will cut Siniora," he said, referring to the prime minister. "*We will cut him!*"

The next day, I took Noah downtown so we could sit and talk with the malcontents. First, though, we had to stop by a Hezbollah propaganda stand so I could buy a "resistance" scarf and go incognito into the tent city.

Don't laugh. I knew what I was doing, and it worked. All the hostile bullshit I had to put up with from Hezbollah's security people vanished entirely as soon as I donned one of their scarves. The men with their sunglasses and earpieces stopped staring at me, stopped tracking my movements, and stopped twitching when I took pictures. They were strikingly obtuse individuals if wearing a scarf was all it took to blend in with the crowd.

Flags, T-shirts, and rearview-mirror ornaments were also for sale. Noah bought the biggest Hezbollah flag in stock. I had to carry it out of the country for him because he didn't want airport security to find *that* in his luggage when he flew back to Israel from Jordan.

A Lebanese woman smirked and asked us where we were from.

"United States," I said.

"And . . ." she said. "You like Hezbollah?" She tried hard not to laugh at us.

"Not really," I said under my breath so the sales guy couldn't hear. "We just want souvenirs because we think it's funny."

She smiled and knowingly nodded.

I had bought a Hezbollah T-shirt in Baalbek the year before—because it was ironic, not because I ever intended to wear it. A Lebanese army soldier watched me hand the vendor ten dollars, and he shook his head sadly in grave disappointment. He was twenty years older than me, and I doubted he would understand Generation X humor even if I explained it. Surely he thought I was a duped useful idiot. I have a whole collection of Hezbollah souvenirs in my office—the T-shirt, a flag, a key chain, even a bracelet. Some people collect refrigerator magnets and stamps. I collect tourist gimcrack from terrorist organizations.

Noah and I paid for our items. I put the scarf around my neck and felt as ridiculous as I must have looked.

Hezbollah's security men left me alone, though, so it was worth it. (Needless to say, I would not have dared to wear that scarf in any other part of Beirut.) Noah did not need a scarf. He had an olive skin tone and an ethnically ambiguous appearance that allowed him to pass as Lebanese, or as someone from anywhere else around the Mediterranean. He wasn't a magnet for the paranoid and suspicious like I was.

He and I walked toward the tent city and passed an angry-looking group of young women on their way out. One narrowed her eyes at me.

"Where are you from?" she said. She looked me in the eye, looked at my Hezbollah scarf, looked me in the eye again, and looked back and my Hezbollah scarf. Then she yelled at me. "Are you from the *States*?!"

"Yes," I said. "We're from the States."

For a second I thought she was yelling at me because she did not like Americans. We were at the Hezbollah encampment, after all. But that wasn't it. She yelled at me because she thought I was a stupid American who supported Hezbollah.

Not everyone who ventured downtown that day supported the "resistance." Some were March 14 supporters who went down there as horrified onlookers.

One of the young woman's friends took her by the shoulders and turned her away from Noah and me. As they began walking away, she nodded her head and flexed her hands as though she were trying to restrain herself and calm down.

A few Westerners in Lebanon actually did support Hezbollah. They were the same kinds of alienated intellectuals who supported the Soviet Union during the Cold War, before communism was universally understood to differ from fascism in only the details. Other Western expats in Lebanon were what you might call "soft on Hezbollah," or defensive on Hezbollah's behalf, even though they weren't outright supporters. I wasn't at all annoyed that this young woman had yelled at me. She thought I was one of those people. It was a reasonable, if wrong, assumption for her to make since I was wearing the scarf.

Noah and I walked the grounds without getting any attitude or even attention from Hezbollah security. We did, however, get some unwanted attention from some of Hezbollah's fans.

Next to the closed-off area where most of the restaurants were located was a small Roman Empire ruin site. It was discovered for the first time in the 1990s when civil war-era rubble was cleared out of the way.

Noah and I leaned up against the railing next to two young Shia women wearing headscarves. Noah snapped a picture. We talked among ourselves—about what I don't remember. I smiled at the two women.

Then an older man walked up to us. He muttered something under his breath in Arabic and plowed his shoulder into Noah's, knocking him sideways. The man could not possibly have known our political views. He was just mad because he heard us speaking English. My Hezbollah scarf didn't ward everyone off. It only seemed to work with the oblivious security people.

"Hi," Noah said to him as though nothing had happened. "What's up?"

I braced myself for anything. Our rude new "friend" said something else unintelligible and stalked off.

Beirut was an open and cosmopolitan city when Hezbollah wasn't occupying the center of it. An encounter like that between a Beiruti and a guest from abroad was all but unthinkable under normal circumstances.

Aside from this character and a few other hostile individuals, Hezbollah's campout was more mellow than it was the first time I saw it. The passion had cooled. Fewer people screamed slogans. Most appeared to have succumbed to some kind of torpor. It isn't easy to be hopped up on protest adrenaline for days in a row. Eventually you have to sit down, eat a sandwich, and smoke a narghile.

The environment downtown was very different from what most Westerners would likely expect from an assault on a capital mounted by an Iranian proxy militia demanding more government power. Prominent figures gave public speeches to roaring applause, not to bullets shot into the sky. College students held teach-ins. Patriotic and Arabic pop music blared through speaker towers. Snack stands were set up all over the place.

"It's like a Phish concert down here," Noah said. "Only it's a Phish concert for terrorists." The only things missing were drum circles and pot. These guys brilliantly copied leftist American political theater. "They'll get a lot more international support this way than if they came down here wearing ski masks and waving rifles around."

We walked the maze of tents and snapped pictures, looking for someone who seemed approachable enough to be interviewed. Few people paid us any mind, and we sat on a curb to drink a soda and smoke cigarettes.

Three young men walked up to us.

"Hello," said the first. He introduced himself as Jad. "Where are you from?"

"We're from the U.S.," Noah said.

"Welcome to Lebanon," he said. "What is your impression?" Lebanese often asked me this question.

"You mean, what do we think of the political situation?" I said.

"Yeah," he said.

"Eh," I said. "We're Americans. We're not the biggest fans of Hezbollah." The contrast between what I said and what I was wearing—the Hezbollah scarf—did not seem to register.

"Where are you from?" Noah said.

"From Beirut," said another of the young men.

"Do you mean the *dahiyeh*?" I said.

"Yes," he said. "From the *dahiyeh*. Have you been there?"

"I have; he hasn't," I said and gestured to Noah. "Cigarette?"

"Please," Jad said.

I gave Jad a cigarette.

"This is your first trip to Lebanon?" he said to Noah.

"Yep," Noah said and sipped from his drink. "It's great."

The five of us discussed Lebanese and international politics. Our conversation was civil and pleasant even though we disagreed about whether Hezbollah was fighting the good fight.

"So," Noah said. "What do you guys think of Iran?"

That was the real question, wasn't it?

"Syria and Iran are helping us," Jad said. "We don't want them to rule in Lebanon. I like drinking and chasing girls and having a good time. We don't want to be like Iran. If Hezbollah tried to make us like Iran, that would be a big problem for us."

They were secular, yet they supported a militia that was loyal to an Islamist police state. Lebanon's Shias had long been politically and economically marginalized by the Sunnis and Christians, so a Shia militia with power and guns seemed like the best thing going. If the leaders of their community had different politics and different priorities, these guys would have likely gone along with that, too. They didn't actually buy what Hezbollah was saying. They would camp out downtown to oust the Sunni prime minister, but not for Khomeini's Velayat-e Faqih.

Two men heard us speaking in English and—once again, and for no other apparent reason—felt compelled to come over and harass me and Noah.

"Where are you from!" the first man yelled.

"United States," I said and looked away from him, uninterested.

He gritted his teeth, leaned forward, and jutted his face next to mine.

"Do you like Bush?" he demanded.

"No," I said calmly. It didn't matter what I thought of the American president. This was the only acceptable answer if I didn't want trouble.

"Do you like *Olmert*?" he said, referring to the Israeli prime minister in a particularly nasty tone of voice.

"No," I said. "*No.*" There was a chance that answering "yes" to *that* question might have been dangerous, but I answered him honestly. Ehud Olmert was arguably the worst prime minister in Israel's history. Huge numbers of Israelis agreed with that assessment, and even many Lebanese I spoke to said they wished Ariel Sharon—who was seriously hated in Lebanon—was prime minister instead of Olmert in 2006.

The guy was obviously spoiling for a fight. Even if I had been Olmert's biggest fanboy, I would have kept my mouth shut at that moment. He was satisfied, though, when I said I didn't like Olmert. So he and his buddy walked off.

An older fat man in a red shirt waddled over. He had the wide eyes of an agitated extremist.

"Gulf Arabs give bombs to Israel to kill my people!" he roared.

This, of course, was nonsense on stilts. Israel didn't receive weapons from Saudi Arabia, Kuwait, or any other Arab country. Don't write off what he said as just another Middle Eastern conspiracy theory, though. An important geopolitical shift had occurred, and he knew it.

Sunni Arab governments—notably those of Egypt and Saudi Arabia—implicitly took Israel's side during the opening days of the July War. And every Arab government in the world except Syria's supported Lebanon's government against Hezbollah. Hezbollah, as a Shia militia fronting the Persians, had no more support in the halls of Sunni Arab power than it had among the Sunnis of Lebanon.

Nasrallah had a new talking point that seemed to be filtering down. He was calling Prime Minister Siniora a tool of the "Zionist Entity." Siniora was continuing the July War on Israel's behalf, Nasrallah said, because he was pushing, albeit weakly, for Hezbollah's disarmament.

Al Qaeda, meanwhile, called *Hezbollah* a Zionist tool because Nasrallah wouldn't allow Sunni terrorists to use South Lebanon as a launching pad for attacks against Israel.

Six Arab governments—Saudi Arabia, Egypt, Morocco, Algeria, the United Arab Emirates, and Tunisia—threatened to pursue nuclear weapons programs of their own to counter Iran's. None of these Arab countries sought nuclear weapons to balance out Israel's. They feared and loathed the Shias of Lebanon, Iraq, and Iran much more than they worried about Zionists, regardless of what they said.

Some analysts were even beginning to wonder if the strife between Sunnis and Shias, whose epicenter at the time was in Baghdad, might supplant the Arab-Israeli war as the region's most defining conflict at some point in the future. At the time, though, the Arab-Israeli conflict was used by both sides of the inter-Islamic divide to score propaganda points against the other.

I was a bit embarrassed on Lebanon's behalf after showing Noah downtown. His first impression of the country was radically different from mine.

Hezbollah had all but conquered downtown. From Noah's point of view, Nasrallah must have looked like the strong horse. The Party of God certainly looked that way from the Israeli side of the border. Most Israelis were convinced they had either lost what they called the Second Lebanon War or that the conclusion was at best a draw. Almost everyone in the world—or in the Middle East, anyway—seemed to believe that.

Noah and I were about to see something, though, that proved everybody was wrong.

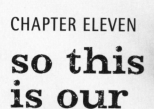

CHAPTER ELEVEN

so this is our victory

How many times can we be
burnt and resurrected?
—LEBANESE POLITICAL JOURNAL

I called up Leena, the Shia woman who showed me around South Lebanon the previous year, and asked if she could meet me for coffee to discuss a return trip to the border. She had taken a number of journalists down there during and after the war, and she knew the area better than almost anyone. Noah and I both wanted to survey the destruction and see what Nasrallah's "divine victory" looked like.

So Leena and I met at a coffee bar in West Beirut's Hamra district just up the street from my old apartment.

"I'm too busy to take you there now," she said. "But you can go by yourself."

Most Beirutis I knew thought it would be a bad idea if Noah and I drove to South Lebanon at that time without at least one local person accompanying us. Unlike Leena, though, none had been down there since the July War. Perhaps they were a bit paranoid, but I didn't want to dismiss what they said out of hand.

"If we get stopped by Hezbollah," I said, "and they call headquarters, we might get in trouble. I'm blacklisted, and they have a file on me in their computer."

"What computer?" Leena said.

I just looked at her for a second, unsure what she meant. Then it hit me.

"Of course," I said and laughed.

The Israeli Air Force destroyed Hezbollah's media relations department, including its paper and electronic files, with building-buster bombs in July. What was left of the office was smashed up at the bottom of a crater in the *dahiyeh*, most likely filled with water and garbage by now.

"I wonder what happened to Hussein Naboulsi," I said, referring to my old nemesis who ran the department. He wasn't my favorite person, but I hoped he hadn't been killed. A small part of me still wanted to talk some sense and moderation into him, although I knew the idea was silly.

"He quit," Leena said.

"He quit the department?" I said.

"He quit Hezbollah," she said.

I just about spilled my coffee.

The previous year, I had asked Leena if she could set up an interview with someone who had quit Hezbollah. I did not care with whom. I just wanted to talk to somebody who used to be an actual member of Hezbollah and no longer was.

She found a guy in the south who said he would tell me anything as long as I wouldn't publish his name. Leena and I set up an appointment with him for lunch in Sidon, a Sunni city where nobody knew him.

He thought better of it after a while. As far as he and Leena knew, only four or five card-carrying members had ever quit the party. If he talked to me even anonymously, Hezbollah could figure out who he was and make him pay for it.

Hussein Naboulsi, then, had joined a very small club.

"I want to talk to him," I said. Suddenly, my urge to buy him a beer (or, more realistically, coffee) didn't seem quite so ridiculous.

"He won't talk to the media," she said. "He'd rather tell his story himself. He's writing a book."

So that was it, then. Leena couldn't take Noah and me to the south, and Hussein would not talk to anyone, let alone me.

Noah and I found someone else to escort us down there—Said and Henry, two men who grew up in the area and came highly recommended as guides. Leena was a Shia, but these guys were Maronites. And they weren't politically neutral like she was.

They picked us up at our hotel first thing in the morning.

Said (pronounced Sah-EED) rode up to the front door on his motorcycle. Henry arrived in his car.

"Good morning, gentlemen," Said said as he shook our hands. "Shall we go in your car?"

"If you prefer," I said.

"Let me drive," Said said. "It is better. We know the best roads to take."

Noah donned his sunglasses, pulled on a light red and black jacket, and climbed into the back next to Henry. I sat in the passenger seat next to Said.

These guys were good. Not only did they know their way around the back roads of the south but they were also battle-hardened veterans of Lebanon's civil war.

They weren't Rambo types. They placed their guns in the glove box. I seriously doubted we would need their services as trained killers or bodyguards. We couldn't shoot our way out of the south in a worst-case scenario anyway. Still, I felt better with them along after hearing from so many people that it might be a bad idea to visit the south while Hezbollah was ramping up its push against Lebanon's government.

Normally, you can drive from Beirut to the Israeli border fence in just over two hours. Lebanon, though, wasn't normal in late 2006, especially not in the south. In July and August the Israeli Air

Force bombed most, if not all, of the bridges on the coastal highway. Reconstruction moved along quickly enough, but snarled traffic had to be rerouted around the construction sites, at times onto side roads too narrow and small to handle the overflow.

Said and Henry had day jobs that had nothing to do with politics, but they also worked part time for a man named Toni Nissi. He labored tirelessly lobbying the Lebanese government and the international community to implement United Nations Security Council Resolution 1559 that mandated Hezbollah's disarmament. Hezbollah hysterically dubbed Nissi's office "the Beirut branch of the Mossad."

After only a few minutes of driving, we crossed Beirut's city limits. To our right was the Mediterranean. To our left was Hezbollah's *dahiyeh*.

"There is Nasrallah now," Henry said from the back seat as we drove past a billboard proclaiming Hezbollah's "divine victory" over Israel a few months before. Every foreign visitor to Lebanon saw billboards like these along the airport road before they reached downtown Beirut. Shortly before the war, I saw one banner draped above the highway—placed there by Hezbollah, of course—that said *All Our Catastrophes Come from America*.

Apropos of nothing, Said asked Noah if he was Jewish.

Noah didn't hesitate. "I am," he said.

Most Lebanese people weren't hostile to Jewish visitors. Some told me they were less anti-Semitic as a whole than Europeans. On some days, I even believed them. I had several Jewish friends who lived there and never once had a single problem with anyone. Noah was the type of person who likely would have answered "yes" to that question regardless. He was no shrinking violet and was angered, rather than intimidated or silenced, by bigots.

Neither Henry nor Said seemed remotely bothered by Noah's Jewishness. I would have been surprised if they were.

"You are welcome, my friend," Said said.

Hezbollah's people, though, were violently anti-Semitic and would surely suspect Noah was Jewish if they stopped us, looked at his passport, and read his first name. There was even a chance they might suspect he was Israeli. The fact that he carried an American passport didn't prove that he wasn't. Lots of Israelis had dual citizenship, and Israeli journalists visited Lebanon once in a while on second passports. Noah lived in Israel, and he worked at an Israeli think tank and magazine. If Hezbollah men stopped and detained us for some reason, as they had detained me and my photographer colleague Dan the previous year, they could have learned all this and more about Noah just by punching his name into Google. I didn't want to spend too much time thinking about what Hezbollah might do to him, or even to both of us, if they thought he was an Israeli spy.

"What do you think about Israel's invasion in July?" I asked Said and Henry.

"Of course, what Israel did wasn't good," Said said. "They only care about themselves. Hezbollah doesn't pay taxes, so the rest of us have to pay for all the infrastructure the Israelis destroyed."

"What do you think about Israel in general?" I said. "Aside from the war in July?"

"I have nothing against Israel," Henry said. "They are good people and they do good for themselves. We need to make peace with everyone. They are open-minded people, but we have had no way to communicate with them since the Syrians came."

"I would love to visit the Holy Land," Said said. "My mother went there when the border was open before 2000. It is a good place. If you want to make peace with people, you can make peace, especially with the Israelis. They just want to live in their country, so it is no problem."

"Is the U.N. doing much in the south?" Noah asked from the back seat.

"The multinational forces don't have the authority to stop Hezbollah unless they are smuggling weapons out in the open," Said said. "The Lebanese army is not taking sides because of the volatile political situation and the violent clashes taking place in Beirut."

United Nations Security Council Resolution 1701,[1] passed on August 11, 2006, mandated Israel's withdrawal from Lebanon and the disarmament of Hezbollah. UNIFIL, the United Nations Interim Force in Lebanon, even sent additional troops to South

Lebanon to assist the Lebanese army and government. Not much changed, though, except for one thing: The government regained at least nominal sovereignty over the border region. The army had a serious presence there for the first time in decades, and Hezbollah was forced to keep a low profile.

UNIFIL was widely assumed to be doing little aside from standing around while Hezbollah reconstituted its weapon stocks for the next round of war. Even though Hezbollah was *supposed* to be disarmed, Israeli intelligence officials later believed Hezbollah had more than twice as many rockets as before the 2006 war began.

Even so, the Lebanese army did confiscate a small number of Hezbollah's rockets smuggled across the Syrian border. Nasrallah demanded the return of those weapons from the army even though Hezbollah's very existence as an autonomous militia was against Lebanese and international law.

Said was right, though, that the army didn't have the authority to disarm Hezbollah. Hezbollah was better armed, better trained, and overall more powerful than the army, which suffered fifteen years of deliberate neglect and degradation under Syrian overlordship. Many of the army's top officers were installed by the Syrians, and they were still loyal to the regime in Damascus. More important were fears that the army would break apart along sectarian lines if orders to disarm Hezbollah were given. Parts of the army split off into sectarian militias during the civil war, after all, and could easily do so again. Roughly a third of the soldiers were Shia conscripts. Many were more loyal to Hezbollah than to the legal authorities.

"The Lebanese army is partly controlled by Syria, not like before 1975," Henry said. "Before 1975, the Lebanese army was pro-Western and neutral toward Israel."

As we left the city and the suburbs behind, apartment towers on the side of the road gave way to soft beaches and the floppy leaves of banana trees. The weather was still warm and sunny even late in the year. Lebanon, as always, looked greener than I remembered it when I was away.

"How badly was the south hit in July and August?" I asked.

Said laughed and shook his head. "You will see, my friend. You will see."

THE ROAD TO FATIMA GATE   179

We passed through the conservative Sunni coastal city of Sidon, where Rafik Hariri was born, and continued down along the shore of the Mediterranean toward the southern city of Tyre.

"What exactly, for the record, do you guys do in your organization?" I said.

"We advise the international community on how to implement U.N. Resolution 1559," Said said. "And we try to convince Lebanon to be less conservative, more open and liberal and democratic. We try to convince the international community that most of us are not fanatics, to make Lebanon a good example for everyone. We want to live our lives as free people like you do in the U.S. and Europe. We have a right."

"The Hezbollah camp downtown is ugly," Henry said. "This is not us. But it shows the world our differences. Most people think we live in a desert and ride camels and are all Muslims."

"Hezbollah is trying to distract the world from Iran's nuclear bomb," Said said, "by making trouble in Lebanon, killings, dissolving the government, and so on. Can you imagine what Iran would do if they got the nuclear bomb? My God. Even right now they do what they want and don't listen to anyone."

A young man stood in the middle of an intersection and waved glossy pamphlets at cars. Said pulled up alongside him.

"What is he handing out?" Noah said and rolled down his window.

"Hezbollah propaganda," Henry said.

Said stepped on the accelerator as Noah tried to grab one of the pamphlets.

"I want one of those," Noah said. But the Hezbollah man kept the pamphlets tightly clutched in his fingers.

"He is selling them," Said said, "not giving them away."

"Oops," Noah said. "I wasn't trying to steal one."

"He doesn't care about money or propaganda," Said said. "He is watching. This is the beginning of their territory. He reports on who is coming and what they are doing."

"Whenever you see something blown up from here," Henry said, "it is because it was owned by Hezbollah people or because Hezbollah had something to do with it."

The Jews love life, so that is what we shall take away from them. We are going to win because they love life and we love death."

In Beirut I saw little round stickers that said *No War* stuck in some of the shop windows. A friend of mine photographed a Muslim woman wearing a conservative headscarf at a rally downtown and holding up a placard that said *War No More*. In the suburbs north of Beirut, an enormous mural on the side of a commercial building urged citizens to *Wage Peace*.

The year before, a series of billboards all over Beirut said *Say No to Anger*, *Say No to War*, and *Say No to Terrorism*. Hezbollah would never have allowed anything of the sort to be erected in their parts of Lebanon, even though I knew lots of Shias who agreed with those sentiments. Almost all of Hezbollah's roadside propaganda was about terrorism, "resistance," and war.

The majority of the people in the south were Shias, but there were some Christian, Sunni, and Druze villages, too.

"The Christians down here are cornered," Henry said. He could have mentioned that the Sunni and Druze were, as well. "They have no freedom of movement. They only have freedom of speech inside their own villages. Outside their villages, they can't speak or talk to the press unless they leave the south."

"They have been a long time under Hezbollah control," Said said. "It's the same scenario as 1975, only with different players."

We drove past a concrete T-wall along the side of the road that had been painted top to bottom with the Hezbollah flag. The contrast between Hezbollah's militant logo, with its upraised AK-47 assault rifle, and the aesthetically pleasing rolling green hills in the background was jarring. It was impossible to forget who ruled the roost in the south.

"Nasrallah will go all the way now unless Siniora and Saad Hariri surrender," Said said. "Only if they surrender will Nasrallah spare them from the final solution."

This struck me as a bit on the paranoid side. Hezbollah could almost certainly win a defensive war against fellow Lebanese, but no one was strong enough to conquer and rule the whole country. "Everyone is against everyone else," President Amin Gemayel famously said[3] during the civil war, "and it all keeps going around and around in circles without anyone ever winning or anything being accomplished."

The totalitarian Velayat-e Faqih doctrine of the Iranian Revolution had quite a few takers in South Lebanon, even so. Portraits of Iran's dead grim-faced tyrant Ayatollah Khomeini and the current "Supreme Leader" Ayatollah Khamenei were as ubiquitous as ever.

As we drove through a small village, an imam screamed slogans in angry Arabic from the muezzin's speaker atop a mosque minaret.

It was a sharp contrast to what I was accustomed to hearing from the mosques in Beirut. In the capital, the muezzin's call to prayer was haunting and beautiful. It sounded spiritual, as though the muezzin himself were no longer tethered to this world. I could make out only some of the words from this southern mosque, but what the loudspeakers broadcast was clearly political and not religious.

"What exactly is he saying?" I asked.

"It is about Palestine," Said said. He listened. "He is saying, 'If we win this fight against the Siniora conspiracy, we will only have Palestine to liberate. We won't have Israel as an obstacle.'"

"They won't have Israel as an obstacle?" Noah said in a bemused tone of voice.

Just then we drove past a Hezbollah billboard atop a small local grocery store that had been punctured with holes by shrapnel from an Israeli air strike. One of the holes passed straight through the center of an image of Nasrallah's turban.

A convoy of Lebanese army trucks passed us on their way north.

"One thing we are worried about," Said said, "is the weakening of the south because the army has to go north. This is part of the plan."

We ventured deeper into the south, into the steep rolling hills dotted with villages and terraced for agriculture that make up the region just north of Israel's border. Few trees grew there. Many places were too rocky for farming, but the region still looked a bit like a tranquil Arcadia.

"It's beautiful here," Noah said. "This would be a great place for an artist's retreat if it weren't so dangerous."

"Beautiful country, fanatic people," Said said.

Most of the villages and towns were more or less intact, at least so far. We only occasionally drove past damaged houses or places where buildings had recently stood. But the farther south we drove, the more destruction we saw.

Dour-looking men stood on street corners and in the middle of intersections and carefully watched all the cars and people who entered the area. A few more on mopeds paid me a considerable amount of extra attention. I had seen similar young men doing the same thing in the Bekaa Valley just south of Baalbek. I didn't feel comfortable taking pictures with them around.

"You see the watchers?" Said said.

"They couldn't be any more obvious," I said. "Can we get out and talk to people around here?"

"I do not recommend it," Said said. "They cannot talk freely. These watchers will come up to us if we get out of the car, and they will make sure anyone who talks to us only tells us what they are supposed to say."

Soon we reached Bint Jbail, Hezbollah's de facto capital in South Lebanon. The outskirts were mostly undamaged, but the city center had been almost completely demolished by air strikes and artillery.

Said parked in the center of what used to be downtown and now looked like a rubble quarry. The four of us got out of the car. Noah and I walked around, dizzied by the extent of the 360-degree devastation.

We were surrounded on all sides by rocks, cinder-block rubble, glass, dirt, and bent rebar. I took a photograph of a dust-covered shoe that I hoped wasn't on somebody's foot when whatever happened to it had happened. The few walls left standing were pocked with shrapnel holes. Pieces of paper and plastic trash were scattered around. A few buildings around the rim of oblivion were only half destroyed, as if the fronts had been violently ripped away and tossed into the rubble pit. What was left of a roof draped precipitously over the sheared-off edge of one building like a curtain of concrete.

Strangely, a medium-sized tree grew amid this desolation. Somebody must have recently planted it.

"The devastation was stunning," Noah later wrote in *Azure*.[4] "The outer ring of the city had been less thoroughly bombed, but in the center there were only a handful of structures that even remained standing, much less intact. It had become a moonscape of pulverized rock. . . . The piles of rubble and crumbling Party of God buildings were in large part monuments to Israel's refusal to let Hezbollah's July provocation go unanswered. I understood that every day since the war, and for many months to come, Hezbollah's prideful warriors would be surrounded by this destruction, would hear the rubble crunching under their feet as they walked, would taste the dust that filled their mouths as they breathed. I wished that every Israeli could experience the feeling that had come over me; from Tel

184 SO THIS IS OUR VICTORY

Aviv and Jerusalem, it looked as if the war had ended ambiguously. Not in Bint Jbail."

"So this is our victory," Said said. "This is how Hezbollah wins. Israel destroys our country while they sleep safely and soundly in theirs."

Nasrallah's declaration of "divine victory" wasn't only belied by the physical destruction wrought on South Lebanon. One hundred sixty-three Israelis were killed in the war,[5] compared with as many as 1,191 Lebanese.[6] Hezbollah claimed it lost 250 fighters; Lebanese and United Nations officials said the number is closer to 500, while the Israel Defense Forces insisted it killed 600.

Three severe-looking men walked up to Said and Henry.

"Who are they, who are you, and what are you doing?" said the man in charge.

"They are international reporters," Henry said. He did not say, and should not have said, that we were *American* reporters. "They are here to document Israel's destruction of our country."

The men seemed satisfied with his answer and left us alone. I was glad Henry and Said were there with us. They were the ones asked to do the explaining rather than Noah and me.

I kept snapping pictures.

"Oh, man," Noah said. "Some real pain got dropped on this place."

We contemplated the destruction in silence for a few more minutes, then got back in the car. Said looked for the road to Maroun al-Ras, the next hollowed-out southern town on our itinerary. The streets, though, were confusing now that so many landmarks no longer existed. Only after a few laps around town could Said reorient himself.

"Three times on the same road, not good," Henry said.

Bint Jbail looked and felt totalitarian. So many people watched us carefully, suspiciously, as we drove past.

Noah could pass for Lebanese much more easily than I could. Of the four of us, I was the eye magnet. He should have been in the front seat instead of me.

If Said was right that the locals weren't allowed to speak freely, assuming they dissented from Nasrallah's party line, it must have felt totalitarian to some of the locals, as well. It wasn't North Korea by any means, but it was what Soviet dissident Natan Sharansky called a "fear society."

I was reminded of what a Shia friend who grew up in the *dahiyeh* had said to me when I asked him what would happen if he stepped into the street and yelled "I hate Hezbollah!"

"I'd get my ass kicked," he said. "No one would do that."

We reached Maroun al-Ras only a few minutes after leaving Bint Jbail. On the way into town, we passed a blown-up car on the side of the road that had nothing left but the rear bumper, the passenger side door, two front seats, and the floor.

Maroun al-Ras was the first Lebanese village seized by the IDF during the war. The scene was familiar—much of the center of town had been reduced to rubble.

One site stood out, though. At the top of a hill overlooking the Israeli border stood a mostly intact mosque surrounded by panoramic destruction. Scaffolding had been erected around the minaret, but whatever patchwork it needed appeared to be finished.

Israel may have overreacted in July and selected targets (the milk factory, bridges in the north, and so on) that should not have been hit, but the stark scene on the hill of Maroun al-Ras demonstrated that the Israeli military did not bomb indiscriminately, as some critics claimed. Unlike Hezbollah, the Israelis were able to hit what they wanted. They were also able to avoid hitting what they did not want to hit. That mosque had obviously been deliberately spared and would not have been standing if the Israelis had resorted to carpet bombing.

"My mother is from Deir Mimas," Said said. "In July, Hezbollah brought their weapons out of the caves and valleys and into the village. My family has a small house there that was burned during the war."

"I'm sorry," I said.

"Eh," Said said. "It's okay. It is fixed now. Anyway, at first Hezbollah fired their missiles from groves of olive trees. Then they got hit by the Israelis. So they moved into Deir Mimas because the other nearby option was Kfar Kila. Hezbollah didn't want the Shia villages hit, so they moved into Christian villages instead."

I wasn't sure that was right, but it was at least plausible. Noah and I stood right across from Kfar Kila during the war. The town was literally *on* the border, only twenty feet or so from the fence next to the Israeli town of Metula. Noah and I saw no damage whatsoever in Kfar Kila, and we were there just one day before the end of the war. We did hear automatic weapons fire in Kfar Kila, though, so there seemed to be some Hezbollah activity even if that activity didn't include the shooting of rockets.

We stopped at a roadside Christian-owned restaurant for lunch. There would be no men from Hezbollah inside. As Said parked the car, he turned the dial on the car stereo.

Scratchy voices in Hebrew came through the crackling static.

"Do you hear them?" he said. "Do you hear the Israelis?"

"Yep," I said. "Those are Israelis."

"We are right next to the border," Henry said.

We went into the restaurant and ordered pizza and sandwiches. The walls were painted white and sparsely decorated with beer signs and the like. Boxes of Kleenex were placed on the tables for customers to use as napkins.

Henry and I sat at a table while we waited for food. Said hovered over us, as did Noah with his camera. We were the only customers.

"We have been screaming about this conflict for thirty years now," Henry said as he dealt himself a hand of solitaire from a deck of cards in his pocket. "But no one ever listened to us. Not until September 11. Now you know how we feel all the time. You have to keep up the pressure. You can never let go, not for one day, one hour, not for one second. The minute you let go, Michael, they will fight back and get stronger. This is the problem with your foreign policy."

"Since 1975 we have been fighting for the free world," Said said. "We are on the front lines. Why doesn't the West understand this? America can withdraw from Iraq, you can go back to Oregon, but we are stuck here. We have to stay and live with what happens."

CHAPTER TWELVE

the siege of ain ebel

> The Western world
> should either defend us,
> or change its name.
> —A LEBANESE CHRISTIAN LEADER
> DURING THE CIVIL WAR

Amid the south's steep rolling hills, a mere handful of miles from the fence on the border with Israel, sat the besieged Christian community of Ain Ebel. It was often said that Lebanon is a victim of geography; few Lebanese were as unlucky as those who lived in Ain Ebel. For decades the people in this village were caught between the anvils of the Palestine Liberation Organization and Hezbollah on one side, and the hammer of the Israel Defense Forces on the other.

Noah and I had arranged to meet with Alan Barakat from the Ain Ebel Development Association. We met him outside a small grocery store owned by his uncle. He agreed to tell us about what happened to his community during the war in July, when Hezbollah seized civilian homes and used residents as human shields.

Ain Ebel was small, and we walked the streets on foot. I didn't see nearly as much destruction as I saw in the Hezbollah strongholds of Maroun-al Ras and Bint Jbail. Downtown seemed intact. In that sense, South Lebanon's Christians were lucky.

Downtown, so to speak, was hardly distinguishable from anywhere else in Ain Ebel. There wasn't much to it aside from a grocery store. I saw only two restaurants—the one outside town where we had just stopped for lunch and a little pizza place around the corner and just up the hill.

The residents were implacably hostile to Hezbollah and always had been. This was not a place where the Party of God could dig in, build bunkers, and store weapons. From Israel's point of view, Ain Ebel was, in military parlance, a "target poor" environment. That did not, however, stop Hezbollah from turning it into a battleground.

"There is a valley just below Ain Ebel," Alan said. "I will take you there later. Until the army came after the war, Hezbollah closed it. It was a restricted military area. They built bunkers there and stored Katyusha rockets and launchers. When the war started, they moved the launchers out of the valley and into our village. When the Israelis shot back, they hit some of our houses."

In Bint Jbail and Maroun al-Ras, whole city blocks were pulverized from the air. Some houses and buildings were merely damaged, but others were blown to their foundations. Nothing remained of whole swaths of these towns but fields of mostly cleared rubble. Hezbollah controlled Bint Jbail and Maroun al-Ras both before and during the war. Its fighters stockpiled rockets and other weapons in houses, turning them into targets.

Ain Ebel, however, was only used as a place to hide and as a place from which Hezbollah could launch rockets at the Israelis. Katyusha launchers weren't placed inside houses. They were, for the most part, placed next to houses. Most of the property damage, then, was caused by shrapnel rather than direct hits.

Most homes in Ain Ebel were simple. A few were made of stone and hearkened back to the days of the Ottoman Empire, but the majority had been constructed more recently. They were neither attractive nor unattractive. They were just basic, though fairly large, houses that wouldn't look out of place anywhere else in the Mediterranean region.

Some were so pocked with shrapnel holes, they looked as if some crazed militiaman had emptied entire magazines of AK-47 rounds into the walls. I saw one home where every last tile had been blown off the roof, and only the metal frame remained.

"No one is helping us," Alan said. "We are paying for all the reconstruction with our own money."

"You aren't getting any of the reconstruction money from Iran?" I said.

"Of course not," Alan said. "Of course Iran is not helping us rebuild our houses."

The Iranian government sent money, via Hezbollah, to at least some Lebanese people whose homes were damaged or destroyed during the war. If Alan was telling the truth, though, that money was not exactly evenly spread.

Reconstruction had progressed more in Ain Ebel than elsewhere, even so. Rubble clearance was the only noticeable improvement in Bint Jbail. Ain Ebel was less damaged, so there was less work to be done.

"Were people still living in Ain Ebel during the war?" I said.

"Yes, of course," Alan said. "Most of us stayed in the village for the first eighteen days."

"Were people still living in the houses that Hezbollah seized?" I said.

"No," Alan said. "Hezbollah only took over houses that had no one in them."

We came across a crater in the middle of a residential street on the edge of town left by an Israeli artillery shell.

"Did anyone here try to stop Hezbollah?" I said.

"How?" Alan said. "We have no weapons. Some people told Hezbollah to leave, but they pointed guns in our faces. 'Shut up, go back in your house,' we were told."

At the southern edge of town was an open field with a direct view to the south. Alan, Noah, and I stood there and looked toward Israel. The border was right there beyond some low rolling hills covered with grass and rock. The scene looked a little like Ireland.

"Hezbollah could have set up their rocket launchers here instead of in town," Noah said. "It's a straight shot into Israel."

"The houses and trees gave them better cover," Alan said. "The valley below, though, gave them even better cover than the village. If that's all they cared about, they would have stayed there."

We walked back downtown. I wanted to find more witnesses who stayed in Ain Ebel during the war.

Noah and I went toward the grocery store owned by Alan's uncle. A poster on the wall outside showed an open hand, palm up in the "stop" position, in front of four strands of barbed wire. Text in Arabic warned children to beware of land mines left behind by Israelis in the 1980s and 1990s.

A convoy of French soldiers from UNIFIL rolled down the street in armored personnel carriers and stopped in front of the store. A handful got out. They wore Smurf-blue berets and carried automatic weapons slung behind their backs. Noah badly wanted to ask them what, exactly, they were doing down there in South Lebanon, but they weren't allowed to speak to us because we didn't have a permit from the United Nations authorizing an interview.

Noah and I followed them into the store. A grim-faced soldier placed five bottles of Lebanon's Château Kefraya on the counter.

"Are those for Hezbollah?" Noah said jokingly. I chuckled.

"No," said the soldier without showing even a trace of a sense of humor.

"The French like to spend time in Ain Ebel," Alan said. "They are welcome here. They feel comfortable. They help our economy. In Bint Jbail, some of the residents make slashing motions across their throats with their fingers when they see U.N. soldiers."

I felt bad for laughing when I heard that. South Lebanon was a hard place. UNIFIL's soldiers weren't allowed to disarm Hezbollah and prevent the next round of war. That would have required their authorization as a combat force. But they did what they could within sharply proscribed limits, and they spent most of their time in a shattered and hostile environment.

Alan's uncle behind the cash register defended the French.

"I feel safer now with them here than I've felt for more than thirty years," he said.

It was easy to find another civilian who stayed in the village during the war. He said he would be happy to talk to me as long as I promised not to publish his name. He didn't even tell me his name, so he had nothing to worry about. I'll just call him Jad.

I turned on my voice recorder.

"So you stayed in Ain Ebel through the whole war?" I said.

"Yes," Jad said.

"At what point did Hezbollah come to the village and fire their missiles?" I said.

"During the war they took some uninhabited houses at the edge of our village and stayed there."

"Uninhabited?" I said.

"Yes, uninhabited," he said. "Nobody was there, so they took them. They were eating in there, sleeping in there, and maybe doing some reconnaissance. They chose specific houses because nobody was living there and nobody would know."

"Did they choose to come to this town for strategic or tactical reasons?" Noah said. "Or was it because it's a Christian town?"

"Strategically, of course," Jad said. "It's a high peak. It is very good strategically. But they could have chosen these parts, these lands. . ." He gestured with his arm toward the valley below, the place Alan promised to take us next. "It would have been more protection for them than this village. So why did they come here? I think it's because it's a Christian village. They do this."

"Did anybody who lives here try to get Hezbollah to leave the village?" I said.

"We don't have any arms," Jad said. "Hezbollah has arms. But there was this incident that happened. Next to a guy's place they were firing Katyushas—you know, missiles. They were firing from the house. This guy went out and said, 'Please do not fire from our home, from in front of our house. My father is very ill and there are some children in the house.' They came to him and said, 'Shut up, go in your house, this is none of your business.'"

What Jad said closely matched what Alan had told me.

Then he told me something off the record. He made me turn off my voice recorder before he would say it. I cannot and will not relay what he told me, but he wanted me to know that the people of Ain Ebel did use secret nonviolent countermeasures against Hezbollah, and that Hezbollah had no idea what was happening. Their countermeasures sounded smart to me, and it seemed as though they were partly effective.

I turned my voice recorder back on, but I didn't realize until later that it was stuck on "pause." So I'll have to paraphrase what he said next.

He told me that eighteen days after the start of the war, a large group of civilians decided it was time to leave Ain Ebel and flee to the north. They were no longer willing to stay while Israel fired back at Hezbollah's rocket launchers. It was too dangerous, and Hezbollah insisted on staying and endangering those who lived there.

So they fled the area in a convoy of civilian vehicles. It was safer, they figured, to travel in a group than to travel alone.

On their way out of the village, Hezbollah fighters stood on the side of the road and opened fire with automatic weapons on the fleeing civilians.

I was shocked, and I asked Alan if he could confirm this. Was it really true? Hezbollah opened fire on Lebanese civilians? Alan confirmed this was true.

"Why?" I knew why, but I wanted a local person to say it.

"Because," Alan said, "Hezbollah wanted to use the civilians of Ain Ebel as human shields."

Fortunately, Hezbollah didn't kill anybody when they opened fire. One person was shot in the hand, and another was shot in the shoulder. This was enough, though, to get the job done. The civilians turned around and went back to the village under Israeli bombardment.

The same story made its way onto the Internet in late July. A Lebanese blogger who went by the anonymous handle N10452 tried to sound the alarm.

"The situation in Ain Ebel is unbearable," he wrote.[1] "Thousands of civilians have fled to the village from nearby villages and more than 1,000 rockets have hit the village. There is no more food, neither clean water and diseases are spreading. Now here comes the most sickening part: Hezbollah has been firing rockets from the village since Day 1 hiding behind innocent people's places and even *churches*. No one is allowed to argue with the Hezbollah gunmen who won't hesitate to shoot you, and I've heard about more than one shooting incident including young men from the village and Hezbollah. Urgent appeals have been done through phone calls from terrified people who wouldn't give out their name fearing Hezbollah might harm or even eliminate them."

"I'm from Ain Ebel," wrote another.[2] "The situation is real bad. People are being used as human shields for Hezbollah to launch rockets. No one dares to stop them, they are threatening the citizens if they argue with them. Hezbollah guerrillas are holding rockets and launching them and then hide between the houses or in the bushes. The people don't have food. For example my uncle lost around 7kg. All they have is to get one small meal a day, *rgheef khibiz*, and 2, 3 cups of water."

New York Times correspondent Sabrina Tavernise reported something similar the next day.[3]

"Hezbollah came to Ain Ebel to shoot its rockets," Fayad Hanna Amar said in Tyre. "They are shooting from between our houses. Please, write that in your newspaper."

One local resident told Tavernise that Hezbollah killed a man who tried to flee Ain Ebel as the Israelis blew up the launchers from the other side of the horizon and from the skies.

Alan then took me, Noah, and Said down into the valley below the village, the previously restricted military zone where Hezbollah fighters built bunkers, dug foxholes, and stashed weapons before they moved their operations into civilian areas.

A local teenager named Victor came along for the ride. He thought it would be cool to check out the area now that someone would show him.

Alan told us to stay on the road because Israeli land mines might still be around. There were, perhaps, more land mines in South Lebanon than there were people.

The road into the valley was made of dirt and large stones. Vegetation looked like Mediterranean scrub bush from a distance, but up close it was clear that some of these "bushes" were three times my height.

"Did Hezbollah build this road?" I asked.

"No," Alan said. "It is agricultural."

Victor spotted some camouflage netting in one of the bushes. He and Noah pulled it out. "Radar scattering," Noah said as he read the tag. "This is American."

He tried to cut the tag so he could keep it as a souvenir, but it wouldn't come off.

The valley did seem like it would have provided better cover for Hezbollah than the village. The sky above was open enough that Katyusha rockets easily could be fired directly at Israel. Camouflaged foxholes and bunkers among the bushes and trees provided much better protection than houses that could be easily spotted by the Israeli Air Force and that showed up prominently on satellite and aerial surveillance photographs. No Israeli ground troops would have wanted to go into that valley without first softening up the area with air strikes and artillery. It was the perfect environment for ambushes and sniper attacks.

The sun dropped quickly below the horizon. South Lebanon is not as high as the Mount Lebanon range in the north, but it's high enough that the cool Levantine air of early winter turned frigid as the light went out of the sky.

"There is a destroyed bunker up ahead," Alan said as he stepped off the road. "Come on."

"Is it safe?" I said. "What about land mines?"

"I have been here before," Alan said. "Hezbollah was here. It should be safe."

So we stepped off the road and walked through a dense grove of olive trees toward one of Hezbollah's demolished fortifications. I walked gingerly and tried to step in the footprints of others.

There was no sound in the valley. I couldn't hear anything but grass and twigs gently giving way under five pairs of feet. Alan was probably right that there were no land mines in the immediate area. Otherwise, Hezbollah would have dug in somewhere else.

But what about unexploded ordnance from Israeli cluster bombs? Those were still lying around. I might as well have stepped on a land mine if I ended up kicking a bomblet by accident.

The faint cold light of dusk illuminated the sky like a backlit screen, but all was dark in the valley on the trail beneath the trees. I tried to imagine what it must have been like if Israeli soldiers walked the same path only a few months before. Some Hezbollah fighters wore the uniforms of the Israel Defense Forces. They used night-vision goggles. They hunkered down in foxholes and waited.

The valley must have been reasonably safe or Alan wouldn't have taken us down there, but the enveloping darkness and the all-too-recent violence made me wonder, although not very seriously, if Hezbollah had really been flushed out and kept out.

The bombed-out bunker was just up ahead under some trees. It was, indeed, very well hidden.

"If I were going to build a bunker," Noah said, "this is where I'd put it."

Nevertheless, it had been hit. And it was hit badly. Anyone hiding inside during the air strike surely would have been killed.

We dug through the rubble. There were a few pieces of rusted metal and splintered wood here and there, but the bunker had been made mostly of cinder blocks that had gone flying in every direction.

"There was a sink," Alan said and pointed to the right of the entrance. "And here is some cable for faxes and phones."

"Look," Victor said. "A lid from a weapons crate."

"Dude," Noah said. "Check out the showerhead."

Sure enough, there was a showerhead at my feet.

It was impossible to tell when the bunker was hit, whether it was at the beginning, during the middle, or at the end of the war. Since there was no evidence that anyone was inside when the strike came, I assumed it was hit in the middle or at the end after Hezbollah had already moved into Ain Ebel.

I'm not a military forensics expert, but everything Alan told me about Hezbollah relocating to Ain Ebel during the war seemed to add up and match the physical evidence I could see. The valley obviously was used as a military area, and so was the village. But the village wasn't controlled by Hezbollah before the war started. Its fighters had clearly moved into Ain Ebel at some point.

196 ⌒ THE SIEGE OF AIN EBEL

We walked back to the car in absolute darkness and drove for a minute or so. Alan parked alongside an open ditch next to the road.

"The Israelis were here," he said. "They left some of their food."

At my feet was an empty can of tinned fish. Some of the words on the can were written in Hebrew.

Alan was right. The Israelis were there, recently enough that no one had bothered to pick up their trash yet. I tossed the can of fish back into the ditch, thinking with a grim almost certainty that they would be back.

CHAPTER THIRTEEN

the solution is in tehran

The solution is
not in Lebanon.
—WALID JUMBLATT

Every one of my Lebanese friends and sources told me to stay the hell out of the *dahiyeh*. Driving down south with locals who knew the back roads was one thing. Poking around in Hezbollah's shattered command and control center was another. In the wake of the July War, the most paranoid party in Lebanon was more twitchy than ever.

That was before I met Sayyed Mohammad Ali al-Husseini, a Shia cleric who outranked Hassan Nasrallah and waged a one-man campaign against the Party of God from right under its nose.

He took me for a ride through the southern suburbs in his sporty SUV outfitted with four-wheel drive and tinted black windows. With his beard, glasses, and turban, he looked a bit like Nasrallah himself, and he drove through the streets like a stuntman in an action movie, thrilling to the high-tech growl of his engine when he depressed the accelerator.

The scene was one of mass destruction and misery. "You can take pictures," he said and flicked a button that lowered my window on the passenger side. "Don't worry. No one will do anything or say anything to you if you are with me."

This was important. Hussein Naboulsi from Hezbollah's media relations department explicitly warned me never to do it. Even local people weren't allowed to photograph their own neighborhood without being detained and investigated by security men from the party. Lebanese citizens in Hezbollah territory fed massive amounts of intelligence to the Israelis, and Nasrallah knew he was at the top of the IDF's hit list.

Al-Husseini wore the black turban of a sayyed—a descendent of the Prophet Muhammad. He could take pictures of anything he damn well pleased, and so could his guests. He was as close to being untouchable as a person could be in an assassination-plagued country like Lebanon.

Our first stop was just a few streets from his house. Entire blocks where twelve-story towers once stood were now craters, some deep enough that you'd break your neck if you fell into them. Thousands of tons of rubble had been carted away, and thousands of tons still remained.

"Did you stay here during the war?" I said and shuddered at the thought of hunkering down while these massive structures exploded around me.

"No!" he said, like I was crazy even for asking. "No one could stay here. Everyone had to leave."

The Israelis dropped leaflets over the neighborhood warning residents to clear out of the way of incoming air strikes. They had to. The *dahiyeh* was vertically packed with tens of thousands of civilians. It was also where Hezbollah concentrated its critical infrastructure and was therefore hit harder than any other built-up place in the country. Israel's government hoped demolishing Nasrallah's stronghold would at least deter future attacks if it didn't destroy the leadership altogether.

It's possible that Nasrallah quietly decided not to start any more fights with his neighbors, but there wasn't much evidence that that was the case. He insisted the "resistance" would continue indefinitely, and he was rapidly replenishing and even upgrading his rocket and missile stocks from Iran via Syria. His constituents cheered him even while thousands lost their homes and even more lived in fear next to shattered apartment buildings towering precariously over the ruined cityscape.

Al-Husseini's fuel ran low, so he pulled into a station to fill up the tank. I stepped out as the attendant inserted the pump. A group of children ran up to the driver's side door and excitedly yelled "Sayyed! Sayyed!" as though al-Husseini were some kind of black-robed Santa Claus figure. The attendant grinned as though he felt lucky to be in the presence of such a great man. If anyone who recognized al-Husseini resented him for condemning Hezbollah, they didn't show it.

He drove me to the place that used to be Hezbollah's media relations department before it was pulverized, where Hussein Naboulsi worked before leaving the party. Nothing remained but a pit the size of a city block. I could not help but wonder: What does a person *do* for a living after quitting a terrorist organization? Work at the local CD store? Host a show on *Al Jazeera*? Perhaps the Syrians would have something for him, though the pay was probably lower.

I swallowed hard as I photographed the devastation, partly because I had been to some of those places while they were intact, but also because the contrast with central Beirut was even more staggering than it used to be.

The Shia experience in Lebanon was diverging from that of the Sunnis, Christians, and Druze more than it had for decades. The *dahiyeh*, like much of the south, was a disaster area. Shattered glass, chunks of concrete, garbage, and twisted rebar were everywhere. It looked as though the place had been hit by a megathrust quake.

Meanwhile, downtown Beirut looked glitzier than I had ever seen it. The city center was in better shape overall than it had been at any time since the early 1970s, despite the war and Hezbollah's encampment. Lebanon's capital was in the midst of a boom, while Hezbollah's "capital" looked as though World War II had just blown through it. The two Lebanons were moving, at great velocity, in opposite directions physically and economically, as well as culturally and politically.

The Shia had always been the most politically and economically marginal of Lebanon's sects, and Nasrallah set them back decades with the ruin and violent catastrophe he called down on their heads. As Lebanese scholar Tony Badran noted, Nasrallah reversed every single gain they had made since the cleric Musa Sadr awakened them from their political slumber during the run-up to the civil war. They needed and deserved better than this, as all human beings do, and could hardly have been saddled with a less deserving *zaim* if one had been imposed on them by their enemies.

Al-Husseini had different ideas, ideas that might have resonated with even conservative Shias if Hezbollah hadn't aggressively marginalized him.

His credentials could hardly be better. Not only was he a sayyed, but he earned a doctorate in religion from the holy city of Qom in Iran. Unlike Hezbollah, though, he used the Koran and the Islamic religion as his foundation for a vision of peace, independence, and democracy for the people of Lebanon.

"I am against the wars and the violence because of my faith," he told me. "Any violence, any terrorism." He handed me the English translation of a book he wrote called *Questions and Answers About Violence and Nonviolence*. "I published this to explain the difference between the religion and those who are pretending to follow the religion. The proof of my words is that Mr. Bush said we must differentiate between the kinds of Muslims. I have faith in peace. That is why I am sitting with you. That I am Muslim and you are Christian doesn't matter because I believe in peace."

His book is short, to the point, and exactly what people in his community needed to hear from someone they trusted.

"I hope that the State Department would invite me and some of my friends to discuss the situation here in Lebanon," he said. "They think the Shia people here are all on Nasrallah's side. That is not right."

It was true, of course, that not every Shia supported Hassan Nasrallah. Even many who did had reservations. His allies in the Amal movement weren't interested in Khomeini's Islamic revolution, nor were they keen on starting wars with the Zionist Entity. Even some Hezbollah supporters were only in it for the social services benefits. They were grateful for support from Tehran as long as Lebanon didn't import its authoritarian ways, and, like most sane human beings, they'd prefer not be "martyred" by Israeli air strikes.

"Because my movement is peaceful," al-Husseini said, "we don't have anybody from outside supporting us. Hopefully you can help. We need support. What did Hezbollah do to become popular up until now? They had four hospitals in the *dahiyeh*. They had thirty madrassas, or schools. They had thirty foundations for supporting work for the people. Also they bring engineers, doctors, and they have plenty of money. They have a TV channel, radio, newspapers, soldiers. They are a country inside a country, a government inside a government. They have all the money. They have the force to do this. Also, in the south it's the same situation. They built hospitals there, and also in Baalbek. Hezbollah pays for the people to build and repair their houses. So the two reasons are money and services. They use those to gather the people around them."

How could the likes of Sayyed al-Husseini compete with Hezbollah's power and wealth? Most Lebanese Shias were unaware that al-Husseini's path was even an option.

Local journalists couldn't interview him. Dissent from the likes of a person like him was intolerable and had to be smashed. Hezbollah issued its threats, and after a two-year car-bombing spree against journalists, threats from a Syrian ally like Nasrallah packed weight.

"If we want to change, we need an alternative," he said. "Here in Lebanon, the Iranian money, for example, is paying for portable water tanks with Iranian flags on them. If you want to take Iran out of Lebanon, you must bring another one with a Lebanese flag on it."

The state had always neglected the Shia regions in Lebanon, and that gave Hezbollah an opening. Once Nasrallah's people muscled their way in, they couldn't let the state provide services without making themselves largely redundant, especially after the Israeli soldiers withdrew in 2000.

Iran's Islamic Republic regime spent hundreds of millions in Lebanon for the same reason. Many Hezbollah dependents thought of themselves as part of a transnational sectarian community with Tehran as its capital rather than a multisectarian nation-state with Beirut as its capital.

"I am Lebanese," al-Husseini said. "I am with Lebanon. My loyalty is to Lebanon. The Shia sect must serve Lebanon. We were born in this country, we live here, we grow here. We must serve and defend its independence and territories. I love Lebanon, and I am ready to serve my country. A man who does not help his country is not good for anything."

Middle East scholar Daniel Pipes[1] once said that "radical Islam is the problem, and moderate Islam is the solution." In 2007, though, the odds that liberal and moderate Shias in Lebanon might defeat Hezbollah in the near term were effectively zero. Sayyed al-Husseini was no match for Hezbollah. He had neither the money nor the profile to compete. Worse, his views got little traction even with those who did hear his message. The only way to beat Nasrallah, or so he came to believe, was through co-option.

He later told Saudi Arabia's *Al Arabiya* news network[2] that he formed his own 3,000-man-strong militia—the Arab Islamic Resistance—that he would use to fight Israel. Everything he said on TV that day was a lie. He didn't have a "resistance" army, nor would he have been able to field one if he tried. This was a desperate Hail Mary publicity stunt. It even worked for a few days, though not the way he intended. He got some attention all right, but practically everyone dismissed him as a liar and a buffoon. He had no credibility as a militia leader since he did not have a militia, and he could never lead a credible peace movement.

Lokman Slim, a liberal Shia activist who worked against long odds for democracy from inside the *dahiyeh*, rolled his eyes when I asked him about this. "Al-Husseini is just an opportunist," he said. "Don't pay any attention to him." Slim and his small band of fellow activists in the community were more honest and reliable, but they were no less marginalized and had no better shot at toppling Hassan Nasrallah than al-Husseini did.

After the war in July and August, and with Hezbollah's ongoing siege of downtown, any effective resistance against the resistance would have to be mounted by Sunnis, Christians, and Druze.

⌒

I booked an appointment with Eli Khoury, one of the most dedicated leaders of the March 14 movement whom I met during the Beirut Spring. He still put in overtime hours while many of his old comrades stayed home and hugged their flags while waiting for the darkening Hezbollah storm to blow over.

He was one of the sharpest political analysts in the country and an informal adviser to a number of political figures, including Druze leader Walid Jumblatt and Prime Minister Fouad Siniora. I went to see him in his postmodern office in the Quantum tower, the nerve center of his various democracy and civil society projects.

"What are you working on these days?" I asked him.

He looked as though he belonged in California with his ponytail and unbuttoned shirt, and he had actually lived in Los Angeles for a while before returning home to Beirut.

"Have you seen our *I Love Life* billboards?" he said and smiled.

I had. They were ubiquitous in the Christian, Sunni, and Druze parts of the country, and their message could not have been simpler. Clean white letters spelled out *I Love Life* in English, French, and Arabic on a red background. Neither Hezbollah nor Amal allowed Khoury's people to place the billboards in the Shia regions, where "resistance" propaganda and portraits of suicide bombers were erected instead.

"Hezbollah intimidates me on their TV channel," he said. "They are calling me a racist now because of this campaign, because I'm implying that they love death."

Hassan Nasrallah himself, though, said Hezbollah's greatest advantage was its romance with death and destruction.

"Most civilizations die by their own hand," my friend, colleague, and Middle East expert Lee Smith wrote in *The Strong Horse*,[3] "a lesson that originates with Ibn Khaldun, whose cyclical theory of history explains that civilizations in their final stages are incapable of defending themselves—in other words, they lose their will to live. The issue with the Arabs is not that they will not fight, but their appetite for warfare disguises the fact that the Arabs are losing their will to live. Never before in the annals of history has suicide played such a large role as it has in the last quarter century of Arab warfare."

Smith's diagnosis may sound over the top, but I'm not sure it is. Khoury's *I Love Life* campaign wouldn't elicit much notice, let alone controversy, in the West, yet it enraged Hezbollah and resonated powerfully with Lebanon's liberals and moderates. Palestinian suicide bombers inspired the term "death cult" to describe the ideology that led young men and even women to annihilate themselves and others, but it was Hezbollah that popularized suicide bombings in the Arab world in the first place.

David Samuels quoted a Lebanese Shia in the *New Republic* who was despondent about the party's necrotic obsessions.[4] "Did Hassan Nasrallah ever have an espresso at a café in Beirut?" the man said. "Did he ever go out to a restaurant and eat a steak? He was talking about death [in a recent speech]. He was asking, 'Have you ever heard of the last moments before death?' You have no idea how terrible these moments are. He was describing the very precise nature of this pain. His point was that the only way to die is as a martyr. He said, 'As you know, everyone dies. So why not choose to die as a martyr, and save yourself the pain of these awful moments between life and death?' I am driving my 2009 car, and this guy is telling me how to die better. Two hours before, I was talking with my financial adviser in Boston. So, practically, you see, this is our problem."

"The whole concept of Hezbollah is to use human shields," Khoury said back at his Quantum Group office. "Not everyone in Lebanon understands this, though, because Hezbollah tries so hard to cultivate an image of decency. Also, politicians here are reticent to say everything they believe. They have to be careful how far they go when they criticize Hezbollah and the Syrians. Sometimes they go back and forth for a while and contradict themselves before they are able to take a firm stand."

We saw this sort of reticence even with Druze leader Walid Jumblatt, who was at that time the fiercest critic of the Syrian-Iranian-Hezbollah axis in the country. Jumblatt actually called for regime change in Syria, and he accused Hezbollah of having a hand in the ongoing assassinations of journalists and members of parliament. He had kept his ties with Hezbollah for a while even after the Syrians left, however, referring to its fighters as a legitimate "resistance" army, saying they should be allowed to hold onto their weapons, and so on. Not until the end of 2005 did Jumblatt's opposition to Hezbollah become absolute.

"The Israelis bombed these bridges all over the country," Khoury said and sighed. "Why? If you want to hit the most important bridge bringing weapons into Lebanon, hit Syria. Why do they want to protect him?"

It did sometimes look, from Lebanon anyway, like Israel was perversely aligned with al-Assad. In the real world this was nonsense, of course, but from a practical point of view, it hardly made any difference. While most Lebanese wanted either regime change or regime punishment in Syria, the Israeli government openly and categorically opposed any such thing. The Israelis dreaded the idea of post-Baathist Syria, fearing the reactionary Muslim Brotherhood might take over in Damascus and transform the country into something like Gaza.

"Ninety-nine percent of our problems are Syrian," Khoury said. "An Alawite government in Syria is good for us. Just not this Alawite government. Anything, even a bin Ladenist government, would be better than the Baath government."

Most Lebanese people I knew, including liberal Shias, would have been perfectly happy had the Israelis bombed Syria after Hezbollah killed and captured their soldiers. A large number of people in an Arabic-speaking country openly supporting an Israeli war against another Arab country would have been something to see. It might have changed forever some of the geopolitical dynamics in the Levant.

"If the Israelis were smarter," Khoury said, "there would be a lot more pro-Israeli opinion in Lebanon. Most of us sympathized with Israel's response for the first couple of days, until they bombed the airport. We thought it was fishy, though, when there was no ground war. They fought the war like it was a Nintendo game. I know the Israelis are careful with their targets, but you never know if the guy flying the bomber over your head at any given moment might miss."

His personal assistant brought him a thin, boring sandwich.

"I'm on a diet," he said as she slid the plate toward him across his desk, "so this is all I get. I eat when I get stressed. Nasrallah makes me gain weight. I put on ten kilos during the war."

"The Israelis were hoping Lebanon would rise up against Hezbollah," I said.

"How are we supposed to deal with Hezbollah," he said, "when Israel's Syrian buddies keep arming them? And when the Israelis themselves can't beat Hezbollah?"

The Israelis used to believe Lebanon would be one of the first Arab countries to sign a peace treaty, but that was before Khomeini's revolution in 1979, before the rise of Hezbollah, before the Israeli-Maronite alliance went sideways, and before Syria's invasion and de facto annexation. Lebanon was still more open to the idea of eventual reconciliation than many, if not most, Arab countries, but it often didn't appear that way from the outside.

"There's an old idea that's been around in Lebanon for a while now," I said, "and I think it confuses a lot of people. Prime Minister Siniora recently said it again, that Lebanon will be the *last* Arab country to make peace with Israel."

"The last Arab country," Khoury said. "This is the statement of those who want to make peace but know that they can't. They don't want to get ganged up on by the Arabs. We are the least anti-Israel Arab country in the world."

Lebanon has some broadly liberal traditions, and many Lebanese are non-Arab Christians who, under different circumstances, might be Israel's natural allies. Even so, some looked no less problematic for Israel and the West than the region's Pan-Arabists and Islamists. Michel Aoun, leader of the predominantly Maronite Free Patriotic Movement, appeared, at least from a distance, like some kind of Christian crypto-jihadist when he forged his tactical alliance with Hezbollah.

"Aoun just wants to be president," Khoury said. "He doesn't give a flying fuck how he gets there, even if he destroys Lebanon. He's positioned himself as the bottleneck so he can be the solution. He learned this well from the al-Assad regime. His intelligentsia is gone. He's left with people who think he is right about everything. Twenty percent of Aoun's people are militant and will do whatever he says. Another 20 percent believe his silly story that Saudi Arabia is trying to take over Lebanon."

Maronites rightly feared and loathed the extreme Wahhabi sect that many wealthy Saudis spent millions of dollars promoting outside their borders, but Aoun was wrong about the Saudis in Lebanon. They weren't trying to take it over, and even if they were, austere desert Islam didn't sell well in this generally open and oftentimes Westward-looking society on the Mediterranean.

Saad Hariri, son of the former prime minister, headed his father's Future Movement party, and *he* certainly was not a Wahhabi. He built mosques, sure, but he was far more interested in secular politics, capitalism, video games on his Xbox console, and justice for his father's murderers.

The Saudis liked Lebanon the way it was. They liked having a decadent playground where they could romp around like playboys without having to travel to Europe, where they felt less comfortable and less welcome.

Aoun had to have some kind of excuse for his alliance with an Islamist militia. He couldn't just blow it off with his Maronite constituents as though it was not a big deal, and playing the Saudi card was no more absurd than anything else he might have come up with.

Nadim Koteich, a liberal Shia who worked as a journalist for Hariri's *Future TV*, explained to me what he thought Aoun was up to.

"Aoun thinks Hezbollah is a wave at its top, at its end," he said. "He thinks the future belongs to the Sunnis, not to Hezbollah. And he thinks that because Hezbollah is at the top of its wave, he can just jump on this wave and take advantage of the power it has at this moment. He knows that in Lebanon, in a region like the Middle East, Hezbollah doesn't have a long-term future."

"But Hezbollah has all the military power," I said. "The Sunnis have nothing."

"You cannot say the Sunnis have nothing," he said. "The Sunnis are the demographic power in the region. The Sunnis are the Saudis. The Shia of the region are like 8 or 12 percent. There is no future for a guerrilla. Yes, Hezbollah is as strong as you can imagine—even stronger—but they don't have a future. If they changed course, if they adapted to international law and accepted the Taif Agreement, they might have a chance, but they would no longer be the Hezbollah we know."

"How will the current situation actually change, though?" I said. "Who is going to stop them?"

"They have to change," he said. "They can't go on like this. You can't be as strong as Hezbollah and as pretentious as Hezbollah without an enemy to fight, without a mission to accomplish. They spend an enormous effort searching for the enemy rather than fighting the enemy. They don't find the enemy. Where's the enemy? Where's Israel? It's not inside Lebanon any longer. The problem, the paradox that every single resistance experiences—and it's bitter—is that they can't continue resisting indefinitely after liberation."

He was right, of course, or at least he'd be in the long run. In the meantime, Hezbollah was still "resisting." Nasrallah could set both Israel and Lebanon on fire whenever he felt like it. He still had the power to bully—and perhaps even topple—Lebanon's government. And Michel Aoun, rather than help ensure Hezbollah's wave had already crested, boosted Nasrallah's stature with a Maronite fig leaf.

Khoury had the most reliable public-opinion data in the country, so I asked him how many Christians actually found Aoun appealing. He used to be one of the most popular Maronite leaders when he commanded what was left of the army and resisted the Syrian invasion in the late 1980s, but his star had fallen since he signed his "memorandum of understanding" with Hezbollah.

"Most Christians are liberal," Khoury said, "and will not be attracted to narrow sectarian parties like the Lebanese Forces except in times of danger. Aoun provided an outlet for these people by being deliberately nonsectarian. The problem with his strategy, though, is that he lost a lot of Christians and didn't gain many Shias. Before Pierre Gemayel was assassinated, Aoun polled at around 37 percent of Christians, but he lost a lot of support since then. We want to replace the March 14 movement with a broader civil society movement. This way we can include the Aounists and isolate the pro-Syrians. Only around 30 percent of the Shias are ready for a movement like this, but the overwhelming majority from all other groups are already there."

"What will it take to get the Shia on board with this project?" I said.

"The Shia are naturally liberal," he said. "They are not, when left alone, interested in jihad. Traditionally they have been secular and leftist. Do you know why they used to be secular leftists?"

I didn't.

"Schoolteachers who were leftists weren't wanted in Beirut," he said, "so they were sent out to small towns in the Shia parts of the country. Then Iran came in and replaced them with Hezbollah. They will come around when Hezbollah is gone. Samir Kassir's Democratic Left used to be communist and pro-Syrian, but now they are militantly anti-Syrian. When political theories fail in the Middle East, they fail hard. People who believed in them have a tendency to support a total opposite point of view later. That's why the Shia will be okay after Hezbollah is defeated."

"Hezbollah will always have some support, though," I said.

"Yes," he said. "Among irrelevant people. The fact that we have some of these silly leftists who support Hezbollah just shows we are a normal country. We are like everyone else. Those people are everywhere. Did you see the protestors in London who said, 'We are all Hezbollah now'? Give me a break."

"What is the solution to this problem?" I said.

It was such an American question. Over time I learned to stop asking it, just as I learned to stop asking about a solution to the Israeli-Palestinian conflict after both Israelis and Palestinians told me to stop it. I was only slowly beginning to understand what every March 14 person knew in his or her bones, that no plausible solution existed for now.

Americans like to believe every problem is fixable. Journalist and author Jeffrey Goldberg referred to this mentality, when it guided American policy in the region, as "solutionism." The Middle East is more fatalistic. Politics have always been violent in that part of the world.

Even the March 14 revolution, nonviolent as it may have been, was backed by the implicit threat of force from America. "I am not Saddam Hussein," Bashar al-Assad said before ordering his troops to withdraw. "I want to cooperate." If the United States hadn't recently toppled Saddam Hussein's regime in Iraq, it's entirely possible that al-Assad would have responded the way his father did to the Muslim Brotherhood uprising in the city of Hama—by killing thousands without flinching and then boasting about it.

Khoury answered my question, though, with a hypothetical solution that might have worked had it been tried.

"The solution to Hezbollah is a United Nations Chapter VII resolution," he said. "Like in Kosovo. When there is a will, there is a way. It will take fighting, though. Hezbollah will not just give up their guns. One thing we can do is bring back General Aoun's old officers. They have guts, and they are multiconfessional."

He pulled out a piece of paper and drew, in a single flourish, a remarkably detailed silhouette map of the country that included most, if not all, of the contours of Lebanon's coastline and land borders. Then he drew circles around the Shia areas in the south and the Bekaa Valley.

"Block off the Shia areas," he said. "Surround them utterly with international troops, like from NATO. NATO can do this if Israel stands aside, withdraws from the [allegedly occupied] Shebaa Farms, and stops all these overflights. Then deploy smartly, and do it slowly. I'm not saying storm Lebanon, go house to house, and kill a bunch of people. Just surround them, block them off from Syria forever, and announce that it's over. Eighty percent of Lebanon would accept this if it's done right, with government and international approval, and if Israel, at the same time, resolves the outstanding issues."

The problem with this, aside from the fact it meant war would return to Lebanon yet again, was that it had no chance of actually happening. The United Nations wouldn't sanction a combat force in Lebanon. Not even during the time of the Bush administration did the United States seriously contemplate such a thing. The Israelis wouldn't surrender to any Lebanese demands—such as a cessation of aerial overflights—unless Hezbollah was first disarmed. Lebanon's Prime Minister Fouad Siniora had no stomach for fighting or authorizing a war against anyone.

Even so, Khoury was right that any solution to the Hezbollah problem would have to come from the outside. Washington, though, couldn't fix it, nor could Jerusalem. The solution would have to be applied in the east, in the land of Ruhollah Khomeini.

⌒

None of Lebanon's *zuama* opposed Hezbollah's agenda more fiercely than the wizened Druze warlord and Progressive Socialist Party leader Walid Jumblatt. He spent most of his time in his Ottoman-era castle at Mukhtara high above Beirut in the Chouf Mountains, but he took time out between meeting European members of the Socialist International at his second house in the capital to meet me for coffee in his salon.

Arranging that meeting wasn't easy. It was more difficult, in fact, than making an appointment with Hezbollah officials. His press secretary repeatedly told me I had dialed the wrong number even though I knew I had not.

He almost convinced me. I actually had misdialed the first time, and the woman who answered laughed uproariously when I asked for an interview with Walid Jumblatt. I didn't think my error was funny until I imagined someone calling me at home in the United States and expecting to speak with Dick Cheney.

Jumblatt's press secretary deflected my inquiry because he didn't know me and because his boss had been getting credible death threats again. Hezbollah's prolonged occupation of downtown Beirut had turned violent on occasion, and several members of parliament had been assassinated since the Syrians left. No March 14 leader was in the mood to take chances.

A mutual friend called and made the appointment on my behalf, drove me to Jumblatt's villa in the heart of the city, and warned me security would be tight at the gate. "The Syrians, Michael, if they catch him they will cut off his head."

Security agents leaped from plastic chairs and aggressively approached me at the entrance. They weren't hostile, as Hezbollah's security agents often were, but they moved fast in case I drew a weapon.

My bulky Nikon D200 hung around my neck from its strap.

"Turn on the flash," said the lead agent after patting me down. "Then point your camera at the ground and take a picture."

I did what he said, proving to him that my camera wasn't a bomb. If he was seriously worried I had rigged it to explode, he would have confiscated it or at least made me step into the street before pressing the button. He seemed satisfied when I handed over my passport. My nationality must have made things a lot easier. Terrorist-cell leaders would have an awfully hard time finding an American willing to assassinate a pro-American member of parliament.

Jumblatt wore a dark suit and waited for me in the shadows of late winter evening on the side of the path leading up to the house. He greeted me coolly, professionally, and a little bit tiredly, as though he had spent most of the day meeting someone or other and would rather put up his feet and knock back shots of arak. Lebanese politics were dangerous and stressful enough when things were calm.

He was by far the most complicated political leader in Lebanon. Though he belonged to the Socialist International, his economic ideas no longer related in any meaningful way to those of Karl Marx. He was sort of a neoconservative insofar as he hailed from the left and credited regime change in Iraq with Lebanon's national interest, yet he went even further than American neoconservatives and called for regime change in Syria. While he was a liberal in the general sense of the word, especially by the Middle East's standards, he was also a feudal lord and former militia leader who lived in an ancestral castle.

"Hassan Nasrallah is officially the representative of Iran's Ayatollah Khamenei," he said wearily as we sat down to talk on his couch. "Khamenei has declared that he wants to overthrow the government and replace it. Syria is becoming a satellite of Iran. They want to use Lebanon as a battleground or as a bargaining card. This is what they have done in the summertime, when they declared the war, when Nasrallah declared the war against Israelis. They want to make Lebanon a satellite of Iran and Syria."

A servant brought us Turkish coffee in cups the size of shot glasses and set them beside finger bowls of pistachios.

"Do you think Hezbollah will ever disarm peacefully," I said, "or will it require force?"

"Nobody in Lebanon said or believed it was possible to disarm Hezbollah by force," he said. "But as a Lebanese I don't accept a state within a state. We have a state within a state. And a separate army, the Hezbollah army, next to the official army. Their intelligence is stronger than our intelligence. They control part of Lebanon without the possibility of the Lebanese state to enter it and enforce law and order. That's the situation."

"So what do you think the solution is?" I said. It was one of the last times I asked that question in the Middle East.

"The solution is not in Lebanon," he said. "The solution is in Tehran."

Walid Jumblatt never called for regime change in Iran as he did in Syria, and I don't think he was trying to coyly suggest it. He was just stating the obvious, that only Iran could solve the problem, whether or not it would actually do so. The Lebanese army and government weren't strong or united enough, Lebanon's Shias weren't about to disown the most muscular *zaim* they'd ever had, the Israelis couldn't engineer political changes in Lebanon through the use of violence or otherwise, and there wasn't a chance the Americans would go in and do it. Tehran's regime, though, at least under its current leadership, would never dismantle Hezbollah. Hezbollah was its most prized possession abroad, the Mediterranean branch of its Revolutionary Guard Corps. No realistic solution existed, not as long as the likes of Mahmoud Ahmadinejad and Ali Khamenei were in charge of the Islamic Republic.

"The solution is in Tehran," Jumblatt said again. "In the summertime they launched a kind of preemptive war against the Americans and the Israelis, and we had to suffer a struggle we don't have anything to do with. We were expecting two million tourists. Nobody came. Now downtown is closed, hotels are closed, nobody's coming from the Arab world, no tourists, that's it."

Jumblatt was something of a radical, but he was not on the Lebanese fringe. He occupied Lebanon's radical center, which is why his answers to questions like these were important. He was a one-man public-opinion barometer.

The Druze are always centrists of sorts. They are a minority in Lebanon, in Israel, and in Syria. There is no Druzistan anywhere in the world and there never will be. Their numbers are too small, and they've learned over time that it's safest to join the political mainstream—which in the Middle East was usually enforced at the point of a gun—to avoid persecution. As Jumblatt's own father explained, the Druze are ever alert and must "gauge their surroundings and choose their words carefully, assessing what must be said and what can be said."

Since March 14, 2005, Lebanon's Druze had been the most solidly pro-American and staunchly anti-Syrian group in the country. If Hezbollah's Secretary General Hassan Nasrallah were really the strong horse he was portrayed to be, Walid Jumblatt would have been his ally whether his heart was in it or not. Instead, he accused Hezbollah's secretary general of collaborating with the car bombers assassinating his colleagues.

"Of course," he said, "we have to say the fighters of Hezbollah did well. Okay? It's a brigade, an Iranian brigade fighting in the south of Lebanon. But it's not Lebanon that won the war. Israelis did not win the war, but they destroyed our country."

"Which country is more dangerous to Lebanon?" I said. "Israel or Syria?"

"Both together," he said and laughed. "Israel and the Syrian regime, okay?"

Saying Syria and Israel were both equally dangerous was, I suppose, the "centrist" position in Lebanon at the time.

"Lebanon is a composition of various confessions and communities," he said. "We are suffering from a huge and quite important Palestinian Diaspora—maybe 200,000 or 300,000 Palestinians here. And we have an aggressive neighbor called Syria. It's safer for us when the Syrians sign a peace with Israel for us to sign a peace with Israel. That's it. We cannot ask to sign a peace unilaterally without having the Syrians first signing the peace."

"During the July War," I said, "you said the Lebanese government was in danger of becoming weak like the government of Nouri al-Maliki in Iraq."[5] It was an ominous thing for him to say. Though al-Maliki's government was legitimately elected by Iraq's people, the only reason it hadn't been overthrown by Sunni and Shia militias was because American soldiers defended it with their lives.

"What I predicted is now a fact," Jumblatt said. "The Lebanese government included the ministers of Hezbollah who have resigned.

The Lebanese government, after all, is a coalition between us and the others. But we have to specify, who are the others? It's not like a coalition in a normal state where you have a coalition with other partners. Here we have a coalition between the official state and the other state. We have a parallel state. So we are not speaking with somebody else who is at the same table on equal terms. This somebody else is aiming a rocket at our heads. Not only guns—rockets. Lebanon is part of this regional struggle from one side—Russia, Iran, and Syria—and from the other side—America, the West, and us. We are unlucky. It's like Poland in 1940 or 1939, divided between the Russians and the Germans."

He laughed darkly, something Lebanese did rather a lot. Sometimes there wasn't much more you could do.

"If the U.S. loses the war in Iraq," I said, "do you think it will be a problem for Lebanon?" The outcome of America's "surge" of troops to Iraq under the command of General David Petraeus was still in doubt when I asked this.

Walid Jumblatt thought for a long time before he answered that question. I could see his mind working cautiously, calibrating his response for multiple audiences as he always did. He said the following very carefully: "It would be bad for Lebanon and for the Middle East if the U.S. withdraws from the region. We will face a different Arab and Muslim world. It is very strange and ironic that even the pro-Iranians in Iraq are asking the Americans to stay. You could write a theater about it. Making the Americans totally withdraw from the Arab world would be a mistake, would be a disaster for the moderates in the Arab world. The radicals and the Iranians would win."

⁓

A few weeks later, in late January of 2007, Nasrallah tired of his experiment with nonviolent protests and decided to act more like the militia leader he was.

Young Hezbollah militants severed the links to Lebanon's international airport with huge piles of rocks and dirt brought in on dump trucks. Masked and hooded men barricaded roads all over the country with thousands of rubber tires and set them on fire. Thick black smoke clotted Beirut's skyline. The airport itself remained operational, but no one could get in or out.

The Lebanese army, divided as always, stepped back and out of the way. Nasrallah promised his people he wouldn't let up until Prime Minister Fouad Siniora was toppled from power.

"Hezbollah thugs armed with sticks, rocks and in some cases guns are storming Beirut neighborhoods," Lebanese political analyst Abu Kais wrote on his blog *From Beirut to the Beltway*.[6] "Some were seen approaching [Hariri's] *Future TV* news building in Raouche. ISF and army troops trying to stop their advance are being attacked. Security forces are being extremely lax and unorganized—intervening only when it's too late. *Future TV* reported that vans carrying covered Hezbollah women are supplying the rioters with rocks. . . . Beirut residents are boiling with anger, and there are rumors of taking up arms against the 'Hezbollah occupiers.'"

In south Beirut's Tariq Jedideh neighborhood adjacent to the *dahiyeh*, furious Sunnis armed with pistols, sticks, rocks, and iron bars tried to break through some of the roadblocks. Masked Hezbollah militiamen defended their positions with automatic weapons. Lebanese army soldiers managed to break up some of these fights without taking sides, at last showing they were at least not entirely useless.

Members of parliament described Hezbollah as "terrorists" and Beirut as "occupied." Even the normally milquetoast and docile Sunni prime minister snapped and accused Hezbollah of "intimidation" and "terrorism."

Violent clashes spread from Tariq Jedideh into other parts of Beirut and even to other parts of the country. Cars were on fire. Entire streets were on fire. People on both sides were shot. Lebanese in the Diaspora watching news footage on television said their homeland looked like Gaza—and it did.

Hezbollah spokesmen liked to say the party modeled its "resistance" to the Siniora government after the March 14 demonstrations, but activists in the Independence Intifada never did anything remotely like this.

Nasrallah wisely called off his "strike." Some of the more militant leaders in the March 14 camp told their people to remain on standby to "lift the siege of Beirut" if Hezbollah refused to stand down and if the army remained on the sidelines.

Hezbollah did, however, stand down. Nasrallah seemed to be at least dimly aware that there were limits to what he could get away with in his crusade, or rather jihad, against the Sunni prime minister. Never mind that Lebanon's government was democratically elected—no sectarian community in Lebanon was allowed to choose or remove the leader of another. Shias couldn't select or deselect the *zaim* of the Sunnis without defeating the Sunnis in war.

Prices of AK-47s more than doubled after the violence in January, according to correspondent Nicholas Blanford.[7] Almost every family in the country owned weapons already, but they'd need to stockpile more if war was coming again. According to Beirut's half-believable rumor mill, Walid Jumblatt's Progressive Socialist Party was expanding its arsenal and training fighters again, and so was Bashir Gemayel's old Maronite militia now turned political party, the Lebanese Forces. Both denied it, and their denials were as plausible as the rumors, but *somebody* was snapping up rifles and ammunition in preparation for something.

The air crackled with sectarian tension, and Tariq Jedideh exploded again two days later when a mere fistfight between students at Beirut Arab University turned into a firefight. Hezbollah brought in gunmen wielding M-16s by the van load to shoot it out with Sunni university students packing pistols.

Hardly anyone in 1975 could imagine that seemingly isolated clashes could spark a civil war that would last for fifteen long years, but that's what happened, and no one in Lebanon had forgotten it. Lebanese army officers could not just stand idly by now that the sectarian monster was stalking the country again, so they clamped down on the city with an after-dark curfew.

"For the third time in almost a year," Michael Young wrote,[8] "Lebanon has averted a civil war, but we're nearing the end of the rope . . . what happened on Tuesday was, in its permutations, pretty much war. . . . And if anything induced Hezbollah to suspend the protests, it was an awareness that if these continued for even a day, war was inevitable. . . . The next time the opposition threatens to do something similar, we might as well load the guns or head for the shelters."

CHAPTER FOURTEEN

guns
in the
capital

Life—soaked in a moving
carcass, and the human
being—poured into a
temple of terror: that is
the Lebanon that they
want for us today.
—ADONIS

War did return to the Land of the Cedars that summer,
but it wasn't the war anybody expected.

Sunni terrorists from a group hardly anyone had ever heard of
before called Fatah al-Islam massacred twenty-seven Lebanese army
soldiers in their sleep outside the gates of the Palestinian refugee
camp of Nahr al-Bared. Hardly any of the militants were Lebanese
or Palestinian. They were fanatical Salafists from all over the place
who had murky ties to Syria's intelligence agencies, and possible ties
to al Qaeda.

The terrorists had embedded themselves in the camp near the
northern city of Tripoli, and when the army laid siege to it, Lebanon
lost almost as many soldiers in the next three and a half months as
the British lost in five years in Iraq.[1]

It was, however, a sideshow—a bloody and frightening sideshow, to be sure, and it underscored that Lebanon was an unstable country that generated armed conflict like weather, but it was a sideshow. A far more significant conflict was coming, one that would decisively shift power in the Middle East away from the American-backed Arab states to the Islamic Republic regime in Iran.

⁓

Lebanese President Emile Lahoud's extended term finally expired in November of 2007 after nine years of service to the al-Assads in Damascus. He left quietly.

The leaders of Lebanon's squabbling factions could not agree on a successor, and the next six months passed like one of the world's longest staring contests. The government's March 14 majority still refused to resign or hand over veto power to the March 8 bloc, Hezbollah still refused to end its occupation of downtown Beirut, and all the while, the presidential palace in Baabda stayed empty.

In the spring of 2008, Walid Jumblatt convinced Saad Hariri and their allies in the Christian parties to shove Hassan Nasrallah hard in the chest. They vowed to disable Hezbollah's vast illegal telecommunications network and fired the head of airport security, Brigadier General Wafiq Choucair. Choucair wasn't a Hezbollah member, but he helped Hezbollah receive clandestine shipments from abroad and monitor everyone who flew in and out of the country.

Hezbollah's parallel telecom system ran from South Lebanon and the Bekaa Valley to the *dahiyeh* and the airport, and it apparently survived the July War intact. According to Telecommunications Minister Marwan Hamadeh—who, if you recall, barely survived a car-bomb explosion in front of his house shortly before Rafik Hariri was killed—the network reached all the way to the city center where government buildings were located.

In early May, Jumblatt said during a press conference that he and Saad Hariri were being stalked by assassins. He added that Hezbollah was surveilling the private jets of Lebanese politicians and foreign dignitaries on runway 17 and was possibly passing intelligence to the car bombers.[2]

A few years earlier, assassins had killed Member of Parliament and *An-Nahar* newspaper publisher Gebran Tueni just hours after he secretly returned on a brief trip home from his self-imposed semi-exile in France. Somebody at the airport alerted the killers he'd landed, and Jumblatt wasn't the only one wondering if it was Hezbollah.

"It has been taken for granted for a long time that Hezbollah controls Lebanon's international airport," wrote David Schenker at the Washington Institute for Near East Policy.[3] "There is much speculation as to the purpose of Hezbollah's surveillance camera, but at a minimum, this asset could assist Hezbollah, Syria, and Iran to monitor the movement of anti-Syrian Lebanese officials, and perhaps even facilitate kidnappings or murders."

The Druze leader, no longer content to resist only Damascus, pushed back hard against Hezbollah's patrons and armorers in Tehran. "Iranian flights to Beirut should be stopped," he said,[4] "because Iranian planes might be bringing in money and military equipment."

Iranian planes certainly were bringing in money and equipment, and none of it ended up in the hands of the government or the army.

"The Iranian ambassador should be expelled," Jumblatt said.[5]

All this was too much for Nasrallah, and he announced on the morning of May 8 that he would hold a press conference that afternoon. A sinking, even cloying, feeling of dread washed over much of the country.

Beirutis cleared the streets as they often did even during the smallest of crises. The Lebanese feared each other, and I even knew some who didn't trust themselves to behave if things went pear-shaped.

The entire country seemed to suffer from collective post-traumatic stress disorder. I'd seen nerve-racked citizens unnecessarily wall themselves up in their homes so many times that I no longer paid it much mind when it happened.

It was easy for me to shrug and assume the best instead of the worst. I hadn't lived through the civil war, and I didn't lug my own portable nightmares around with me. I was also out of the country this time on assignment in Eastern Europe. From a distance, the latest news hardly even appeared to be news.

But it was about to.

"The [government] decisions," Nasrallah said,[6] "are tantamount to a declaration of war, and the start of a war on behalf of the United States and Israel."

Then Lebanon came apart.

∽

Hamra is the most diverse neighborhood in Beirut. It's the most diverse neighborhood in the country, in fact, and probably the most diverse in the Middle East. It's on the western side of the city and therefore predominantly Sunni, but it's also effectively a "college town" wedged between the American University of Beirut and the Lebanese American University. Substantial numbers of Christians, Druze, Shias, and foreigners—including Jews—live there alongside the Sunnis. Everyone gets along reasonably well most of the time, and you can fool yourself into believing the Middle East is more peaceful and tolerant than it is if you spend enough time there.

Achrafieh on the predominantly Christian east side is a little more polished and feels a lot more Western, but Hamra is more interesting, as it's the closest thing Lebanon has to a microcosm of itself. Cafés, all-night bars, and even brothels are right around the corner from mosques, which are just up the street from churches, which themselves are only a twenty-minute walk from a Jewish synagogue that was being restored with some of Saad Hariri's money.[7]

Most of Hamra's residents may have been March 14 Sunnis, but every political ideology relevant to the region, from communism to American-style neoconservatism, had champions there. This was the place where all of Lebanon's sects and ideas came together, and with so many intellectuals, college students, professors, journalists, and foreigners, it was no less international than Tel Aviv or Jerusalem. You could drink with the enemy there. Western Jewish Zionists could argue politics over coffee or beer with Hezbollah supporters. I personally know three dual-national Israelis who sneaked in on second passports, and I have no doubt there were others. Nonconformists who didn't fit in well in Damascus or Cairo loved Hamra as much as Westerners who found themselves alienated, understimulated, or both in cities like New York and London.

Charles Chuman, my Lebanese American friend who gave me a tour of Hezbollah's *dahiyeh* the first time I went down there, lived in the neighborhood on the top floor of the Mayflower Hotel just a few streets over from my old apartment. He spent the morning of May 8 in his office where he worked as a media and political analyst, but he didn't want to stick around long after Nasrallah announced the upcoming press conference. Most of his coworkers left at lunch and were not coming back. Crossing the city was a major hassle already. Hezbollah and its allies in the opposition were "on strike" and were burning tires again.

A few of his American friends casually went to their favorite cafés or to the gym, but most Lebanese people went home and shut their doors, as did Charles.

When he set up his laptop in the living room so he could keep working from home, a spooky feeling came over him. Normally he wouldn't be able to hear much over the roar of traffic and the blaring of car horns, but the city was as quiet as if it were three o'clock in the morning.

Nasrallah's face filled his TV screen, but Charles wasn't listening. He left the volume down so he could concentrate on his work, but he did not need to listen. Instant message windows opened up on his laptop.

"Oh, my God," wrote one of his friends. "It's going down."

"Hezbollah," said another, "is invading Beirut."

Then the gunshots started.

They were in the distance at first, most likely in the neighborhood to the south, somewhere in Verdun, perhaps near the Bristol Hotel. Charles could have walked there in ten minutes, but the shots were sporadic, and it was hard to tell if someone was just firing into the air or if this was for real.

It was for real.

The distant cracking of gunshots mushroomed into a terrifying crescendo. The firing wasn't sporadic anymore; it was constant, and so was the screaming.

He closed his curtains, bolted the door, and moved his laptop into the hallway between the bedroom and kitchen. Floor-to-ceiling windows were about to turn his living room into a death trap.

He called the front desk downstairs on his cell phone.

"What's going on down there?" he said.

"It's fine," said the man at the desk as though nothing was out of the ordinary.

"What do you mean, it's *fine*?" Charles said. He could barely even hear the man's voice over the gunfire, and the ground floor had floor-to-ceiling windows just like his apartment.

"Just don't go outside."

"Okay," Charles said in disbelief. "Whatever you say."

The instant he ended the call, his phone rang again. It was one of his friends in America.

"Look," he said, "I'm fine, don't worry, but I have to hang up. I need my phone."

He tried placing one call after another to friends elsewhere in the city hoping they could tell him what was happening in front of their own houses, but he heard a recorded message every time telling him in Arabic that all the circuits were busy.

The Internet was his only line out to the world.

"Dude, it's f**kin scary," one of his friends who lived near the International College wrote to him using Facebook. "Snipers across from my house just got rocket launchers."

Civil war veterans told him what to do.

Stay in an interior room or a hallway. Lie down in your bathtub if the gunshots get close. Keep the hell away from the windows, and for God's sake, close the curtains. Be nice to the doorman. Don't go anywhere unless you know where the snipers are.

His phone rang. According to the caller ID, it was one of his distant cousins who lived in the mountains northeast of the city.

"Charles! It's the opening night of White, mate. I can get us in, we've got to go."

White was a fashionable club reopening for the season on top of the An-Nahar building downtown.

"Um," Charles said, "we've got a little bit of a war going on over here."

His cousin couldn't see Beirut from his house and obviously wasn't paying attention to the news or to anyone else.

Charles heard several men wearing boots run up the stairs and go out onto the roof, and he had an idea what they were doing.

"I have to go," he said and ended the call.

Saad Hariri's house in Qoreitem was a few minutes' walk toward the south, and Prime Minister Fouad Siniora lived just a few streets to the north. Charles could almost see each of their homes from his balcony. His building would make an excellent sniping position.

He thought he heard men out in the hallway. Someone could easily kick through the flimsy lock on the front door, so he tiptoed into the kitchen to get out of the way.

His refrigerator and cupboards were almost empty. He was supposed to make his weekly trip to the grocery store the day before, but he got home late and blew it off. So he sat on the floor by himself, wary of whoever was out in the hallway and up on his roof, listening to automatic weapons fire in front his building, amazed that the front desk guy told him everything was just dandy, and he had no food or water.

His friend Rama lived downstairs with her roommate. They presumably had a stocked kitchen, and he desperately needed some company.

He crept to the door and pressed his ear up against it. The hallway sounded quiet, so he slowly unlocked the bolt, turned the knob, and pushed the door slightly ajar. He heard the suction sound of a rocket-propelled grenade launcher firing, the shattering of a plate-glass window, and a choir of car alarms, but no one seemed to be in the hallway.

He darted downstairs to Rama's apartment.

"Charles!" she said as she opened the door. "Jeez, come in."

She was the young Syrian American woman who also accompanied me on my first trip to Hezbollah's *dahiyeh*.

Charles collapsed into her couch. Her Jordanian American roommate was there with her boyfriend, Hassan.

"I know some of those people out there," Hassan said. "They're with Amal and the SSNP."

So it wasn't Hezbollah outside, at least not on their street.

Amal, recall, was Lebanon's secular Shia party and Hezbollah's junior partner in the March 8 coalition. The SSNP was the Syrian Social Nationalist Party, a minuscule but violent pro-Syrian militia that had been around since before Lebanon even existed as an independent republic.

Charles peered behind the curtain and saw young men with guns running up the street.

"A guy I know from the university escorted me over here," Hassan said, "but his friends are riding around on scooters and shooting up everything. All the pro-Hariri stores are getting shot up. They aren't trained. They don't even know what they're doing. They're just shooting at everything."

Charles stayed for dinner before returning to his own apartment and getting back on the Internet.

His American acquaintance Vince had been in the country for three months and was one of the oddball Westerners who washed up in the country every so often. Nobody really knew what he was doing there. While he said he was studying Arabic, he never seemed to take classes. Some thought he might work for the CIA, but Charles just thought he was weird.

"I want to head over to Captain's Cabin," Vince typed in an instant message, "and check on Andre."

Captain's Cabin was a popular bar among the expat crowd, and Andre had been running the place since the civil war.

"Don't do it," Charles typed back. "Don't try to go."

But Vince signed off and seemed to have left.

Charles called Andre and was relieved when the call was patched through.

"I'm okay," Andre said, "but tell Vince *not* to come here. Shit's going down. It's crazy. There's fighting outside, and I won't be able to let him in if he shows up."

Militiamen banged on Andre's door with the butts of their rifles and demanded he open up, but they couldn't get in because he lashed it shut with the same metal bars he'd used to barricade himself inside during the civil war. He ended up spending the night there and, like just about everyone else, hardly slept.

Vince's apartment was only a few blocks from Captain's Cabin, and Charles's apartment at the Mayflower was just a street over from Vince's, but these kinds of distances are enormous in war zones. You can really only run "safely" from one position to the next if it takes less than three seconds.

Urban combat environments are much more dangerous than open battlefields. Combatants can conceal themselves on roofs, inside cars, behind dumpsters, and within apartments. Anyone can be shot at any moment from any direction. If you're there and you're a civilian, you damn well better act like a civilian.

Do not carry a weapon. Do not carry anything that even looks like a weapon. If you're driving a vehicle and you accelerate toward a checkpoint, you should expect to be shot.

If all the other civilians have cleared off the street, get off the street, close your shutters, turn off your lights, and be quiet.

Vince ran toward Captain's Cabin.

An SSNP militiaman carrying a rocket-propelled grenade launcher stopped him.

"*What* are you doing in Lebanon!" the militiaman demanded.

Vince put his hands up, apologized, and slunk back inside, but he still didn't get it. He parted his curtains, opened his window, leaned out, and pointed his camera at the men with the guns.

An SSNP fighter, possibly the same one who had just stopped him, fired a rocket-propelled grenade straight at his window. Vince saw it flying right at him and dived into the kitchen. The explosion vaporized his air conditioning unit, blew a hole in the exterior wall, and set everything in his apartment on fire.

Nobody shot at Charles's building. Somebody on the Mayflower's staff seemed to have paid someone off or had the right connections. Both the hotel and apartment wings were untouchable. The Napoleon Hotel was likewise untouchable.

Charles called the front desk.

"Look," the guy downstairs said. "Don't worry. Really. Just don't go anywhere. You'll be perfectly fine if you stay here. Oh, and by the way, we have room service."

They had room service?

Charles wasn't hungry. He had already eaten at Rama's, but he was thirsty. And while the hotel charged several dollars just for a small bottle of water, if there was ever a time to pay extra for Evian, this was it.

The gunmen outside were aligned with Hezbollah, but they weren't Hezbollah. That meant they were more dangerous. Hezbollah's fighters missed entire Israeli cities with their wild Katyusha rockets, but they were crack shots with a rifle. They hit what they aimed at.

Amal and SSNP militiamen were barely trained, angry young men who saw the current political crisis as their chance to reenact the civil war. They sprayed bullets all over the place. They fired at people, at storefronts, into the air, even into the Mediterranean. They shot up just about everything. Several of Charles's friends, all of them noncombatants, said they found bullets on their balconies and inside their houses.

He collapsed from sheer exhaustion around four in the morning and even managed to sleep for a couple of hours.

During the July War he dreamed about politics, that he was a member of Lebanon's parliament searching desperately for a diplomatic solution. This time he dreamed of himself in a vibrant city he loved that was about to be washed away by a biblically proportioned tsunami.

⌒

Hamra was just one of West Beirut's neighborhoods, and it was farthest from Hezbollah's stronghold. It therefore made sense for local Amal and SSNP members to take over that one. Every neighborhood to the south was closer to the *dahiyeh*, and some were directly adjacent. Hezbollah could hit them as fast and as hard as the Israel Defense Forces could cross the border into South Lebanon. From the time the gunmen were given the "go" from the boss, they only needed minutes or even seconds to get into position.

Advance teams burst from brand-new black SUVs and moved in perfectly executed formations. Witnesses saw two men in each squad carrying mint-condition AK-47s, one a rocket-propelled grenade launcher, another a sniper rifle, and the last a tripod-mounted machine gun.

They stood out markedly from the ragtag gangs of kids shooting up Hamra.

These men were professionals, and they looked it in their dark green shirts and black combat fatigues. They knew how to run, where to take cover, how to carry their weapons, how to aim and fire their weapons, and how to hit what they aimed at.

"They weren't just running down the street," one witness told me. "They sent out scouts, and they knew how to take cover. They clearly knew how to handle their weapons, especially compared with the SSNP guys riding around on Honda scooters with their guns on their laps while talking on their cell phones. There's no way Hezbollah would do that."

The journalist Nir Rosen secured permission to embed with Hezbollah fighters while they patrolled West Beirut. "It felt just like being on patrol with young American soldiers in Dora in December," he said to counterinsurgency expert and former U.S. Army Captain Andrew Exum.[8] "They operated that well, moved that well, and were as young as American soldiers on their first tour."

Saad Hariri's *Future TV* station was near the top of their target list, and they brought engineers with them who knew exactly which lines to cut to disable the satellite feed. When they left the scene to shut down the *Al-Mustaqbal*, *Al-Sharq*, and *Al-Shiraa* newspapers, masked SSNP men firebombed the station with Molotov cocktails, burned it to the ground, and put up a poster of Syria's Bashar al-Assad on the ruins.

"I have learned," Nasrallah said,[9] "through experiences, that we should not say 'the Siniora government.' Siniora is a poor man, an employee. We should say 'the government of Walid Jumblatt.' When Jumblatt wants to remove the airport security chief, he does. This decision is a declaration of war by Jumblatt on the resistance and its arms for the benefit of the U.S. This decision has uncovered the truth behind this team and their loyalties and behavior during the July War."

"This is a characteristic of totalitarian parties," Jumblatt said in response.[10] "You are either under their command or a traitor."

"Any hand that reaches for the resistance and its arms will be cut off," Nasrallah continued.[11] "Israel tried that in the July War, and we cut its hand off. We do not advise you to try us. Whoever is going to target us will be targeted by us. Whoever is going to shoot at us will be shot by us."

Samir Geagea, leader of the Lebanese Forces party, was furious that he and his men had surrendered their weapons at the end of the civil war while Hezbollah had not. The resistance, he said,[12] "uses revolutionary means of violence and fire, which turns Hezbollah into another Mahdi Army in the streets and alleys of Beirut."

Of course, Hezbollah wasn't the only militia on the rampage in Beirut at the time, but Amal and the SSNP could never get away with shooting up the capital without Hezbollah's protection and blessing. In return, Amal and the SSNP gave Hezbollah political cover by soaking up some of the blame.

SSNP spokesperson Maan Hamieh spun it the best he could.[13] "The coordination between the SSNP and Hezbollah is very spontaneous and on the ground," he said. "It does not need an operation center." He admitted, though, that his party shared Hezbollah's goals, and that his own men were really just helping. "Hezbollah has a significant role in this. It is like a compass for everyone."

After shutting down West Beirut's media, Hezbollah hit Saad Hariri's house in Qoreitem just south of Hamra. Gunmen fired an RPG at the gate and broke into the complex. Hariri's bodyguards from the Secure Plus company were no match for an Iranian-trained revolutionary militia, and they scattered when Hezbollah shot at everything in front of the house and seized control of the entrance and exit.

Hamra, Qoreitem, Verdun, and other parts of northwestern Beirut fell almost at once. The resistance met precious little resistance in those "bourgeois" middle-class neighborhoods full of college students, shoppers, and tourists. Farther south, however, in gritty working-class Sunni areas nearer the *dahiyeh*, Hezbollah found itself with a fight on its hands—especially in Tariq Jedideh.

Tariq Jedideh was the kind of place Humphrey Bogart's character Rick Blaine in *Casablanca* warned a Nazi officer about when he said, "There are certain sections of New York, Major, that I wouldn't advise you to try to invade."

There were more firearms than people in Lebanon, even in the most progressive of areas. Almost every family in the country had at least one rifle stored in a closet somewhere. They knew from bitter experience that their neighborhood could be attacked at any time while impotent state security forces cringed and stepped out of the way.

Hezbollah couldn't take Tariq Jedideh. Nasrallah may have even regretted that he tried. Hariri told the neighborhood's residents to stand down, but instead they threw everything they had at their attackers and either killed or repulsed every last one of them. They were furious that Hariri ordered them not to fight back, especially after proving they were up to the job.

This meant two things.

First, Hezbollah was secure in its strongholds but vulnerable when it stepped outside. Nasrallah may have been stronger than everyone else, but he was not strong enough that he could easily conquer and rule the whole country.

Meanwhile, moderate Sunnis like Siniora and Hariri would have to become war leaders if the conflict continued, or they would risk being swept aside as irrelevant.

⟶

Lebanon's first civil war was a short one. Sunni Arab Nationalists in thrall to Egypt's Gamal Abdel Nasser hoped to attach Lebanon to the United Arab Republic, a brief union of Egypt and Syria. A larger bloc of Maronite Christians resisted, and President Camille Chamoun even tried to rig an election. A nation cannot hold itself together when a third of its population wishes to be annexed by another.

The second civil war was a long one. This time, Yasser Arafat's Palestine Liberation Organization formed a state within a state in West Beirut and South Lebanon and used it as a launching pad for terrorist attacks against Israel. Again, Lebanon's Christians resisted, as did Lebanon's Shias. The second civil war was actually a series of wars triggered by that first fatal schism.

This conflict resembled both the first and the second. With Iranian money and weapons, Hezbollah built its own state within a state in South Lebanon and the suburbs south of Beirut and used it as a base to wage war against Israel. Hezbollah also wished to violently yank Lebanon from its pro-Western and pro-Arab alignment into what Lee Smith began calling the Iranian-led Resistance Bloc, an agenda roughly a third of the population supported.

No country on earth can withstand that kind of geopolitical tectonic pressure.

Hezbollah may not have overthrown the government outright, but the invasion of Beirut was still a coup d'état. It was, literally, a blow against the state.

"The Hezbollah rampage in Lebanon," Noah Pollak wrote in *Commentary*,[14] "should make it obvious to any sentient observer that Hezbollah's claims to democratic political legitimacy have always been intended only to manipulate the credulous. Participation in politics requires the willingness to persuade your foes, to compromise, to stand down when you don't get your way. But there is no record of Hamas or Hezbollah ever observing such restrictions: the moment Hezbollah was confronted with political pressure, it responded not within the political sphere, but with warlordism. . . . In the streets of Beirut, with Kalashnikovs and RPGs, Hezbollah is making it abundantly clear that its participation in Lebanese politics ends when Hezbollah is asked to submit to the state's authority."

Until May of 2008, Hezbollah existed both inside and alongside the state. After attacking Beirut, Hezbollah showed the Lebanese that it existed above the state, the parliament, the police, and the army. No members of Hezbollah or its affiliates were arrested or prosecuted for murder, arson, or terrorism as they would have been in any other country in the Middle East, including Syria, Iran, and Iraq.

The army was too weak to protect the country from external threats and too divided to protect the country from internal threats. The previous summer it could barely win a fight against a few hundred foreigners it had completely surrounded in a refugee camp.

Americans at the time were training and equipping Iraq's army to protect the government in Baghdad from Syrian- and Iranian-sponsored terrorist groups, but al-Assad's regime had sabotaged Lebanon's armed forces for more than a decade and staffed it at the highest levels with Damascus loyalists who had yet to be purged. Not every officer, though, was corrupt. Brigadier General Ghassan Balaa and forty of his fellow officers sent resignation letters to army commander General Michel Suleiman to protest, as they put it,[15] "the way the military handled the latest violence."

"What has happened in the streets of Lebanon," Suleiman said,[16] "is a real civil war that no national army in the world can confront. Major states encountered such wars and its armies could not contain the fight." On the contrary, he said, the armies "disintegrated" just as Lebanon's did under similar circumstances in the late 1970s.

He rejected his officers' resignations.

The restrained rhetoric Lebanese citizens were accustomed to hearing from most of their leaders, along with the erstwhile prevailing mentality of precarious coexistence, all but evaporated.

"Hezbollah has gained control over Beirut," Member of Parliament Ahmad Fatfat said,[17] "and has caused a Sunni-Shia conflict that will be extended for years."

"If no compromise is reached, we will be facing a long internal war," said Suleiman Franjieh,[18] former member of parliament and leader of the small Marada movement in Northern Lebanon aligned with Hezbollah and the Syrians.

No sect was allowed by law or social contract to bully or rule the others. The system, when it worked, provided uniquely Lebanese checks and balances. Hezbollah overthrew it. And when the system was overthrown, as it had been in the past, some Lebanese in every sectarian community were willing and able to fight as viciously as the militias and death squads in Fallujah and Baghdad. That may have been the only reason Hezbollah didn't storm the Grand Serail, the Ottoman-era military headquarters where Prime Minister Fouad Siniora kept his office.

The SSNP, though, was pissing in corners all over Hamra. They flew their spinning red swastika flag all along the main shopping street and threatened to kill anyone who dared take it down.

Meanwhile, fighting exploded in Tripoli, a more conservative city than Beirut and the stronghold for Lebanon's small but fiercely committed Sunni Islamist community. Clashes had been breaking out once in a while between Sunni and Alawite gangs, but now entire neighborhoods were at war with each other.

A few local SSNP gunmen joined in and learned the hardest way imaginable that the Sunnis of the north were not like the Sunnis of

Hamra. An armed gang loyal to the government chased an SSNP squad into their local headquarters, surrounded them, charged inside, shot them, dragged them outside, and mutilated their bodies with axes.

Most Sunnis did what Saad Hariri told them to do and stood down even though they felt humiliated. Nobody, however, expected them to sit still for long while being attacked. The violent counter-resistance in Tripoli and Tariq Jedideh saw to that.

Sunnis in the rest of the Middle East wouldn't sit idly by for long either.

"As the Christians learned to their detriment during the 1975-1990 war," Michael Young wrote,[19] "fighting the Sunni community in Lebanon is tantamount to fighting the Arab world. The Northern Islamists have been awakened, and with them Sunni Islamists every-where in the region and beyond who will rally to do battle against the [Shia] apostate."

"In the eyes of many Lebanese," Andrew Exum wrote,[20] "the resis-tance is now an occupying power. How will Hezbollah—which has in the past divided the world into the oppressors and the oppressed—adjust to the ugly new reality where they are seen as the former?"

Hezbollah, though, was a guerrilla army, not an occupation force. Counterinsurgency was not in its toolbox. Nasrallah would find himself with a deadly serious problem if he tried to emulate Hamas in Gaza and violently seize the whole country. A popular Sunni blogger named Mustapha bluntly wrote what everyone must have been thinking on his website, *The Beirut Spring*.[21] "Expect the fight for Beirut to begin in earnest later," he wrote, "with the distinct trademark of an occupied population: Hit and run."

"Unleashing the sectarian monster can seem like a good idea to Islamists allied with the Future Movement and to the Saudis," he continued,[22] "but they had better think twice before letting that genie out of the bottle. . . . Before we know it, extreme elements can manipulate the sense of victimhood some Sunnis would have and target Shia symbols with terrorist operations that would unleash the same god-forsaken death spiral that exists in Iraq. We don't have to go through what Iraq has suffered to realize that al Qaeda is not really what the Sunnis want for their protection."

Most Lebanese Sunnis only supported liberal leaders like Siniora and Hariri as long as they were not in danger. They wanted the army for their protection rather than something that looked like al Qaeda, but that didn't stop Fatah al-Islam fighters from infiltrating the country the previous year and blowing up Northern Lebanon. And a spokesman for whatever was left of the group issued a statement saying they'd stand by Lebanon's Sunnis.

Just a few months before the Nahr al-Bared conflict began, another radical Sunni group calling itself the Mujahideen in Lebanon made bloodcurdling Iraq-style threats of its own against Hezbollah.

The "zero hour" was approaching, its communiqué said, for Lebanese Shias who would no longer be permitted to have their own "entity" inside the country. "Blood will flow like rivers," they said. "Prepare your coffins and dig your graves. The hurricanes of the Mujahideen are coming to Lebanon."

⌐

Just moments after Nasrallah finished his speech, Royce Hutson saw Hezbollah fighters running up the street toward his house. They had already moved into position; the speech was their green light to go.

He was a visiting professor at Beirut's Lebanese American University and had already grown accustomed to working in countries torn asunder by conflict. That's what brought him to Lebanon in the first place. He enjoyed teaching social work at Wayne State University in Michigan, but he felt a bit restless after a while and set out to edgier places where he could make more of a difference, first in Haiti and now in Lebanon.

His apartment was bang on the front line in the Caracas neighborhood near Hariri's *Future TV* station before the SSNP scorched it. He had a terrific view of the invasion out his picture windows before he pulled the curtains closed and ducked into his hallway as Charles had done.

Several of his friends and colleagues lived three doors down in an apartment building housing teachers at the International College. He'd rather move in with them than spend days lying prone in his hallway, so he persuaded his doorman to let him out during a lull.

No one was on the street. Every door and window was shut, and every car was punctured with bullet holes.

The International College building was only three doors away, but it may as well have been miles.

He ran. He ran with everything he had. He ran with everything he had and with his hands over his head, screaming "don't shoot, don't shoot!" until he made it inside and, gasping, slammed the door shut behind him.

Not five minutes later, the street exploded again with another barrage of automatic weapons fire that didn't let up even once for more than four hours.

"I was so glad to be at the International College building," he told me. "I wanted to be around foreigners. I knew Hezbollah wouldn't target us. At least I didn't think they would target us. I also didn't want to be alone while going through that kind of thing."

There was no formal Sunni militia in West Beirut, but Hezbollah did meet some resistance from locals who had prepared for a day they knew was coming.

"They were passing out AK-47s right outside my friend Susan's building," he said. "There was this old half-abandoned narghile market that never had any business. I always wondered what was up with it. Now I know. It was a weapons depot."

He was right that Hezbollah wasn't interested in killing, kidnapping, or even harassing foreigners at that time. Hezbollah was at war with the Sunnis. He wasn't naive or right by sheer chance. Unlike some Westerners who lived in Beirut's luxurious bubble, he had been to the south, and not as a tourist.

He spent a year directing a project down there and had lost track of how many times Hezbollah got in his face while he conducted his research. Every single one of the surveyors working for him had been detained at least once.

Two Lebanese army soldiers once stopped his car while he was on his way to the Château Kefraya vineyard in the Bekaa Valley with a friend visiting from Detroit, and he was sure they were aligned with Hezbollah. One called Royce and his friend filthy Americans as the other stalked in circles around the car while repeatedly chambering and unchambering a round in his rifle.

Anti-American as Hezbollah's fighters undoubtedly were, they couldn't be bothered with the likes of Royce and his British, American, and Canadian colleagues. The only people shooting at Hezbollah at the time were West Beirut's Sunnis.

Most teachers at the International College were terrified, even so. Two were hosting their mothers who had come to Beirut during the glorious spring months for vacation. The university president called and offered to put them on buses to Syria. Unlike Royce, most weren't accustomed to living and working in anarchic regions or war zones. Lebanon wasn't like Iraq or Gaza, where violence and misery were near constants. Much of the time, you could pretend it was a normal, if slightly ramshackle, country on the Mediterranean if you squinted at it and didn't think about politics much.

At least they had food. It was always wise to stock up with a week's worth of food and water in Lebanon. After they pooled all their resources, Royce thought they might have enough to get through a month.

He wasn't the type of person who wanted to be put on a bus to Damascus like a refugee, so he called his regular car rental company.

"If I want to take a car out of here," he said, "will you give me one?"

"We're in the middle of a war here."

"Yeah," Royce said and laughed. "I know. That's why I might want a car."

"You know war damage isn't covered by the insurance, right?"

"I understand," he said.

The plan was to cram as many people into a car as humanly possible, drop it off at the Syrian border, and figure out how to return it after the guns cooled—however long that might take.

When he checked his e-mail, he found a message from the U.S. Embassy listserv advising American citizens to get out of the country. Eight hundred dollars or so could pay for a water taxi to Cyprus from the Maronite port city of Jounieh. The Canadian

Embassy had more practical advice. If the combatants start firing mortars, go below the fourth floor. If they stick to small-arms fire, stay above the fifth.

Our mutual friend Charles called him. He also wasn't interested in spending the next several days in his hallway or his bathtub, especially after he heard men in heavy boots on his stairs and his roof.

"Charles!" Royce said. "I'm at the International College building and we're having a potluck. Do you want to come over?"

It was almost a stupid question. Royce risked his life running three doors down the street, and Charles lived a half mile away.

But Charles made it.

⌒

Aside from four hours of sleep, Charles had been on his phone and computer nonstop for more than twenty-four hours. If the electricity went out, he'd be more isolated and frightened than ever, and he'd have no idea what was happening anywhere but on his own street. His world would become deadly and small, but he didn't know where he should go.

He called Royce.

"I'm at the International College building and we're having a potluck," Royce said. "Do you want to come over? We have the whole building here."

Charles knew that building well. Several of his friends lived over there, and it was just a few doors down from Royce's place. The apartments were huge. They had plenty of room for him if he could figure out how to get through a half mile of checkpoints now that there was a lull.

He rifled through his closet and found a T-shirt that looked vaguely like the SSNP flag in dim lighting. The SSNP logo is a spinning red storm or swastika, and his T-shirt showed a spinning tire, but it was close enough in the dark. So he donned it along with some black pants, stepped out onto the street, and pretended that's where he belonged. He was the right age, had the right build, dressed the part, and feigned a look like he'd punch anyone who got in his way. The sun had gone down. If he stayed in the shadows, he just might pull it off.

He grimly nodded at SSNP gunmen manning a checkpoint. They nodded back. It was working. And it continued to work. Nobody messed with him. Hardly anyone even looked at him twice.

Ten minutes later, he knocked on the door.

"Wow." Royce said as he opened up. "You actually made it."

Few of the resident teachers noticed he looked like an SSNP militiaman. Most probably didn't even know what an SSNP militiaman looked like, and they weren't about to hit the streets and find out.

Most were frightened out of their minds, but Royce and a few others kept it together. This was Charles's second Lebanon war. He was starting to get used to it. The war muscles in his mind were toughening up.

Because he was half Lebanese and had been in Beirut longer than anyone else, they dubbed him the expert and pumped him for information.

"Look," he said. "Nobody knows which direction this is going to take. It could be over in a couple of days. The best thing you can do is just stay inside and keep your shutters closed."

They felt better having someone tell them they'd be okay, though Charles had no way of knowing they'd be okay. Outside was a war zone. Lebanon wasn't okay.

Everyone brought a different dish to the potluck and felt relieved to have been given a task. Preparing a meal and cohosting a dinner party less than thirty-six hours after the start of a war on your street is an accomplishment.

Thomas Friedman captured the surreal quality of Lebanon's civil war in his classic work of reportage *From Beirut to Jerusalem*. In the first chapter, he quotes a hostess at a dinner party in a house near the Green Line who notices her distinguished guests are getting impatient and hungry. "Would you like to eat now," she asks casually while a ferocious battle rages outside the window,[23] "or wait for the cease-fire?"

Human beings can adapt to just about anything, but it takes time. Older generations of Lebanese fortified their emotions, their minds, and their nerves, but Charles and Royce attended a dinner party for foreigners, many of whom were more accustomed to tranquil North American suburbs than to Beirut even when the city was calm.

They discussed their anxiety responses as they ate. No one could just sit down and read a book, not with gunshots ringing out on the street.

Some responded by cleaning. They cleaned everything they could get their sponge on. If they had been putting off cleaning the oven, they cleaned the oven. Some wiped down the same counter-tops over and over again.

Others, like Charles, let his apartment get dirtier while he consumed and shared as much information over the Internet and telephone as he could.

He noticed that some responded brilliantly to the crisis and knew exactly how to take care of themselves even if their personal lives were a mess. Others who normally had it together buckled under the stress and had to be held by the hand.

Most couldn't sleep without alcohol. An extraordinary amount of alcohol was consumed in the building that night, but nobody acted like they were drunk. After finally crashing from booze intake and exhaustion, most didn't stay down for long, and they went right back to their anxiety-relieving activities as soon as they woke up again.

Charles told himself he felt calm, but he clenched his teeth so hard in his sleep that it hurt just to talk in the morning.

He and Royce stepped outside the next day. Somebody had given the "all clear" sign. Neither had any idea who or how these things happened.

Glass crunched under their boots. Nobody smiled. Children ran around collecting spent bullet casings. Most restaurants and shops remained closed while the owners knocked out the rest of the broken glass from their window frames and swept it up.

Charles ran into a couple of friends who gave him a double-take. He hadn't brought a change of clothes with him the night before and was still wearing the shirt and pants that made him look vaguely like a thug from the SSNP.

The Lebanese army moved into the area, and some of the soldiers didn't even try to hide their disgust when they saw him. If Charles really were a member of the SSNP, he'd have more authority on the street than they did. They couldn't shoot anybody, nor could they arrest someone for shooting somebody. They couldn't do much of anything but deter looters.

"I need to get home," Charles said to Royce. "I want to take a shower, and I have got to get out of these clothes."

So he went back to his apartment, thinking for the first time that the violent stage of the crisis might finally be over.

It wasn't.

CHAPTER FIFTEEN
götterdämmerung

We cannot go back to
how we lived with them
before. . . . Every boy here,
his blood is boiling.
—HUSSEIN AL-HAJ OBAID

Hezbollah fighters stormed out of the *dahiyeh*, charged up the foothills of the Chouf Mountains, and battered the predominantly Druze region of Aley with mortar rounds and artillery fire. Amal and SSNP gunmen trapped Walid Jumblatt in his West Beirut house while his Progressive Socialist Party leaders in the mountains rounded up young men of fighting age and placed them into defensive positions.

There hadn't been a lot of actual fighting in West Beirut. For the most part, Hezbollah, Amal, and the SSNP went in with guns blazing and seized it. The Druze in the Chouf, though, fought as though Hezbollah threatened them with extinction.

The overwhelming majority of Lebanon's Druze backed Jumblatt and his Progressive Socialist Party, but a tiny minority sided with Talal Arslan's so-called Lebanese Democratic Party, which was in league with Hezbollah and the Syrians. The Aley district was

Arslan's stronghold, such as it was, so Hezbollah made a peculiar decision in choosing that Druze city of cities to try to invade. If Nasrallah expected Arslan's men to help out, he was mistaken.

Jumblatt, one of the most adept Lebanese political leaders alive, knew just how to play this. He ordered all fighters loyal to him to surrender to Arslan and hand over their weapons. They did. Lebanese scholar Tony Badran[1] pointed out this wasn't a sign of weakness but "a shrewd move by a master tactician."

In times of genuine danger, sectarianism trumps every political position that has ever existed in Lebanon. Arslan had his tactical alliance with al-Assad and Hezbollah, but he wasn't about to let an Iranian-backed Shia militia burn down his cities and murder his people. His men refused to accept Jumblatt's surrender. They switched sides, and the two repelled Hezbollah's invasion together. Residents were wounded and killed, houses were firebombed, women and children as well as men were left homeless, but Hezbollah failed to conquer even an inch of the Chouf.

Badran noted a parallel development in the north.[2] Omar Karami, who was briefly prime minister during the Syrian occupation, "lamented the 'deep wound' that has occurred between Sunnis and Shia, and told Hezbollah that if this becomes a sectarian fight, then we have two choices: to either stay home, or fight with our sect."

Political alliances have their limits, and Arslan's people and Hezbollah discovered theirs. Hezbollah suddenly found itself with no friends at all in the mountains overlooking the *dahiyeh*. Together, Jumblatt and Arslan could have turned Hezbollah's command and control center into a shooting gallery from their perch on the high ground.

The Druze are among the fiercest of warriors, and everyone in Lebanon knows it. They are well known in Israel, too, where they often serve in elite units of the Israel Defense Forces and suffer lower-than-average casualty rates in battle. Most of Israel's Sunni Arabs abstain from military service, but Druze Arabs are loyal to the Jewish state and will fight for it. There's a reason two of the Middle East's religious minorities—Maronite Christians and Druze—live in Lebanon's mountains in significant numbers. Attempts to invade and subjugate them are ill-advised, very likely to fail, and therefore rarely attempted by even large armies. Geography preserves these micro-civilizations. Lebanon wouldn't even exist as an independent republic if it were a plain instead of a mountain range.

"People love to talk about how Jews and Israelis feel an existential threat," Charles told me in the aftermath of all this, "but what about the Druze? They are such a small community. There are only a few hundred thousand of them in Lebanon. All the Druze in the world were watching what was happening in those mountains."

"What happened in West Beirut was a given," Lee Smith wrote.[3] "According to a report from the pro-Hezbollah Lebanese paper *Al-Akhbar*, this coup had been planned well in advance, and its mastermind was the recently assassinated Hezbollah commander Imad Mughniyeh. The government may in fact have forced Nasrallah to show his hand at a time of its choosing, not his. Hezbollah's walkover in Beirut came as a surprise to no one; nor did the performance of the army, except perhaps the Bush administration which must now reconsider the amount of money it has spent on equipment and training for the Lebanese Armed Forces."

The Economist Intelligence Unit noted[4] that "the military setback in the Chouf has served notice that Hezbollah has little chance of expanding its area of operations at the expense of other groups." That was true, but it didn't matter that much. Hezbollah didn't need to expand. Nasrallah just needed impunity, and he got it when he proved to his internal enemies that he could rampage through the streets of Beirut whenever he wanted, and nobody—not even the national army—could stop him.

"The U.S. has failed in Lebanon and they have to admit it," Jumblatt said to Andrew Lee Butters at *Time*.[5] "We have to wait and see the new rules which Hezbollah, Syria and Iran will set. They can do what they want."

Lebanese political analyst Abu Kais admired Hariri's borderline pacifism and Jumblatt's strategic and political acumen. They may have handled this as smartly as they could. Hezbollah sullied its name and reputation again while they preserved theirs. When it was over, however, he concluded—and he hardly had any choice—that despite the resistance in Tariq Jedideh and Aley, "the dark age of Hezbollah is upon us."[6]

⌐

Royce got a ride out of West Beirut. His journalist friend Matt Nash swooped in from the east side of the city to pick him up. Somehow they made it through all the checkpoints.

Nobody rescued Charles.

When the shooting picked up in Hamra again, he called three young women who lived in an apartment two streets away—Dana from Lebanon, Sara from Syria, and Hala, a Palestinian. All were dual nationals and carried American passports.

"I'm going to try to leave in a taxi," he said, "and there's room for all of you if want to come with me."

He packed his most precious personal belongings into disheveled boxes, thinking there was a real chance he'd never see anything he left in his apartment ever again.

"Please call a taxi," he said downstairs at the desk.

"Where do you want to go?"

"Achrafieh," he said. "And then to the mountains."

Almost everyone Charles talked to in Hamra hoped to flee to Christian areas even if they weren't Christians themselves. His Sunni and Syrian friends didn't think Achrafieh in East Beirut was far enough. They wanted to go all the way to the Christian hinterlands. That's where they'd be protected. Even Sunni women who wore hijabs and were obvious Muslims at one hundred yards yearned for the Christian hinterlands. Nobody would shoot at them there. They might get dirty looks from a couple of people, especially under the circumstances, but Lebanon was an open country, and everyone would know displaced Sunnis weren't terrorists or invaders, but refugees.

Hala, Dana, and Sara walked over and met Charles in the lobby. The sound of gunfire wasn't as terrifying anymore, and since nobody was shooting on their particular street at that particular moment, there was no sense in getting overly worked up about it.

As soon as they left in the taxi, gunshots cracked from just a few hundred yards to the right, and militiamen began closing streets. The driver slammed the accelerator into the floor and drove the wrong way down one-ways.

There wasn't a chance they could punch all the way through to the east side without clearing one checkpoint or another. The key now was to pick which one looked easiest.

Dodgy-looking men with guns up ahead covered their faces with keffiyehs and balaclavas and flew the SSNP's swastika. They were more dangerous and sadistic than even Hezbollah, and the driver nearly crashed fishtailing the car around a corner.

"Okay," Charles said and laughed nervously. "I guess we won't be taking that road."

Directly ahead was another checkpoint staffed by clean-shaven young men contentedly smoking cigarettes and flying the Amal insignia. This was the checkpoint they wanted. Some March 14 Lebanese still held out hope that the secular Shias of Amal would tire of Hezbollah's Iranian masters. Some thought that's what would almost have to happen eventually. Amal's counterparts in Iran had turned against the likes of Mahmoud Ahmadinejad and Ali Khamenei long ago.

"Sorry," one of the young Amal men said to the driver. "You can't drive through here."

They had their orders. They weren't really allowed to say anything else. But this was Lebanon, where rules were often downgraded into suggestions.

"Listen, *Habibi*," the driver said. "I've got three girls and their brother here. Their parents are in the Gulf. They're worried and they want their kids in Achrafieh."

"Okay, okay," the militiaman said and waved them through. He didn't inspect the car or ask any more questions.

"That was easy," Charles said.

"We got lucky," the driver said and wiped his forehead with a handkerchief.

Crossing to the Christian side of the city—a mere forty-minute walk from the center of Hamra—was like driving four days into the past. Nothing at all was out of the ordinary. Shops were open. Traffic was normal. People were out on the street. Nobody was shooting at anybody, and nobody seemed concerned in the slightest that anybody might start.

The driver pulled over next to the Starbucks at Sassine Square and asked for twenty dollars.

"That's outrageous," said Sara, the young woman from Syria. Normally the ride would have cost five.

"It's fine," Charles said and paid. "He just got us out of a war zone."

The girls got out. Charles continued into the mountains. Because he was heading into the secure Christian heartland, his driver charged him the usual rate. He blew out his cheeks and felt fifty pounds lighter as they approached Rabieh, a rather posh area on the side of the mountain near the American Embassy, where his journalist friend Habib had prepared a spare bedroom.

The next day he had lunch with one of his relatives down in Dbayeh, one of Beirut's northern suburbs on the beach just south of Jounieh. The Christian areas were untouched by the war, but Christian thoughts weren't.

"The Christians," Charles told me, "were thinking, 'Wow. Look at them. They're at it again.' Things were going crazy in Beirut, and there were constant references on TV to the battle on 888 Hill in the Druze mountains. There are Christians in those areas, too. We didn't know how long we could hold out before the fighting spread everywhere."

The fighting didn't spread everywhere. It didn't even last very much longer. Lebanon's government caved. Walid Jumblatt whipped Nasrallah's boys just outside Aley, but even he caved. His people fought fiercely and well, but their numbers were small, and they no longer had a logistics infrastructure that could sustain them throughout a protracted conflict. Hezbollah had Syria and Iran, the Sunnis had most of the Arab world at their back, but the Druze, like the Kurds, had no friends but the mountains.

Hezbollah won. And that, as they say, was that.

⌒

When Charles returned to Hamra, Beirut felt like another city. Everything was trashed, the ground seemed to list sideways, and the SSNP flags were still flying.

Hezbollah had previously left that part of the city alone. There seemed to be an unspoken agreement that it was off-limits, if not outright protected, but *khallas*, that was finished now. The entire western half of the capital, including the vast majority of the city's hotels and resorts, was cast into the shatter zone.

Young people drifted apart from each other. The political divisions between March 14 and March 8 strained friendships during the Beirut Spring and wounded them severely after the July War. Hezbollah's invasion of Beirut damn near shot them through the brain and the heart and finished them off for good.

"It became a real emotional battle," one resident said. "Anybody who wasn't Shia was hating the Shia. Even my Syrian friends were saying the next time they saw their Shia friends, they were going to punch them in the face, even if their Shia friends were with March 14."

Rising sectarianism was hardly just a "street" level phenomenon. The *zuama* felt it, too, or at least had to pander to it.

Former Member of Parliament Khaled Al-Dhaher blasted away.[7] "Since the army and the security forces are incapable of defending our sons, our religion, our faith, and our liberty," he said, "we in the Islamic Gathering have decided to launch a national-Islamic resistance, in order to protect Lebanon and defend its people, and in order to prevent the Persian enterprise from getting its clutches on an Arab capital, because the people who have occupied Beirut belong to the Persian-Iranian army."

Lebanon's divided Christian community sat out the fighting. Perhaps the only reason they remained divided was because they sat out the fighting. Free Patriotic Movement leader Michel Aoun had been hemorrhaging Christian supporters for years thanks to his cynical alliance with Hezbollah, and he would likely lose nearly all of them if Hezbollah blew up Christian cities or neighborhoods. If Nasrallah didn't understand that from the beginning, he almost surely figured it out when his Druze allies turned on him in the Chouf.

"I finally understand why the Lebanese don't have civic trust," Charles said. "The people who lived next door wanted to kill me over politics. I didn't really know the Hezbollah people. They were mostly from the *dahiyeh*. But some of the people who lived in a building just down the street from me were with Amal and the SSNP. They intentionally terrorized us. We all tried to hide it, but everyone on the street was full of rage."

He'd hardly left his comfort zone in the Beirut bubble since the July War ended two years before, and by the time the May conflict started, he had all but forgotten about the rest of the country. He knew there were lots of poor people without much education even in Beirut, but he didn't move in those circles.

"When all these militiamen came out of the woodwork," he said, "I first wondered where on earth they all came from. A lot of people said they were from the *dahiyeh*, but no. Not all of them."

Many Hamra residents were indeed in denial about this at first. Few wanted to believe they were being shot at by some of their neighbors.

"These guys were the ones whose faces you don't normally look at," he said, paraphrasing the philosophers Emmanuel Levinas and Jean-Luc Marion, "the ones who just sit in the alleys, who don't have jobs and just hang out all day. They sit around, you walk by, you glance over, but then you keep walking because they're just five schlubs sitting there doing nothing. You see that all the time in Lebanon, guys without jobs and without anything to do, bullshitting all day long, consuming stupid sectarian rhetoric, and getting in fights with each other. They don't generally cause problems for the neighborhood, but when they do, it's a *big* problem."

Though he spent most of his time in the bubble, he still wasn't all that surprised Hezbollah invaded Beirut. Anyone in Lebanon who didn't live in a complete state of denial knew a foreign-sponsored militia and international terrorist organization with armed resistance as its raison d'être could never be trusted to keep its guns in the armory. What shocked him the most—what shocked a lot of people the most who hadn't lived through the civil war—was what he learned about human nature.

"People I knew," he said, "stopped looking at me as a person. I became a political position in human form. They stopped thinking of me as Charles and could only see me as a function of politics. And they took up arms against me. Instantly. Everything I held dear in Lebanon and in my neighborhood was destroyed. All the trust I had was destroyed. You can work really hard at being nice and being friendly, and you can do it for years, but when they decide they want to kill you, they'll do it."

Royce wasn't surprised that Hezbollah invaded, either. He studied conflict for a living and wouldn't even be in Lebanon if the country were stable. The very day he got off the plane, assassins killed Kataeb Party Member of Parliament Antoine Ghanem in Beirut's Sin al-Fil neighborhood with a car bomb. Hezbollah's occupation of downtown had already been in place for months, and the war against Fatah al-Islam in the north was well under way. What did surprise him, though, was how quickly his neighbors chalked the whole thing up to the new normal.

"They call it the May events," he told me, "which is such a euphemism. Imagine if that happened in America. They were saying, yeah, well, that was the events of May, that was weeks ago. I saw this in Haiti. Most people may not want war, but they're used to it. When you see it as an outsider, it's horrific, but for them it's just Tuesday."

For Charles, though, and for plenty of others I knew, it could never be Tuesday. More than half the friends I made in Lebanon in early 2005 relocated to the United States, the European Union, or Dubai by 2008.

Charles left, too. "Hezbollah proved they're willing to attack other Lebanese," he said after he moved from Beirut to Chicago.

"Nobody else is interested in their ideology," another Hamra resident told me. "And they'd rather kill us than talk to us about it."

⁓

"Nasrallah is like Ariel Sharon!" Saudi Foreign Minister Prince Saud Al-Faisal said at an Arab League conference shortly after the fighting died down.[8] "They both invaded Beirut. The legitimate government in Lebanon is being subjected to an all-out war. We, the Arab world, cannot stand idly by as this happens."

When Faisal said "the Arab world," he meant, of course, the Sunnis. The Shia Arabs of Hezbollah and the Alawite rulers of Syria were the enemy.

"We must do whatever it takes in order to stop this war and save Lebanon," he continued, "even if this requires the establishment of an Arab force that will quickly be deployed there, thus protecting the existing legitimate government."

Nothing remotely like this, however, happened.

Leaders from Lebanon's warring parties met in Doha, Qatar, on May 21. Ostensibly they were there to negotiate a compromise, but what they really did was hash out the terms of surrender. Nasrallah walked away with everything in his pocket. Brigadier General Wafiq Choucair had already been reinstated as the chief of airport security, and the government agreed to leave Hezbollah's telecoms network alone. And now March 8 got its "blocking third" veto power in the cabinet. Nasrallah spent eighteen months trying to wrench that out of his enemies' hands with civil disobedience and mostly nonviolent protests, and he failed. Yet it was his after less than a week of armed "resistance" in the streets.

It didn't bode well for Lebanon's future. Hezbollah had no incentive to limit itself to peaceful opposition when war yielded better results, and yielded them instantly.

"No victor, no vanquished," is a formula civilized Lebanese leaders use to peacefully resolve conflicts with each other, but Nasrallah was not a civilized leader. He was a terrorist.

Sure, some nice-sounding things were put into the Doha Agreement.[9] "The parties commit to abstain from having recourse or resuming the use of weapons and violence in order to record political gains," for example. Hezbollah also agreed on paper to the following: "Reasserting the commitment of the Lebanese political leaders to immediately abstain from resorting to the rhetoric of treason or political or sectarian instigation."

But this was just blather. There wasn't a chance Hezbollah would tolerate another attempt by the government to clamp down on its war-making or surveillance capabilities. Nasrallah would again accuse them of treason and would again declare war.

Army commander Michel Suleiman was chosen as a "compromise" president, at last filling the vacancy left behind by Emile Lahoud. Suleiman wasn't the venal pro-Syrian toady Lahoud had always been. He was only *moderately* pro-Syrian, and he was much more of a gentleman. While clearly an improvement and hardly a would-be tyrant himself, he wasn't what March 14 had in mind as a replacement for al-Assad's yes-man in Baabda.

Nasrallah permitted majority leaders to portray the Doha Agreement as a compromise so they could save face, but everyone understood that he won. No Arab force landed in Beirut to shore up the government, and the region's Sunnis had to face up to the fact that they were no longer dominant in the Middle East. The agenda in their part of the world was now being set by the Persians and by the Israelis.

The governments of Egypt and Saudi Arabia made it clear that they weren't on Nasrallah's side during the opening days of the July War, and that was when Hezbollah was shooting at Jews. Now that Iran's private army was at war with Lebanon's Sunnis, Sunni leaders elsewhere would have to think long and hard about which side of the Persian-Israeli conflict they'd have to come down on if and when all the stops were pulled out.

What they decided was something few, if any, Middle East experts during the previous several decades would have expected. But as Middle East blogger Jesse Aizenstat wrote,[10] "There's nothing like a fanatical band of Persian cats to bind the Semitic tribes."

CHAPTER SIXTEEN

the mystic
in his
bunker

We are this East's saints
and its devils, we are its
cross and its spear, we
are its light and its fire.
—BASHIR GEMAYEL

Cold winter rain off the brooding Mediterranean lashed the sides of the mountain in sheets. My driver rubbed condensation off the inside of the windshield with a cloth while the van's tired wipers struggled to keep up on the outside. Lebanon is a dense country, almost entirely lacking in wilderness, and the lower elevations north of Beirut are chockablock with apartment towers, but we found ourselves on a rare lonely road winding its way through trees and grass as though we were approaching a hermitage.

The driver stopped in front of a swing gate, where five men wielding AK-47s waited in dripping ponchos.

"We get out here," he said. "They will take us the rest of the way."

I accompanied a small group of Western journalists and foreign-policy analysts to a meeting with Lebanese Forces leader Samir Geagea, a pillar of the March 14 coalition whose alliance with Saad

Hariri and the Future Movement proved more durable over time than any other.

As its name implies, the Lebanese Forces was founded as a militia during the civil war. Geagea seized command in 1986 from his rival and onetime ally Elie Hobeika and transformed the organization into one of the most formidable fighting forces in Lebanon. Most of its members and supporters were Maronites, and they fought hard against Syria's invasion and conquest. Competent fighters as they may have been, they were too weak and too few to stave off defeat and de facto annexation forever, and they surrendered their weapons at the end of the war.

Like some of the other warlords from that era, Geagea matured into Lebanon's version of a regular politician in the early 1990s. Unlike most of the others, however, he continued resisting the Syrians when Hafez al-Assad's regime broke one promise after another. It was clear almost from the beginning that the Syrian ruler had no intention of leaving the country and letting its people govern themselves.

In 1994, Syrian authorities ordered their Lebanese subordinates to frame Geagea for setting off a bomb in the Our Lady of Deliverance church in Zouk that killed nine people. He was acquitted in the church bombing, but the accusation voided his inclusion in the general amnesty for crimes committed during the civil war. The court found him guilty on several counts from that period and gave him four life sentences in solitary confinement.

He was released almost at once after the Syrians were thrown out in 2005, and he happily reunited with his wife, Sethrida, who was herself elected to parliament as the head of the party in the election that June.

I stepped out of the van and into the rain, squinting as the wind blew water into my eyes.

"Bonjour," said one of the guards, using a greeting common among Lebanese Christians.

"Hello," I said, both to return the greeting and to let him know which language I spoke.

German shepherds sniffed me and my colleagues for explosives while the men with guns patted us down. Our hosts would not even send a car until after we had been cleared. They knew, of course, that Western journalists weren't a threat to them or to Geagea, but if they started relaxing their security posture under certain conditions, somebody might eventually figure out a way through. Geagea's men couldn't let their guard down for even one second, not after so many assassinations and car bombs had nearly decimated the March 14 bloc in parliament.

I had spent enough time in the Middle East by that point that the region and its logic had changed me. Most people I knew back in the States, especially in my hometown in the Pacific Northwest, would have felt a little unnerved being frisked by men wielding rifles who were not the legal authorities. I actually felt better around men with guns than I did around unarmed civilians, as long as those men were politically friendly.

In the 1970s, many Lebanese liberals, intellectuals, and other sensitive types who hate war ended up supporting or even joining militias. Political violence has been the norm in the Middle East as long as humans have lived there, and the Lebanese state was far too weak to protect its citizens from it. Men and women had to look out for themselves or take shelter behind those willing to commit violence for them. Western civilians would eventually do the same if the police effectively ceased to exist and their neighborhoods turned into war zones.

Each major sectarian community fielded at least one militia during the war. Because they might be killed for what was printed next to "religion" on their identity cards, almost everyone eventually had to go to their corner, and their corner was chosen for them at birth.

I hated Lebanon's sectarianism and wished to be above it all as a foreigner, but I couldn't change it, nor could I entirely opt out of it. I had friends from every sect in the country, but because I was baptized Catholic as a child, the Maronites were "my people" whether I liked it or not, even though I am not religious. That's how they saw me, anyway, and it guaranteed my protection when I traveled among them.

An official Lebanese Forces van approached from the road above. The guards opened the swing gate. My colleagues and I piled into the back.

My friend and colleague Lee Smith sat on my left. We met in 2005 shortly after he moved from Cairo to Beirut. He relocated to the Middle East after al Qaeda's assault on his hometown of New York City, hoping to figure out what on earth compelled more than a dozen well-educated people to kill themselves and almost 3,000 others by flying hijacked jetliners into our buildings. Like me, he was swept up in the euphoria of the Beirut Spring and thought 2005 was a terrific time to be an American in the Middle East.

It *was* a great time to be an American in the Middle East. He ended up as a sort of refugee in Syria, however, when the Israelis invaded in 2006 during their failed attempt to crush or cripple Hezbollah. He then moved on to Jerusalem, where he began wrapping up years of research and experience that went into his brilliant but bleak book *The Strong Horse*.[1]

To my right sat Jonathan Foreman, reporter at large for an outstanding new magazine in Britain called *Standpoint*. This was his first trip to the Levant. He would learn the hard way how Lebanon had changed since Hezbollah's armed assault on the capital, when he and I were attacked in Beirut by some of the most dangerous people in the entire country. But I'm getting ahead of the story. First we had our meeting with a former militia commander.

The Lebanese Forces headquarters had an expansive, even spectacular, view of the Mediterranean from so high above sea level that it enjoyed its own microclimate. It was colder in winter but above the suffocating summer humidity. The structure itself looked more like a concrete compound or even a bunker than an office, but it was new and had a bit of style—as much as such buildings can be said to have any style. It looked vaguely futuristic and could have even worked as a set in a science-fiction movie. Sparta might have constructed something like that if it had twenty-first-century building materials and money to blow.

Square-jawed security men at the door confiscated my cell phone and camera, and they traded my digital voice recorder for a pencil and paper. I normally tape interviews so I can quote my subjects precisely, but this time I'd have to furiously scribble down notes. Some of the guards were built like weight lifters, and their rifles looked new. They were polite enough, as people in the Middle East usually are, but at the same time, they were the types you would not want to mess with unless you had a small army.

A young woman escorted me and my colleagues to a modern conference room without windows. Somebody had prepared coffee and sandwiches for us in advance. The Lebanese Forces leader sat alone at the head of the table and introduced himself. His bald head and mustache made him look vaguely like a police officer.

"I was a medical student at the American University of Beirut when the war suddenly erupted," he said. "I tried to continue studying medicine, but was stuck at the campus in Hamra, a Muslim area. So I had to stay at the university in the dorm and eat in the cafeteria."

Poor Hamra, my old neighborhood. Hezbollah's invasion in May brought it right back to 1975.

"I took night classes and couldn't go home," Geagea continued. "Just to get up the coast to Jounieh, you had to fly to Syria and then go the rest of the way by sea. It took twenty-four hours."

Jounieh was a thirty-minute drive from Hamra when there was no traffic.

Joining a militia wasn't something he ever imagined he'd do, but that was true of almost everyone who eventually did.

"I went home to Bcharre," he said, "and joined a citizen militia to fight Palestinian invaders in our towns. We called ourselves the Lebanese Christian Resistance. We were not a regular army. The population rallied around us, especially in the early years of the war."

You can't fully understand Geagea without first understanding the roots of his movement and its civil war-era founder Bashir Gemayel.

The idealistic yet ruthless Gemayel united a number of disparate Christian militias under his command and dubbed them the Lebanese Forces in the late 1970s. Their raison d'être was the same as so many others in the Middle East at that time: resistance. But the Lebanese Forces was not founded to resist Israel or the West. It was founded to resist Yasser Arafat's Palestine Liberation Organization and the Syrian soldiers sent to divide and conquer the country by

Hafez al-Assad. And the Lebanese Forces, hard as it was to believe in 2009, waged their battle of resistance in a political and military alliance with the State of Israel.

Gemayel was elected president in August of 1982, the same month the Israel Defense Forces vanquished the PLO from its stronghold in West Beirut. It was extraordinary that a Christian allied with Israel managed to land in the highest office in an Arabic-speaking country, but he did. The Israeli leadership was ecstatic. They thought peace with their northern neighbor was finally at hand, that their ground invasion and occupation of Lebanon was paying political dividends as well as security ones. They had not yet learned that their ability to transform Lebanese politics in their favor, either violently or diplomatically, was effectively nil.

The election of Bashir Gemayel was, of course, controversial. Arafat and the PLO were banished to Tunisia, but local Sunni militias loyal to the Palestinian cause hadn't gone anywhere. Syrian soldiers still occupied parts of the country. *Israeli* soldiers still occupied parts of the country, saying they'd stick around in Beirut at least until after Gemayel signed the peace treaty and established some kind of order.

The president-elect gave a speech to supporters at the Kataeb Party headquarters in Achrafieh on the east side of Beirut shortly before he was to be sworn in. "To all those who don't like the idea of me as president," he said, according to Thomas Friedman's account,[2] "I say, they will get used to it." Just a few minutes later, Habib Shartouni of the Syrian Social Nationalist Party blew him to pieces with a remote-controlled bomb planted in his sister's apartment upstairs.

Gemayel, before he was killed, was an ardent Lebanese nationalist. He once described his political mission as "ten thousand four hundred and fifty-two square kilometers," the size of the country.

But he was an ardent Lebanese nationalist at a time when Lebanese nationalism was still perceived by most Sunnis, Shias, and Druze as a Maronite project.

"Let us proclaim that if Lebanon is not to be a Christian national homeland," he said in a famous speech,[3] "it will nonetheless remain a homeland for Christians. Above all a homeland for Christians, though one for others as well if they so choose a homeland to be protected and preserved, in which our churches may be rebuilt at the time and in the manner we desire. Yasser Arafat has transformed the church of Damur into a garage. We forgive him, and though they defiled, sullied, and pillaged the church of Damur, we will rebuild it. Had we been in Egypt or Syria, perhaps we would not even have had the right to rebuild a destroyed church. Our desire is to remain in the Middle East so that our church bells may ring out our joys and sorrows whenever we wish! We want to continue to christen, to celebrate our rites and traditions, our faith and our creed whenever we wish! We want to be able to assume and testify to our Christianity in the Middle East!"

You might say the Lebanese Forces even appeared to be superficially similar to Hezbollah in some ways during its civil war period. Both were sectarian militias founded in the spirit of resistance against a hated foreign occupier, and both forged a military and political alliance with another foreign occupier. Hezbollah sided with the Iranians and the Syrians against the Israelis, while the Lebanese Forces sided with the Israelis against the Syrians and Palestinians. Both fought ruthlessly against rivals in their own communities.

There were as many differences, though, as there were similarities. The Lebanese Forces never went through a theocratic phase, nor were they ever directly controlled by their foreign sponsor. They fought as hard against the Syrian occupation as Hezbollah fought against the Israelis, but they never denied Syria's right to *exist*. They never vowed to destroy Syria, nor did they commit acts of terrorism in Syria or attack Syrian interests abroad as Hezbollah did to the Israelis. They also, unlike Hezbollah, turned over their weapons at the end of the war and transformed themselves into a nonviolent political party. The Taif Agreement that ended the war demanded no less, and the Lebanese Forces were one of its signatories.

They upheld their end of the bargain even when the Syrians didn't.

"The first president after Taif was Rene Moawad," Geagea said. "The Syrians killed him when he didn't implement it the way they wanted after they began to erode the agreement. Syria was supposed to leave Beirut and Mount Lebanon in 1992 and leave all of Lebanon in 1995."

The Taif Agreement looked great on paper, though the Christians were despondent that many of the powers of the president—whose office was reserved for a Maronite—were transferred to the Sunni prime ministership. Damascus couldn't control the Sunnis as easily as it could the Shias, but the Christians were even less pliable. A weak president served Syria's interests, so Lebanon got a weak president. Even so, Moawad was assassinated after seventeen days in office.

Much of the rest of the agreement was pretty good, though. The Syrian military was supposed to begin a phased withdrawal as Lebanese security forces came back on line and grew strong enough to keep peace themselves. All militias were to be disarmed. Perhaps most important of all, Lebanon was declared[4] "a sovereign, free, and independent country and a final homeland for all its citizens." There would be no more occupations, no more warlords, and no more loyalties to countries beyond Lebanon's borders.

Yet the Syrians wouldn't leave, and Hafez al-Assad let Hezbollah hold onto its weapons, saying the Party of God was not a militia any longer but a resistance movement fighting Israeli occupation in the South Lebanon border area. No pressure was put on the Shias to abandon their loyalty to their Persian coreligionists ruling Iran. On the contrary. Hezbollah could claim fealty to Tehran as long as it also worked with Damascus, which was convenient enough since Syria and Iran were close allies anyway. So Lebanon was not sovereign. Lebanon was not free. Lebanon was not yet a final homeland for all its citizens.

"The Syrian pretext," Geagea said, "was that the Lebanese state was not ready to safeguard the security of the country. Whenever it was time for them to withdraw, we had security problems. Then the Lebanese puppet government asked Syria to stay, and the security problems went away. This happened over and over again."

Geagea and his men surrendered their weapons like they were supposed to, but they didn't go along quietly with everything else the Syrians had in mind. They gave Ghazi Kanaan a serious headache, in fact. He was the chief of Syrian military intelligence in Lebanon at the time, and he practically ran the country himself from his headquarters in Anjar through a network of bribed, cajoled, and bullied party heads and officials.

"The Lebanese Forces," he once said,[5] "are like a germ that must be eliminated."

So Geagea was arrested on trumped-up charges, and he spent more than a decade by himself in a cell beneath the Ministry of Defense, not to be released until after the Syrians had been evicted.

"After eleven years in solitary confinement," he told me, "how can a person emerge the same? The first year I realized that this would be deep and long lasting. I had to adapt. I couldn't assume anybody would ever let me out. Six square meters was the whole world. I had to build a life there."

And build a life there he did. What else could he do? They wouldn't even let him read newspapers, let alone communicate with his supporters outside. His wife, Sethrida, could visit, but the two never had any privacy, and they weren't allowed to talk about politics.

"Since I was a child," he said, "I was interested in saints and hermits and the mystical life, so I returned to that road. The guards didn't allow me any communication, but they did let me read theology and philosophy books, which suited me well. Bit by bit I built a small world inside. My biggest difficulty was when they took me from my cell to the hospital or to the court. It bothered me. It took me out of my spiritual world. I studied Christian, Muslim, Hindu, and Buddhist mystics. I went around the whole world. It took me seven years."

I had ideas about Geagea before I met him, ideas that I had picked up from media reports over the years; from history books; from broad-minded Lebanese Christians discomforted by his earlier behavior and instinctively opposed to militias; from some of his own party's past bloody deeds that I was uneasy with for my own reasons; and even, to a lesser extent, from what his enemies said about him. I found myself softening a bit as he talked, though. The doctor-turned-warlord seemed to have metamorphosed yet again. It could have all been a put-on, of course, but at the same time, eleven years in solitary confinement had to have some kind of effect on a person.

"This was the major event of my life," he said. "I went into another dimension which is much more vivid than anything that goes on in this one. When they say everything is known to God, it's not bullshit. All our unconsciousness are linked together. Whatever goes on in this dimension is related to what happens in that one. I suddenly became very concerned about what I would do if they liberated me. I was safe inside myself. I had hundreds of books in my six square meters."

The Syrians still loathed him, of course, and Hezbollah feared him. He opposed the Iranian-led Resistance Bloc a bit less stridently than Walid Jumblatt, but unlike Jumblatt, he had done so consistently without ever having let up. Jumblatt had been pressured into appeasement before, and he might be pressured again. Everyone knew Geagea could not be. He would rather go back to prison or face a firing squad.

"I could have fled with my wife before I was arrested," he said. "It was my personal choice to stay and risk prison. I am of the warrior archetype, and we do not flee. We confront. I would not have felt at ease with myself if I fled the country."

I could understand why Hezbollah and the Syrians thought this man could be a serious problem for them. His reputation might even have influenced their decision to leave Christian areas alone when they rampaged through Beirut the previous May. It was hard to say.

It was also hard to say, though, what he and his party could actually do to stop Hezbollah if they tried. Unlike Saad Hariri and Hassan Nasrallah, Geagea had no foreign allies. No one would come to the rescue of the Lebanese Forces. Everyone in the country had access to light weapons, but Geagea's men no longer had anything that could be called an arsenal with a straight face. There wasn't a chance any country in the world would sponsor them as a proxy, not even the United States, especially now that George W. Bush was no longer in office.

Not even the Israelis were looking for allies in Lebanon. They wouldn't have found any if they tried. Geagea might not survive twenty-four hours if his party again reached out to Jerusalem. His ability to resist the resistance was severely proscribed.

He wasn't as downbeat as he could have been.

"I am not confident about the future in the short run," he said, "but the Syrian and Iranian regimes are ultimately doomed."

He had to be right about that much, at least. No dictatorship lasts forever. Westerners know this instinctively, as we replaced our own autocracies over time with democracies. Middle Easterners know it instinctively, too, though for slightly different reasons. In that part of the world, all rulers fall to another in the end, even if they are replaced by rulers who are no better.

Lee Smith surely knew what the Lebanese Forces leader was talking about. In his book *The Strong Horse*,[6] he described the pattern of Arab history set out by the brilliant medieval-era Tunisian historian Ibn Khaldun, who explains how, as Smith put it, "history is a matter of one tribe, nation, or civilization dominating others by force until it, too, is overthrown by force." Once group cohesion starts to fade, Smith wrote, "the regnant civilization becomes easy pickings for a younger one still adhering to its martial ethos." One ruler after another "[rises] in the desert to replace his predecessor and rule until he, too, is put down by a more vital force."

It may seem obvious that this was how history worked in the Middle East and North Africa, at least during the medieval era when Khaldun wrote his *Al-Muqaddima*.[7] That's how history worked in Europe at that time, as well. That's how history worked pretty much everywhere until liberal democracies were established to smooth transitions of power in the more fortunate parts of the world.

No one could seriously believe that the Syrian Baath Party or the Khomeinist regime in Iran would still be in power after another 500 years. One way or another, al-Assad's and Khamenei's governments would, Ozymandius-like, follow the communists, the Latin American generals, the Shah, the Arab kings of Libya and Iraq, and so on, into oblivion.

Something just short of that had already befallen the Lebanese Forces. They themselves once indisputably ruled parts of Lebanon, including the side of the mountain where Geagea hunkered down in his headquarters. The Lebanese Forces, in a way, was no longer the Lebanese Forces.

I asked him how his political views had changed since the war and his own loss of power.

"My old vision was one of separation between Christians and Muslims," he said. "But now? I don't know. Lebanese who want to live together should abide by that vision. I wanted a federal state, but now? No. I am open to whatever the people decide they want."

Nothing generated suspicion of the Lebanese Forces among Syria's and Hezbollah's supporters like its former alliance with Israel. Some Lebanese Forces members told me in no uncertain terms—anonymously and off the record, of course—that they still admired Israelis and secretly thought of themselves as Israel's friends and allies. Not all Lebanese Forces members felt this way or would admit it, however, and I couldn't get Geagea to even hint at it obliquely.

"Our relationship with Israel was not a deep relationship," he told me. "It was a relationship of convenience. The PLO was much more powerful than us. We were squeezed and had to look elsewhere for arms and training and support. We were obliged to go to the Israelis. Our relationship peaked when the Israelis drove the PLO out of Beirut and Bashir Gemayel was elected. It fell apart after Bashir was killed."

It was a careful answer. He did not have the latitude to say anything more, assuming he even wanted to say anything more. Hezbollah might push to put him on trial for treason or even have him assassinated if he described an alliance with Israel in anything other than the past tense. Many of his Sunni allies would also have been troubled by that kind of talk, and some might even break ranks.

Lee Smith asked Geagea why he thought the Lebanese Forces had such a bad reputation with Western journalists—an excellent question. I was a bit suspicious myself when I first arrived in the country, partly because I disliked even former militias on principle, but also because his party was at times described as fascist. No self-respecting Westerner would dare write anything positive or even neutral about fascists.

But how accurate was that label? The word "fascist," over time, lost much of its meaning. It was so often used as an epithet instead of a properly understood and sparingly applied noun. Only totalitarian parties can be fairly described as fascist. Otherwise, the word is no more than a slur, like "pig" for "policeman."

"When Christians defended the first republic," Geagea said, "some journalists thought we were like the apartheid regime in South Africa. There were abuses on our part in the war, but less than the Palestinians and the Syrians, even though the Syrians had a regular army and we were just a militia. After 1982, the Israeli media also turned against us because they thought we betrayed them. Our bad reputation continued after the war because I was arrested and subjected to trials while the others were not. Most journalists didn't know these trials were rigged by the Syrians. It even took the embassies a while to figure it out."

Did that answer the charge? I'm afraid it did not. At the same time, though, I never heard anyone in the Lebanese Forces say anything that could fairly be described as totalitarian. They could be parochial and use obnoxious sectarian rhetoric to denounce their enemies, but almost every party in Lebanon was guilty of that from time to time, and it would be absurd to say they were all fascists just for that reason. Besides, if anyone in the country deserved a label like that, it was Hezbollah and the Syrian Social Nationalist Party. Their ideologies really were totalitarian.

Still, the Kataeb militia—which was aligned with the Lebanese Forces during the war—committed an infamous massacre in the Palestinian refugee camps of Sabra and Shatila, and it did so with Israelis in a background support role. Between 300 and 3,000 people were killed, depending on who you want to believe. Many, if not most, were civilians. It triggered the largest political demonstration in the entire history of Israel, and it brought about the downfall of Defense Minister Ariel Sharon. Most Western journalists, including me, wouldn't forget it.

There was more to complain about. During the war, Geagea and the Lebanese Forces fought other Christians and even, incredibly, the Lebanese army under the command of General Michel Aoun—which partly explained why Aoun had recently established a *modus vivendi* with Hezbollah and the Syrians. Aoun had to sidle up to one old foe or another whether he liked it or not, and he decided it would not be his old nemeses Samir Geagea or Walid Jumblatt.

So the Lebanese Forces was hardly innocent, even if it did take the international press a bit longer than it should have to realize the group had mellowed out during peacetime like most of the others. One could say all kinds of unpleasant things about every armed faction during the civil war with considerable justification. Many Lebanese liberals did, and the most idealistic were dismayed that the Independence Intifada wasn't able to toss out the whole lot of them along with the Syrians. What made leaders like Hariri and Siniora so admirable to so many, whatever else you might say about them, was that they had no dried blood under their fingernails. They were practically pacifists, which was not something you could say about many Sunni Arab leaders in the Middle East.

What kind of people made up the Lebanese Forces was an important question. It wasn't enough that they were Christians opposed to Hezbollah. Antun Saadeh, founder of the Syrian Social Nationalist Party, was a Christian. Michel Aflaq, one of the founders of the Baath Party, was a Christian. If the Lebanese Forces had even latent fascist tendencies, they might become a genuine menace if hostilities broke out again. Surely the radical Sunnis in the Nahr al-Bared camp would be a serious problem if they were turned loose against Hezbollah. They were the types to hate and kill Shias for being Shias, just as they were the types to hate and kill Jews and Americans for being Jews and Americans. No one in the West should hope to see a Christian version of that sort of force emerge in Lebanon to counter Hezbollah.

"I told the Kataeb and the Lebanese Forces that they should change their names," Lebanon Renaissance Foundation founder Eli Khoury told me. "They sound like they've come out of the 1940s." He did not, however, think it was fair to dismiss them as fascists. "They saw that the number of Christians in Lebanon was decreasing. And they dug in because the region was on fire. They want to preserve themselves."

Many, if not most, Lebanese Christians still worried about their future in an Arab and Muslim region. How could they not? It had been decades since they were the majority in their own country. A plurality of Lebanese who emigrated were Christians. Palestinian and Iraqi Christians had been fleeing the region for years. Coptic Christians in Egypt lived as second-class citizens. The Middle East has always been a hard place for minorities. The only thing that may save Lebanon's minorities in the end is that every sect in the country is a minority.

Geagea, though, wasn't as concerned as some of the others. He took the long view.

"I am not too worried about the future of Christians in Lebanon," he said. "We have survived much worse. When the Mamluks invaded, they massacred us, demolished our homes, and burned down our forests. The world is much more open now. We will be okay."

The world changed. Lebanon changed. Geagea himself apparently changed. He still thought of himself as a confrontational warrior, but he was no longer a warlord. He and his men no longer shot at their enemies, not even when Hezbollah, Amal, and the SSNP laid siege to Beirut. They almost certainly would pick up their rifles again if their neighborhoods, streets, and homes were invaded, but they hated the very thought of it now. Geagea himself hated it more than some of his followers. Prison and age seemed to have massaged most of the violent impulses out of him, and there was always, despite appearances, a part of him that was haunted by war.

"There is an image I cannot get out of my mind," he said to Lebanese journalist Giselle Khoury.[8] "One time there was a meeting held in Aley between the Progressive Socialist Party officials and ours. I was in the jeep. It was the winter of 1983. I saw a girl of six, seven, or eight years old, blonde, walking barefoot in the rain and playing. The image remained in my mind all the time. She was playing in all her childhood innocence. I asked myself, what if the bombing started? Isn't it possible that a bomb could kill, disfigure, or injure that child? The image of that girl is still in my mind even now."

He and his party did nothing when Hezbollah invaded Beirut. Neither the Party of God nor its Amal and SSNP allies attacked Christian areas, but that's not the only reason. Geagea didn't want to fight in the civil war either. He resisted resisting for years before he enlisted.

"I was twenty-one when the war started," he said to Khoury.[9] "I was a student at one of the most prestigious universities in Lebanon, the American University of Beirut. I wasn't in the streets playing marbles. My major was one of the hardest—medicine. When the war started, I was in my fourth year. And despite the war, I continued two more years. I'm saying this because it's not true that we're responsible for the war. The whole situation and conditions in Lebanon led to the war, a violent and harsh war as you saw. Some of us chose to stay out of this war, and that was their choice, but it wasn't the best choice for me. One should do his best to prevent his society from facing war, but if a war starts without him doing anything to help start it, he must defend himself and his society. And when peace comes, he should do his best to make peace."

Hezbollah and the Syrians feared him politically, as they should have, but they had little to worry about militarily as long as they left his people alone and didn't seize power outright. Prison taught him patience, and living in the east gave him longtime horizons.

"Hezbollah is a transient phenomenon in the history of Lebanon," he told me. "We cannot judge whether coexistence is possible because of Hezbollah. Coexistence will be between Christians and Muslims, not between March 14 and Hezbollah."

Nasrallah's army surely was a transient phenomenon in the history of Lebanon. The Iranian regime would one day either fall or reform itself out of all recognition, as Mao Tse-tung's Chinese Communist Party finally did. Ali Khamenei's overseas brigade in Lebanon wouldn't last long, at least in its present form, after its patrons in Tehran were overthrown or replaced.

Geagea, however, no longer sounded like the kind of man who thought he would ever again try to overthrow or replace anyone.

"The one who wants life to be straight and true should not avenge himself or hold a grudge against anyone," he said to Khoury. "I barely got out of prison and didn't have time to do anything, and the ones who put me in jail are now in jail themselves. He should let everything go by itself and justice will be done."

He sounded like a Taoist, almost. If this was what Hezbollah's fiercest Christian opponent was saying, Westerners no longer needed to worry about their own coreligionists in Lebanon acting like Iraqi- or Bosnian Serb-style death squads. The mystic in his bunker might make an excellent companion to be stuck with in a foxhole, but he had no intention of digging one ever again.

Hassan Nasrallah—as long as he left the Christians alone—had little to fear from his Maronite countrymen.

CHAPTER SEVENTEEN

the arabist in his palace

> You are not our Lord.
> —FOUAD SINIORA TO
> HASSAN NASRALLAH

A man in Jerusalem once summed up Middle Eastern politics for me in one sentence. "If someone in this region isn't afraid of you," he said, "you will do what he wants." This was hard for me to hear as a Westerner, but I couldn't deny the Middle East had its own set of rules.

Hassan Nasrallah had little to fear from Samir Geagea. He had even less reason to fear the Sunni prime minister. Fouad Siniora was a bit like Rafik Hariri in some ways, only with less charisma, less money and power, and more hang-ups. He was one of the least imposing figures in the entire Middle East, an arthritic gazelle among young and fit lions.

After studying business administration at the American University of Beirut, he embarked on a distinguished career in Levantine capitalism and politics. His work at Citibank, the Lebanese Central Bank, and in Hariri's corporate empire led to his job as Lebanon's finance minister in the 1990s, and the March 14 bloc in parliament chose him as prime minister after the election in 2005.

As a staunchly pro-business free-trader, Siniora was, unlike most Pan-Arab Nationalists, entirely uninterested in and even hostile to economic socialism and the bullying state apparatus that came with it in his part of the world. He paid his respects to the revolutionary regimes in Syria and Libya, and even to Nasser's Egypt and Saddam Hussein's Iraq, but he broke with them sharply when it came to the day-to-day business of economics and governance. He had his detractors, but any suggestion that he was a tyrant was hysterical. Most Arab countries had way too much government, but Lebanon hardly had any.

I finally had a chance to meet him in his office in the Grand Serail, a beautifully restored palatial Ottoman-era military headquarters overlooking downtown. He wore a perfectly pressed charcoal-gray suit and tie, and he came across a bit stiff, his handshake limp, his crooked smile a little perfunctory.

He was a liberal in the general sense of the word, but at the same time he was loaded down with ideological dead freight common among Sunni Arabs of his generation. Few people described him as fresh, though he actually was compared with the likes of Bashar al-Assad and even Egypt's more reasonable Hosni Mubarak. He filed off the rough edges of his Nasser-era Pan-Arabism, making his view of the world suitable for the modern sort-of democracy he partially governed.

Michael Young described Siniora brilliantly and concisely in *The Ghosts of Martyrs Square*.[1] "He saw himself as a quintessential Arabist politically and culturally, but an Arabism shorn of the radicalism of yesteryear, of any renovatory yearning; his Arabism was that of the courts and presidential palaces, with their old men, wedding cake furniture, and sealed windows, an Arabism of ornate compromises and weighty silences, of coagulated immobility."

"Let me tell you something and put things straight," he said as he sat down and folded his hands on the table in front of him. "Lebanon is an Arab country. It has a sense of belonging to the causes of the Arab world, but at the same time, Lebanon cannot carry the burden of the whole Arab world on its shoulders."

He spoke for the overwhelming majority in his Sunni community when he said that, but not for the majority in his country. Many, if not most, Maronites couldn't give two figs about Arabism or its causes. Hezbollah, at the same time, was perfectly willing to shoulder as much of the Arab world's burdens as possible for the street cred its Shia constituents needed in a region with an otherwise hostile Sunni majority.

He did, however, know how to speak for the majority and sound like a statesman instead of a sectarian *zaim* when he had to.

"Lebanon is composed of so many groups," he said. "It is like a piece of mosaic of different colors that live in harmony together without a single dominant color. For a long period of time it has been a place of refuge and belonging. For millennia it has been a crossroads and has played a role in the interface between the west and the east, the north and the south. It has developed certain ways of behavior and ways of life, certain principles and values—democracy, openness, tolerance, and moderation."

Tolerance was something the Middle East painfully lacked, and Siniora felt this acutely. He was, like his country, an exception in his part of the world. He even thought the likes of Hezbollah deserved tolerance, and he was endlessly patient and generous with that tolerance, something Hezbollah did not appreciate and did not reciprocate.

"This mosaic is beautiful as long as it fits well together," he said. "If, for one reason or another, the glue that brings the pieces together is loosened, something else happens. It doesn't mean you should curse the loose piece of mosaic. You should try to add a little more glue to make it work."

Siniora was facing one of liberalism's greatest dilemmas—how much do the intolerant deserve tolerance? He was perhaps a tad less naive, though, than he sounded. He realized Lebanon's greatest virtue was also its weakness.

"The glue comes loose," he said, "because of the pressures and the passions coming in from the outside. Lebanon is an open country and a democracy where people can speak their minds, so some use the country as an arena for fighting the wars in our region."

Friends and colleagues who knew him warned me not to mention the Palestinians. Apparently, he liked to lecture foreign journalists about Israel for as long as an hour if given the chance. Still, it was as difficult to talk about Lebanon without bringing up Israel as it was to ignore Syria and Iran. In any case, he started in on Israel without being prompted, and as soon as he did, it was difficult to steer him back to anything else.

"Our only enemy up until now is Israel," he said. "We don't want to have any other enemy. Syria is a sister country. We want to make the best of the situation with Syria, but on the basis of full respect for our freedom and independence, for our special character-istics and features, for our values."

He had little choice but to say about Israel what his Sunni con-stituents wanted to hear, but there was nothing pro forma about it. I knew Lebanese Sunnis and Shias who weren't obsessed with Israel the way he was, and I even knew a few who quietly sympathized to an extent with the Israelis, but theirs was a distinct minority position, and they kept quiet about it in public. Siniora may as well car bomb himself before saying anything nice about Israel, but I doubted he'd have much nice to say anyway. He seemed entirely uninterested in destroying his southern neighbor, and he was especially uninterested in using Lebanon as a launchpad for Iranian missiles, but that hardly meant he had to like Israel.

"The occupation is responsible," he said, "for restraining devel-opment and adaptation to change in the Arab world."

It would have been more accurate to say Arab despots used Israel as an excuse for restraining development and adaptation to change in the Arab world. Al-Assad justified his dictatorial "emergency" laws on his state of war with the Zionists, but Dubai managed to prosper and grow and adapt despite Israel. Dubai even did a little business with Israelis and allowed them to visit. Tunisia was a perfectly lovely place, and none of the problems it did have had anything to do with Israel. Iraq's problems were catastrophic, but Israel had no more to do with them than Brazil.

If Siniora had as much power as al-Assad had in Syria, Leb-anon might look like an Arab version of Greece or even Italy. Israel wouldn't get in the way. The Israelis wouldn't even think about Leb-anon much, just as they rarely thought about Cyprus except when they went there on holiday and peaceably ate next to Lebanese tourists in the same restaurants. What held Lebanon back—and Siniora knew this perfectly well—were the totalitarian anti-Zionist forces inside and outside his country that wished to turn the Arab world's Riviera into a garrison state.

"In the years before 1948," he said, referring to the year Israel declared independence from the British Mandate, "I was a kid. I come from the city of Sidon. We had plenty of Jews, and we were living together, doing business with them. All the coups d'état in this region, all the revolutions, all the problems, all the bloody confrontations were influenced by Palestine, the presence of so many Palestinian refugees, and the continuation of the occupation that has been in place for the past sixty years. I'm not saying there aren't other issues in the region, but this is the main one. There are others, yes—political, social, economic, lack of adaptation—but this problem is getting worse."

Hezbollah was not fighting Israel when its gunmen rampaged through Beirut the previous May. Syria was not fighting Israel when it occupied Lebanon and assassinated journalists and members of parliament. Iran was not fighting Israel when it murdered dissidents, and Iraqi insurgents were not fighting Israel when they massacred civilians with car bombs. And while the Israelis fought Hezbollah ineptly in 2006, they never targeted Siniora or his government. On some level he knew this, even if he could not admit it in public, especially after Hezbollah denounced him as a "Zionist hand."

Nasrallah's hatred of the prime minister made perfect sense. If the whole Arab world were like Siniora, the Arab-Israeli conflict would wind down in short order. There would be no militias, no death squads, no suicide bombers, and no rocket wars. Arabs and Israelis don't have to like each to live near each other in peace. Turkey and Greece worked out a way to quietly coexist near each other despite feelings of mutual hostility, and they're both even members of NATO.

Siniora hoped to work toward a similar *modus vivendi*, one step at a time, with the Israelis. He hinted at it in public, but Syria, Iran, and Hezbollah would not let him discuss a separate peace before the rest of the Arabs went first. The most he could ask for was a nonviolent cold war.

"We want to go back to the Armistice of 1949 with Israel that was restated in the Taif Agreement," he said. "Israel has to understand that its security cannot be achieved through the use of power or force. As to my vision of Lebanon, we are ready for peace with the other Arab countries, not before them."

Recall what Lebanon Renaissance Foundation head Eli Khoury told me about what Siniora meant when he said this. "This is the statement of those who *want* to make peace but know that they *can't*. They don't want to get ganged up on by the Arabs. We are the *least* anti-Israel Arab country in the world."

Even so, Siniora blamed Israel more than the Arabs for making peace difficult. He seemed to think that if Israel turned to pacifism, the problem would be solved, though pacifism so far had not worked at all well for him.

"Sparta was the nuclear power of its time," he said. "Figuratively, I'm saying. What happened? What's left of Sparta? Nothing. There are two examples where Israel resorted to force in order to solve problems and ended up complicating the problems. In 1982 they invaded Lebanon hoping to finish the Palestine Liberation Organization. They came in. They even occupied Beirut, hoping that with force they could do whatever they wanted, but they laid the seeds for Hezbollah. Then in 2006 they came to Lebanon hoping they could finish Hezbollah, but ended up with Hezbollah becoming stronger, with longer-range missiles and a larger number of missiles."

All that was true, but it didn't logically follow that refusing to use force would somehow work better. Siniora had to surrender to Hezbollah, but Israel didn't.

Siniora was so traumatized by the civil war that he clung to pacifism like a life raft. Many Europeans reacted similarly after the continent all but destroyed itself in the inferno of World War I, and an even larger number reacted that way after the second round against the Axis a few decades later. Siniora, though, sounded and acted like a man who wouldn't defend himself even from someone breaking down his door with an ax.

Pacifism only works when it's reciprocated. Holland could afford to be more or less pacifist because it was surrounded by European Union countries with a similar disposition. Lebanon and Israel faced hostiles who used violence as a matter of course.

Unlike Israel, though, Lebanon's government was so weak, it had few other options. March 14 would almost certainly lose a fight with Hezbollah, and Lebanon absolutely would lose a war against Israel. Picking a fight with a more powerful adversary is rarely a wise decision. Siniora was many things, but he was not reckless, and he was not stupid.

At the same time, the only way to survive as a liberal anomaly in a violent and authoritarian neighborhood is to fight back when attacked. That's what Israel did. Siniora was right that the Israelis had yet to solve their problems this way, but Israel endured as a democracy in a sea of autocracy while Lebanon couldn't.

Siniora might have seen things differently if his government were stronger than Hezbollah. He did, after all, send the Lebanese army into battle against Fatah al-Islam in Nahr al-Bared in 2007. He wasn't opposed to the use of force then. Hezbollah, though, had him effectively cornered at gunpoint with his hands over his head. Nonviolence was his only practical option.

"Is there a solution to the Hezbollah problem?" I asked him. "Do you have any idea how you can integrate them into the mainstream by either disarming them or making them a subservient part of the army?"

"First of all," he said, "we do not have the word *disarm* in our vocabulary." He sounded annoyed and slightly offended. "Violence is not the way. We want ultimately to engage in dialogue, open dialogue, and try to find a way at the end of the day that protects the people, even Hezbollah. That way is the state. The state has to come back and be fully in charge. The Lebanese government can't be dragged into a war without being consulted."

I did not mean to suggest he go to war with Hezbollah. He'd lose. Everyone in Lebanon knew he would lose. Many in his Sunni community were frustrated that he didn't want them to defend themselves when they were attacked on their own streets, but even they knew starting a war of disarmament would end in disaster.

"It is not possible for me to start a war against my countrymen in order to disarm them," he said, "while at the same time they argue that the enemy is occupying a part of my country."

He meant the Shebaa Farms, that tiny uninhabited sliver of land that the United Nations said was actually Syria's.

"I don't want to disarm my countrymen," he said. "I want to convince them. I want to have a dialogue with them and get them to agree to give back sovereignty to the state. But in the meantime, the basic illness is the occupation."

He kept going back to that, even after Hezbollah shot up Hamra, his own neighborhood, while the Israelis left him alone. I sometimes had the feeling he spoke at a forty-five-degree angle to the truth, as Middle Eastern leaders so often did, but perhaps he really believed that.

Most Sunnis elsewhere in the region thought Iran—and by extension its proxies—was the larger of the two problems. Like him, they lacked the strength to project power beyond their own borders, and in many cases they lacked the strength to even defend themselves. The Saudis and Kuwaitis relied on the United States to protect them from Saddam Hussein, and none of the Arab states could stop or even slow Iran's ascent to hegemony.

They were horrified by the creeping realization that they may have to rely on the Israelis for that. Washington, it seemed, was in no mood to take a hard line on Iran's nuclear weapons program even though that's what most Arab governments wanted.

The Sunni Arab states made it clear to everyone who was paying attention in 2006 that they tacitly supported Israel, at least initially, in the July War when they publicly condemned Hezbollah for starting it. The war was fought in an Arab country, but it was a proxy war between two non-Arab powers. Lebanon merely provided the battle space. One U.S. diplomat even told Lee Smith that the governments of Egypt and Saudi Arabia were privately thrilled when Israel initiated its counterattack.

David Samuels put it bluntly in *Slate:*[2] "Israel has effectively become the hired army of the Sunni Arab states." *Somebody* had to resist the resistance. Israel may have been everyone's last choice, but either Jerusalem would lead the resistance or nobody would.

This was all but unthinkable for Siniora and the rest of the Sunnis of Lebanon. Israeli resistance meant bombs fell in their country, and incompetent Israeli resistance meant Lebanon suffered for nothing.

A few weeks before I spoke to Siniora, the Israelis had finished fighting a small war in Gaza against Hamas to put a stop to Qassem and Grad rocket attacks in the cities of Sderot and Ashkelon. Egyptian President Hosni Mubarak took Israel's side even more blatantly than he did during the July 2006 war, announcing in advance that under no circumstances should Hamas be allowed to win the war against Israel.

The *Times* of London even said Riyadh gave Israeli war planes permission to fly through Saudi air space en route to Iran's nuclear weapons facilities.[3] The story could have been bogus. Israeli Prime Minister Benjamin Netanyahu denied it. He'd have to deny it even if the story were true, however, to prevent diplomatic pressure on the Saudis to reverse their decision.

John Bolton, the former U.S. ambassador to the United Nations, wouldn't have been a bit surprised if the story was true.[4] He thought the news was "entirely logical." None of the Arab leaders he talked to, he said, "would say anything about it publicly, but they would certainly acquiesce in an overflight if the Israelis didn't trumpet it as a big success."

According to the *Financial Times*, a majority of citizens in eighteen Arab countries thought Iran was more dangerous than Israel.[5] In that sense, Fouad Siniora was wildly out of step with the Sunni Arab mainstream in the Middle East for focusing so relentlessly on Israel. Yet he was, a bit paradoxically, less stridently anti-Israel than mainstream Sunni Arabs who thought Iran was an even bigger problem.

According to a report by the Washington Institute for Near East Policy,[6] a substantial number of Saudi citizens supported military action against Iran. A third of Saudi respondents said they would approve an American strike, and a fourth said they'd back an *Israeli* strike. This was extraordinary. Supporting Israel was taboo in the Arab world, and that went double when Israel was at war. This was not the sort of thing most Arabs were comfortable admitting to strangers, yet one-fourth of Saudis surveyed were willing to do so. The percentage who privately felt that way was almost certainly higher.

Iran's rulers constantly threatened Israel with violence and even destruction because they knew the Arabs were against them. The ancient conflicts between Sunnis and Shias, and between Persians

and Arabs, were far more important at the end of the day than a sixty-
year-old conflict between Israelis and Arabs. The Iran-Iraq war in
the 1980s killed orders of magnitude more people than all the Arab-
Israeli wars put together. The Iranian leadership needed to change
the subject to something they and the Sunnis agreed on. Ever since
Ruhollah Khomeini seized power in 1979 and voided Iran's treaty
with Israel, regime leaders believed they'd meet less resistance while
amassing power for themselves in the region by saying, "Hey, we're
not after *you*; we're after the Jews."

It wasn't enough anymore. Even apocalyptic anti-Zionism and
the arming of terrorist organizations that fought Israel weren't
enough anymore. Most Arabs simply did not believe Mahmoud
Ahmadinejad and Ali Khamenei when they not-so-cryptically sug-
gested that their nuclear weapons would be pointed only at Israel.
By a factor of three-to-one, Saudis believed Iran would use nuclear
weapons against either them or another state in the Gulf region
before using them against Israel.

With only a handful of exceptions, the region had been firmly
controlled by Sunni Arab regimes since the dissolution of the
Ottoman Empire, yet all of those governments had become second-
rate regional powers at best. The political agenda in the Arab Middle
East was now being set by non-Arabs in Jerusalem, Tehran, Washington, and Ankara. Syria's Bashar al-Assad helped set the regional
agenda as the logistics hub in the Iranian-Hezbollah axis, but he was
a non-Muslim Alawite, not a Sunni, and he was doing it as a mere
sidekick of the Persians. If all that weren't enough, the Sunnis now
depended on the hated Israelis to defend them, and they weren't
even sure the Israelis would ever go through with it.

Tehran hoped to convince Sunni Arab governments to do more
than just issue boilerplate denunciations of the "Zionist Entity."
Ahmadinejad and Khamenei wanted them to actually join the Iran-
led resistance and fight Israel like they used to, before Egypt and
Jordan signed peace treaties. Instead, Sunni Arabs outside Lebanon
and Syria were falling in behind their Jewish enemies, though they
dared not admit it in public.

"The area has suffered a great deal of wars and losses," Siniora
said, "and it's high time to go to peace. It's in the interest of the

Israelis more than anybody else. It has been proven in history that the best security for any country is its ability to build good relations with its neighbors, no matter how many weapons you have in your arsenal."

Few would argue with that, but no one could plot a plausible course from here to there. The Israelis tried everything, and nothing worked—not dialogue, not diplomacy, not a peace process, not withdrawal from occupied territory, and not war. Everything would become rapidly worse if Iran developed nuclear weapons, but Siniora had no idea how to stop that from happening.

"We do not believe in having nuclear weapons in the Middle East," he said. "We also don't believe in using force to disarm or attack Iran. We are against the use of force. We believe it's the origin of the problem."

While Siniora was an outdated throwback to the 1960s in some ways, he was also, at the same time, way ahead of his peers. Many in the Middle East preferred war. There is no getting around this. Millions pumped their fists, thrilled to resistance, and lionized martyrs. Siniora wouldn't stand for it, but he couldn't stop it.

"We believe," he said, "at the end of the day, that this country cannot be ruled except through openness, dialogue, and understanding each other. We cannot satanize others. What has been developing over the past few years is what prevailed in the Middle Ages, where the world was composed of two camps, the camp of the devil, and the camp of the angels and righteous. The problem is that everybody thinks that he is in the camp of the righteous and that the others are the devil. We don't believe that. The world is not like this."

His beautiful vision for Lebanon stood little chance while his country was bullied by ruthless totalitarians abroad and their proxies at home. The Arabist in his palace was a tragic and lonely figure, a premature liberal, a democrat before the Middle East was safe for democracy. He stood in Hezbollah's way, not as a barricade, but as a speed bump.

"We do not believe in violence," he said. "We don't believe in weapons of any kind, not even a stick."

CHAPTER EIGHTEEN

the warlord in his castle

> How dangerous emperors
> are when they go mad.
> —WALID JUMBLATT

I met up with British American journalist, essayist, polemicist, and literary critic Christopher Hitchens at the Bristol Hotel, where the nascent March 14 coalition met to plot against the Syrian occupation authorities in the weeks before Rafik Hariri was killed. Hitchens hadn't been to the country since right after the civil war ended, when Beirut was a howling wilderness of bullet-pocked and mortar-shattered towers.

"I hardly recognize the place," he said. "I would not have thought it possible that the city could look like it does now."

As a former revolutionary socialist, he pounced at the chance to join me and a handful of others for lunch with former revolutionary socialist Walid Jumblatt, especially since Lebanon's Druze leader had so recently been involved in a shooting war with religious totalitarians—the kind of enemies Hitchens most loved to hate. Hitchens had gotten himself into a spot of trouble with his old comrades on the political left by championing the American invasion of Iraq, and though he was hardly enamored of Israel's botched war in 2006, he nevertheless felt a keen sense of solidarity with those who struggled against the likes of Hezbollah.

"Jumblatt," he said, "is one of the Middle East's real revolutionaries," which was partly true, but not entirely true. Sometimes and in some ways Jumblatt was a real revolutionary, while at other times and in other ways he wasn't at all. To understand him, you have to understand the Druze, and in order to understand the Druze, you have to understand what it was like to be a minority in Lebanon and in the Middle East generally.

In the late 1980s, Saddam Hussein waged a war of racial extermination in the Kurdistan region of Iraq. Iran's Baha'i community had been mercilessly persecuted by the government in Tehran ever since Khomeini replaced the Shah. The vast majority of Jews living in Arab countries were expelled to Israel, and many in the Arab world still hoped to expunge them from the region entirely. Egypt sidelined Coptic Christians as second-class citizens, and many Christian women in Iraq felt compelled by violent gangs of Islamists to wear headscarves even though the law didn't require it. Libya's Muammar al-Gaddafi repressed the indigenous Berber minority, and the Shias of Saudi Arabia lived under the boot heel of fanatical Sunni Wahhabis.

The Druze minority communities in Lebanon, Israel, and Syria devised a survival formula that worked better than most. They're weather vanes. They calculate. They, even more than other Arabs, side with the strong horse.

In Syria, the Druze supported al-Assad—not because they liked him, but because he was the boss. Israeli Druze were fiercely loyal to the Zionist state and fought harder than most Israeli Jews against the likes of Hamas and Hezbollah in elite IDF units. Many Palestinians considered them traitors.

It was trickier for the Druze people of Lebanon. Politics there had always been vastly more complicated, but you still usually could tell who had the upper hand locally and even regionally because the Druze were most likely their allies.

Those who followed Jumblatt's political trajectory since Hariri's assassination knew that many thought of him as a Lebanese neoconservative. The description was apt in some ways. He was the head of the Progressive Socialist Party, yet neither he nor it were socialist any longer. He had moved from the political left to the political right—in Western terms, anyway—which was basically what it meant to be a neoconservative.

During Lebanon's civil war, he accepted backing from the Soviet Union. His home in the mountains was still decorated with posters and knickknacks from Communist Russia. Much later, in 2005, when he became one of the leaders of the Independence Intifada, he retroactively threw his support behind the Bush administration's war against Saddam Hussein in Iraq. He even half-jokingly asked the White House to send car bombs to Damascus.[1]

You could say—and many did say—that he changed because the political center of power and gravity changed. When Arab Nationalism and fervor for the Palestinian cause swept Lebanon before and during the civil war, his family championed both. When the Syrians ruled in Lebanon, he went along with that, too—not that he was happy about it. When Lebanon later turned against Syria, he helped lead the charge.

None of this meant every idea in his head was cynically calculated to best represent the "centrist" position. Nor did it mean the rest of the Druze didn't sincerely feel what they said they felt. Jumblatt and his people were complicated. He wasn't a revolutionary in the usual sense, but he wasn't strictly a weather vane either.

The man was a bundle of contradictions who couldn't be easily pigeonholed or even described. He was a quasi-feudal warlord, yet at one time he worked with the Soviet Union. He was an anti-Syrian revolutionary, yet he once collaborated with Syrian power. He masterfully gamed the sectarian system to his advantage, yet at the same time he hated that system because it restricted his power. (Since he wasn't a Maronite, Sunni, or Shia, he could never hold any of Lebanon's three most powerful posts.) He threw himself behind the Palestinian cause and had no warm feelings for Zionism, yet he fiercely opposed all who fought Israel.

He hosted me, Hitchens, Lee Smith, Jonathan Foreman, and a handful of others at his home in the small town of Mukhtara. He lived there in luxurious Ottoman splendor with a view out his windows of the Chouf Mountains around him. You might call his home a palace or a castle, but you would not call it a house. It's hundreds of years old and big enough that you could get lost in it if you wandered around on your own. Much of the interior was a museum for living in, decorated with real Roman Empire sarcophagi. Hundreds of antique rifles and swords adorned the walls. Ancient artifacts from all over the Eastern Mediterranean were professionally displayed in built-in glass cabinets. His library was bigger than many bookstores, and I noticed an entire shelf holding decades' worth of *Foreign Affairs* magazine bound specially for him in leather. He kept a pistol and two full clips within easy reach on his desk atop the current *New York Review of Books*.

"You know one thing I really like about Lebanon?" I whispered to Jonathan Foreman.

"What's that?" he said.

"Cultured warlords," I said. "You won't find anyone or anyplace like this in Iraq or Afghanistan."

Jumblatt's mountain home was more luxurious than any normal man ever dare wish for, but he looked distinctly ill at ease. He lived in breathtaking opulence, but with a sword of Damocles over his head.

"How can we control our own destiny," he said after inviting us to sit in his salon, "when we have a state within the state called the state of Hezbollah? When we have open borders to all kinds of traffic and weapons and people from Syria to Lebanon? Hezbollah has said it before and will say it now: 'Thank God the Revolutionary Guards in Lebanon defend the interests of the Iranian Revolution.' As long as we have this Syrian regime next door, we won't have a sovereign Lebanon."

He could have added that there could be no sovereign Lebanon as long as the Khomeinist regime existed in Tehran, although he implied it. Lebanon regained some of its sovereignty after the Syrian military was driven out in 2005, but the Cedar Revolution in Lebanon had yet to defeat the Iranian Revolution in Lebanon.

"You did a good job in Iraq," he said, "so why don't you do the same thing in Syria? Yesterday, one of our guys was assaulted in Beirut. He died today, and I have to go this afternoon to cool things down. We are living with action and reaction. We could respond by attacking a Shia, and it will again become a vicious circle. The Lebanese army is doing its best, but it is unable to impose its authority, its dominance. It's unable to fix up being a part of the state of war and peace, unable to look at carloads of weapons coming into Lebanon. Next to Hezbollah you also have the Palestinian bases inside the camps. There are, I think, facilities for all kind of hostilities hiding in bunkers and in tunnels."

Jumblatt was no friend of Israel and never had been, even though his coreligionists who lived in Israel were. It was clear, however, that in 2008 he had a serious problem with everyone who actually fought against Israel and would opt out of the Arab-Israeli conflict entirely if he could. Lebanon suffered far more death and pain and destruction from that conflict than any other country around.

"The other issue is the Shebaa Farms," he said, "which are not Lebanese. Officially, legally, they are not Lebanese. They were taken from the Syrians in the late 1960s, and by pretending that they are Lebanese we are still hooked into the Arab-Israeli conflict. The Shebaa Farms are still under U.N. Resolution 242. And we have nothing to do with the 242 Resolution, because in 1967, Lebanon did not go to war against Israel. The Syrian and Iranian policy is to hook Lebanon into the 242 Resolution and the Arab-Israeli conflict. If you look back to the so-called Baathist theory or ideology from the Atlantic to the Gulf, they have never accepted the fact that Lebanon would be independent. Never accepted that."

Jumblatt's history with the imperial Baath government was a long and twisting one. He recounted to us one of his favorite anecdotes, one he told most journalists who interviewed him. Shortly after his father, Kamal, was assassinated, he was summoned to Damascus by the ruthless Hafez al-Assad. When he meekly objected to what the Syrian ruler expected of him, al-Assad smiled and wolfishly said, "Walid, you remind me so much of your dear father."

And so he surrendered. Before either principle or politics, his first order of business was his own survival and that of his family and his community.

"I was obliged to fix up a cynical compromise," he said, "because I needed allies and I needed routes for weapons and ammunition. At that time I had an important ally called the Soviet Union. The Soviet Union saved me. It trained my people. I had a small militia and they supported me through Syria. So, of course, I shook al-Assad's hand. I knew that he killed my father, but I tried to forget for some time."

"When was the first time that you publicly accused Syria of killing your father?" Christopher Hitchens said.

"From 1977 until, let's say, 2000, I had to keep silent," Jumblatt said. "In 2000, I challenged the Syrian president, and the patriarch of Lebanon said it's time for the Syrians to get out of Lebanon. That was a crucial year because the south of Lebanon was liberated from Israel. Hafez al-Assad died in June. I was accused by the Syrians of betrayal and treason. Later on we had to postpone our language. We still have some among us who take the romantic approach of Arab Nationalism. And later on came September 11 and the news that the Americans were about to invade Iraq."

"You said the intervention in Iraq might have been helpful for the March 14 movement," Hitchens said. "Would that still be your view?"

Whether it was true or it wasn't, quite a few Lebanese thought the invasion of Iraq convinced al-Assad he might be destroyed if he did not get out of Lebanon.

"It depends now on the outcome," Jumblatt said, "after America reduces its troops in Iraq. There are some signs in the last week that again the terrorists are blowing themselves up and trying to create chaos. It's a very unstable situation. If there's no compromise between the powers surrounding Iraq—meaning the Iranians, the Turks, plus the Americans—I don't know how Iraq can be stable. Also the Syrians, unfortunately, have been importing jihadists to the Damascus airport and exporting them to Iraq, where they blow themselves up to go to heaven. Barack Obama should be careful. He should be careful here and in Iraq. And he should be much more careful, of course, in the land that nobody was able to conquer, Afghanistan."

Unfortunately, Obama administration officials, like so many others before them from both the Democratic and Republican parties, failed to understand Syrian foreign policy. They figured what al-Assad wanted most was the return of the Golan Heights, as he so often publicly claimed, and that he felt compelled to seek an alliance with Tehran against both his wishes and his real interests. The truth about the Middle East, though, was often concealed behind misdirection and bombast. What Arab leaders said publicly only rarely lined up with what they thought privately.

"Assad doesn't care about the Golan," Jumblatt said. "Suppose we go ultimately to the so-called peace. Then later on, what is the purpose of the Syrian regime? What is he going to tell his people? Especially, mind you, he is a member of the Alawite minority. This minority could be accused of treason. It's not like Egypt or Jordan, whereby the government has some legitimacy. Here you get accused of treason by the masses, by the Sunnis. So using classic slogans like 'Palestine will liberate the Golan with Hezbollah' is a must for him to stay in power.

"I had a friend at the time—he is still my friend—when I was in Syria. He was the chief of staff of the Syrian army and is now living in Los Angeles. He was quite an important guy and honest with the media. He was a Sunni from a big family in Aleppo. And when Hafez al-Assad was about to fix up the so-called settlement through Bill Clinton, and before they met him in Geneva, a prominent Alawite officer in the Syrian army came to al-Assad and said, 'What are you doing? We will be lost if you make peace. We will be accused of treason.'"

The U.S. and France all but brought the hammer down on Syria after Rafik Hariri was killed, but French President Jacques Chirac—one of Hariri's personal friends—was replaced at the helm by Nicolas Sarkozy. The Israelis thought Sarkozy an improvement, but the Lebanese didn't. The new French president thought isolating Syria diplomatically was counterproductive and that engagement might yield better results. The United States government came around to Sarkozy's point of view when Barack Obama replaced George W. Bush. Both hoped to lure al-Assad away from his alliance with Iran and into the nominally "pro-Western" Sunni Arab mainstream.

Jumblatt thought the idea was preposterous. "The interests are too interconnected between the Syrian regime and Persia," he said. "And I think Persia is now stronger."

Syria had been cunningly outwitting Americans and Europeans for decades, and most Western leaders seemed entirely incapable of learning from or even noticing the mistakes of their predecessors. Al-Assad cared not a whit for peace or the Golan. In his privacy of his own mind, he may not have cared much for Ahmadinejad and Khamenei, but he needed terrorism and a simmering state of war just to survive.

No basket of carrots Barack Obama or anyone else could offer would change his calculation of his own strategic interests. His weak military and Soviet-style economy would instantly render his country as geopolitically impotent as Yemen if he scrapped his alliance with Iran, Hamas, and Hezbollah. In 2009, though, he was the most powerful Arab ruler in the Levant. Because he contributed so much to the Middle East's instability and started so many fires in neighboring countries, he managed to make himself an "indispensable" part of every fantasy solution Western diplomats could come up with. He wouldn't be where he was without Iranian help, and that help would become more valuable than ever if and when Tehran produced nuclear weapons.

The alliance worked for both parties. While al-Assad's secular Arab Socialist Baath Party's ideology differed markedly from Khomeini's Velayat-e Faqih, "resistance" was at the molten core of each one. Syria's and Iran's lists of enemies—Sunni Arabs, Israel, and the United States—were identical.

Syria was no more likely to join the American-French-Egyptian-Saudi coalition than the U.S. was likely to defect to the Syrian and Iranian side. Trying to peel Syria away from the axis of resistance was like trying to pry East Germany out of the Soviet bloc before the Berlin Wall came down.

Al-Assad wasn't just a state sponsor of terrorist groups fighting Israel. He also, as Jumblatt said, aided and abetted terrorists and insurgents from all over the Middle East who were willing to die in Iraq. It was a brilliant move, frankly, so long as the Americans were bogged down and felt reluctant to fight back. Al-Assad could effectively "deport" the most dangerous radical Sunnis from his own country to Iraq, where they would make trouble for somebody else, and he could earn street cred in the rest of the Arab world as a result.

There was a third rationale, too, that was perhaps the most sinister.

"For Assad and the Alawis," Lee Smith wrote in *The Strong Horse*,[2] "the Iraqi insurgency amounted to a debate over the nature of the Middle East. The Bush administration thought that the region was ripe for democracy and pluralism, and that its furies could be tamed by giving Middle Easterners a voice in their own government. Syria countered that the Middle East could only be governed through violence. Its support for the insurgency was, at least in part, intended to give Washington no choice but to put away dangerous ideas like Arab democracy."

All this served Iran's interests, as well.

"Before the American invasion," Jumblatt said, "the overthrowing of Saddam, we had an Arab state between us and the Persians called Iraq. Now the Persian Empire is in Lebanon."

"Will Lebanon change if Iran gets nuclear weapons?" I said.

"It will not change," he said. "But it will give the Iranians more prestige, of course, with their allies. It will provoke a series of armaments—an arms race—in Saudi Arabia, maybe Egypt. It will be crazy. We will have bombs everywhere."

"Are you concerned about a replay of what happened up here on the mountain?" Lee Smith said, referring to Hezbollah's aborted invasion of the Chouf the previous May.

"They can do anything on the mountain," Jumblatt said. "Just twenty miles from here you have the area of Jezzine, which is the second line of defense of Hezbollah. What is left of Jezzine is, of course, in a Christian area. Still, in ten years' time or maybe more, it will be a Shia area. Five hundred years ago it used to be Shia. On this side, you have my old supply lines from the Bekaa Valley. They are cut, but they are there. And they have Beirut's southern suburbs. They can squeeze anything through, and it would be foolish on my behalf to go to a so-called civil war. This is why last time, when the clashes started, I did my best to stop the clashes. Anybody can fight when they are squeezed. Anybody can fight. But we don't have supply lines. We don't have weapons. We will end up emigrating from Mount Lebanon. To where? The sea? No. To Syria."

That was the Druze nightmare—to be driven from their lands to live out their lives as refugees with no rights or future. Nothing much mattered when held up to this.

"Hezbollah inflicted the Israeli army with big losses," he said. "And they were good fighters. But, of course, three years later, I don't think doing the same thing would be very popular in the south of Lebanon. It's not every day that you can rebuild your house. The fighters of Hezbollah can hide. They have caves; they have their own expertise. But they also have got to be accountable to the population."

How could Jumblatt laud Hezbollah when he knew as well as anyone else that Nasrallah brought the Israelis into Lebanon through his own militant foolishness? It was partly because he felt compelled to do so by the dictates of Lebanon's internal politics, but also because his family's long-standing dedication to the Palestinian cause all but precluded him from saying anything nice or even neutral about Israel.

"My past," he said, "my political heritage, from my father to myself, was to defend the Palestinian cause. Okay? And my father, although he was killed by the Syrians, was killed because he was defending the Palestinians in Lebanon."

"Is there any realistic way to either disarm Hezbollah or integrate them within the state and the army?" I said. "Or will this problem go on and on?"

"I think it will go on and on and on," he said. "I think so. Unless—if you ask them, most of the Shia will give up their weapons in exchange for a political price. The political price will be maybe reshuffling of the actual Lebanese system. More power to the Shia community within the Lebanese sectarian system. At the same time, because, I mean, they are proud to have defended Lebanon against the Israelis. After the war in Gaza, they said, 'Look, now you are asking us to surrender our weapons? Are you crazy?'"

"Israelis wouldn't even come into Lebanon if Hezbollah wasn't kidnapping or shooting them," I said.

"They have invaded several times with excuse and without excuse from 1978 up until now," he said. "They came clear to Beirut.

Nothing has changed in Israel. Now it's Nasrallah; before it was Yasser Arafat."

"But if Hezbollah was disarmed," I said, "or integrated into the state and the army, and the border was quiet, they wouldn't come back here. I mean, why would they?"

"The people of the south," he said, "think the weapons of Hezbollah are protection against Israeli incursions."

That much was true. Supporting Hezbollah as a deterrent was perfectly logical if you believed Israelis wanted to invade Lebanon so they could expand their borders, steal Lebanon's water, or for some other nefarious purpose. The problem with this, however, was that there was no constituency whatsoever in Israel for anything of the sort. It was a conspiracy theory, a fantasy, and it was a fantasy that started wars and got people killed.

"You talk about the increasing strength of Hezbollah and the difficulty of your own supply lines," Jonathan Foreman said. "Is there any way to strengthen the position of Hezbollah's opponents? Is there any way you and others can become stronger in relation to Hezbollah?"

"There is no way," Jumblatt said. "Again, it would be suicidal and an endless civil war without any results. I'm concerned this very afternoon about the kidnapping and death of one of my Druze community members. We have to prepare for funerals tomorrow. And tomorrow there is this big Hezbollah celebration in the *dahiyeh* for [assassinated Hezbollah commander Imad] Mughniyeh. The Shias will come from the south to Beirut through some areas where we have Druze. I have been told now by the army that they have caught some people, and I hope they found who killed this guy. The people of Hezbollah are much more organized. It's a regular army."

He offhandedly mentioned "the obsolete and backward mentality" of some of the Maronites.

"Is that the socialist Jumblatt speaking?" Hitchens said.

We all laughed, including Jumblatt, but Jumblatt laughed a bit darkly and sadly.

"The socialist Jumblatt died a long time ago," he said. "He died with my father. He had a dream with the leftist parties to change Lebanon. It was my father's vision to change the system. This is also

294 ~ THE WARLORD IN HIS CASTLE

one of the reasons why he was killed. He was seen by the Arab world as backing the communists."

"Can you say a few words about what the Progressive Socialist Party means to you and what you might mean for them?" Hitchens said.

"My father studied in Europe at one time," Jumblatt said. "As a member of a minority, he wished to achieve equality. He said it's time to abolish the sectarian system in Lebanon. It's time to have social justice; it's time to redistribute land. He started with his own land because we were at that time one of the biggest feudal families of Lebanon. So he started with his properties. My mother told him, 'Well, okay, but wait until you reach power.' My father said he had to be equal, like others. The sectarian system was against his wishes. And he paid."

I wanted to ask him how much of the Jumblatt family land was redistributed to poor Druze in Lebanon; if any, in fact, had been redistributed. He seemed to have plenty left, and his home would likely be a tourist attraction if it weren't his private residence.

He had to cut our time short, however, after his cell phone rang and he was told about a crisis that had to be defused at once.

As he said earlier, a Druze man had just died after being attacked by Hezbollah supporters. Enraged Druze citizens wanted revenge, and they set up roadblocks on the highway to exact it. They stopped every vehicle on the road from Beirut to Damascus and checked ID cards—a disturbing echo of the civil war.

When they identified individuals as Lebanese Shias—not Hezbollah members, but ordinary Shias who may well have detested Hezbollah—they dragged them from their vehicles and beat them, gangland-style, on the side of the road with long wooden sticks.

Jumblatt ordered his men to seal the roads leading into and out of the Chouf. We would be allowed out, but no one was allowed in. And he raced to the scene in a convoy and put a stop to the beatings at once.

It was the right thing to do, of course, not only on general principle, but to stop the tit-for-tat cycle of violence before it spread. Wars can start over this sort of thing in his country.

There was also more to it than that. He had mellowed with age and was no longer as ruthless as he once was. "He did not want Shia blood on his hands," Abu Kais wrote.[3] "This I believe. It took him a long time to wash off Christian blood." He hadn't undergone as powerful a transformation as Samir Geagea, nor was he a pacifist like Fouad Siniora, but he was, or at least he seemed, a bit more liberal in the general sense of the word than he was during the war when his men engaged in a sectarian cleansing campaign against Maronites.

The biggest reason of all, though, wasn't so lofty. His weakness had been exposed during the conflict in May. Druze fighters could defeat Hezbollah in a short war on their home turf. They proved that. At the same time, Hezbollah proved it could sever the roads leading into their territory. A long war could easily starve Lebanon's Druze of bullets and food.

Jumblatt had to run fresh calculations after that happened. An election was coming up. He needed March 14 to win, but he might not have the luxury to stand by Geagea's and Siniora's side for very much longer. If he was going to pivot—and he knew he might have to pivot—it would be all the more difficult with Druze gangs beating innocent Shia civilians with sticks on the road to Damascus.

The warlord in his castle was slowly but inexorably preparing himself and his people for another surrender. Abu Kais may have sounded slightly hysterical during the conflict in May when he said that "the dark age of Hezbollah is upon us," but he was right.

CHAPTER NINETEEN

a hurricane in the land of the cedars

> For them, the real danger has always been independent thought—against which they can only muster media that threaten, crowds that threaten, and security services that best them both by implementing the threats.
> —MICHAEL YOUNG

Hamra was cooked.

It looked like my same old neighborhood on the surface, but it had been violated. The ground no longer felt stable. Beirut's most cosmopolitan and international district felt much like my house once did after a burglar had broken in. What happened to Hamra, though, was much worse than a mere breaking and entering. Hezbollah and its militant allies shot the place up and killed people.

Christopher Hitchens, Jonathan Foreman, and I set out from our hotel, the Bristol. Christopher needed a new pair of shoes. Jonathan needed a shirt. I needed a coffee. So I led the way as the three of us strolled down to Hamra Street, where we could buy just about anything.

On the way I told them how the Syrian Social Nationalist Party had a serious presence there now. During the invasion in May, its members had placed their spinning swastika flags up on Hamra

Street itself, one of the city's premier places to shop. Those flags stayed there for months. No one dared touch them until Prime Minister Fouad Siniora ordered city employees to take them down.

It was a warning of sorts—or at least it would have been heeded as such by most people. I didn't go looking for trouble, Jonathan was as mild-mannered a writer as any I knew, but Christopher was brave and combative, and just hearing about what had happened riled him up.

When we rounded a corner onto Hamra Street, an SSNP sign was the first thing we saw.

"Well, there's that swastika now," Christopher said.

The militia's flags had been taken down, but a commemorative marker was still there. It was made of metal and plastic and had the semipermanence of an official *No Parking* sign. SSNP member Khaled Alwan shot two Israeli soldiers with a pistol in 1982 after they settled their bill at the now-defunct Wimpy café on that corner, and that sign marked the spot.

Some SSNP members claimed the emblem on their flag wasn't a swastika, but a hurricane or a cyclone. Many said they couldn't be National Socialists, as were the Nazis, because they identified instead as Social Nationalists, whatever that meant.

Most observers did not find this credible. The SSNP, according to the *Atlantic* in a civil war-era analysis,[1] "is a party whose leaders, men approaching their seventies, send pregnant teenagers on suicide missions in booby-trapped cars. And it is a party whose members, mostly Christians from churchgoing families, dream of resuming the war of the ancient Canaanites against Joshua and the Children of Israel. They greet their leaders with a Hitlerian salute; sing their Arabic anthem, 'Greetings to You, Syria,' to the strains of 'Deutschland, Deutschland über alles'; and throng to the symbol of the red hurricane, a swastika in circular motion."

They wished to resurrect ancient pre-Islamic and pre-Arabic Syria and annex Lebanon, Cyprus, Jordan, Iraq, Kuwait, Israel, and parts of Turkey and Egypt to Damascus. Their vision clashed with Hezbollah's, but the two militias had the exact same list of enemies and they were both Syrian proxies, so they worked together.

Many Lebanese believed members of the SSNP were the ones who carried out many, if not most, of the car-bomb assassinations in Lebanon on behalf of the Syrians since 2005. In December of 2006 some of their members were arrested by the Lebanese army for storing a huge amount of explosives, timers, and detonators amid a large cache of weapons. Then-party leader Ali Qanso responded,[2] saying, "We are a resistance force, and we use different methods of resisting, among which is using explosives."

Christopher wanted to pull down their marker, but couldn't. He stuck to his principles, though, and before I could stop him, he scribbled "No, no, Fuck the SSNP" in the bottom-right corner with a black felt-tipped pen.

I blinked several times. Was he really insulting the Syrian Social Nationalist Party while they might be watching? Neither Christopher nor Jonathan seemed to sense what was coming, but my own danger signals went haywire.

An angry young man shot across Hamra Street as though he'd been fired out of a cannon. "Hey!" he yelled as he pointed with one hand and speed-dialed for backup on his phone with the other.

"We need to get out of here now," I said.

But the young man latched onto Christopher's arm and wouldn't let go. "Come with me!" he said and jabbed a finger toward Christopher's face. These were the only words I heard him say in English.

Christopher tried to shake off his assailant, but couldn't.

"I'm not going anywhere with you," he said.

We needed to get out of there fast. Standing around and trying to reason with him would serve his needs, not ours. His job was to hold us in place until the muscle crew showed up in force.

"Let go of him!" I said and shoved him, but he clamped onto Christopher like a steel trap.

I stepped into the street and flagged down a taxi.

"Get in the car!" I said.

Christopher, sensing rescue, managed to shake the man off and got into the back seat of the taxi. Jonathan and I piled in after him. But the angry young man ran around to the other side of the car and got in the front seat.

I shoved him with both hands. He wasn't particularly heavy, but I didn't have enough leverage from the back to throw him out. The driver could have tried to push the man out, but he didn't. I sensed he was afraid.

So my companions and I got out of the car on the left side. The SSNP man bolted from the front seat on the right side. Then I jumped back in the car and locked the doors on that side.

"He'll just unlock it," Jonathan said.

He was right. I hadn't noticed that the windows were rolled down on the passenger side. The young man reached in, laughed, and calmly unlocked the front passenger door.

I stepped back into the street, and the young man latched once again onto Christopher. No one could have stopped Jonathan and me had we fled, but we couldn't leave Christopher to face an impending attack by himself. The lone SSNP man only needed to hold one of us still while waiting for his squad.

A police officer casually ambled toward us as though he had no idea what was happening.

"Help," Christopher said to the cop. "I'm being attacked!"

Our assailant identified himself to the policeman. The officer gasped and took three steps back as though he did not want any trouble. He could have unholstered his weapon and stopped the attack on the spot, but even Lebanon's armed men of the law feared the Syrian Social Nationalist Party.

A Lebanese man in his thirties ran up to me and offered to help.

"What's happening?!" he said breathlessly as he trembled in shock and alarm.

I don't remember what I told him, and it hardly matters. There wasn't much he could do, and I did not see him again.

"Let go of him!" I said to the SSNP spotter and tried once more to throw him off Christopher.

"Hit him if you have to," I said to Christopher. "We're out of time, and we have to get out of here."

"Back to the hotel," Christopher said.

"No!" I said. "We can't let them know where we're staying."

Christopher would not or could not strike his assailant, so I sized the man up from a distance of six or so feet. I could punch him hard in the face, and he couldn't stop me. I could break his knee with a solid kick to his leg, and he couldn't stop me. He needed all his strength just to hold onto Christopher, while I had total freedom of movement and was hopped up on adrenaline. We hadn't seen a weapon yet, so I was pretty sure he didn't have one. I was a far greater threat to him at that moment than he was to us by himself.

Christopher, Jonathan, and I easily could have joined forces and left him bleeding and harmless in the street. I imagine, looking back now, that he was afraid. But I knew the backup he'd called would arrive any second. And his backup might be armed. We were about to face the wrath of a militia whose members could do whatever they wanted in the streets with impunity. Escalating seemed like the worst possible thing I could do. The time to attack the young man was right at the start, and that moment had passed. This was Beirut, where the law of the jungle can rule with the flip of a switch, and we needed to move.

I saw another taxi parked on the corner waiting for passengers, and I flung open the door.

"Get in, get in," I said, "and lock all the doors!"

Traffic was light. If the driver would step on the gas with us inside, we could get out of there. Christopher managed to fling the man off him again. It looked hopeful there for a second. But seven furious men showed up all at once and faced us in the street. They stepped in front of the taxi and cut off our escape.

None wore masks. That was an encouraging sign. I didn't see any weapons. But they were well built, and their body language signaled imminent violence. We were in serious trouble, and I ran into the Costa Coffee chain across the street and yelled at the waiter to call the police.

"Go away!" he said and lightly pushed me in the shoulder to make his point. "You need to leave now!"

This was no way to treat a visitor, especially not in the Arab world, where guests are accorded protection, but getting in the way of the Syrian Social Nationalist Party could get a man killed, or at least beaten severely. Just a few months before, the SSNP attacked a Sunni journalist on that very street and sent him bleeding and broken to the hospital in front of gaping witnesses.[3] A Lebanese colleague told me he was brutally assaulted merely for filming the crew taking down the SSNP flags as Siniora had ordered. "He didn't do anything to them," she said. "He just filmed their flag."

Christopher was encircled by four or five of them. They were geared up to smash him, and I reached for his hand to pull him away. One of the toughs clawed at my arm and left me with a bleeding scratch and a bruise. I expected a punch in the face, but I wasn't the target.

Christopher was the target. He was the one who had defaced their sign. One of the guys smacked him hard in the face. Another delivered a roundhouse kick to his legs. A third punched him and knocked him into the street between two parked cars. Then they gathered around and kicked him while he was down. They kicked him hard in the head, in the ribs, and in the legs.

Jonathan and I had about two and a half seconds to figure out what we should do when one of the SSNP members punched him in the side of the head and then kicked him.

Christopher was on the ground, and Jonathan and I couldn't fend off seven militiamen by ourselves. I was reasonably sure, at least, that they weren't going to kill us. They didn't have weapons or masks. They just wanted to beat us, and we lost the fight before it even began. I could have called for backup myself, but I didn't think of it—a mistake I will not make again in that country.

Then the universe all of a sudden righted itself.

Christopher managed to pull himself up as a taxi approached in the street. I stepped in front of the car and forced the driver to stop. "Get in!" I yelled. Christopher got in the car. Jonathan got in the car. I got in the car. We slammed down the locks on the doors with our fists. The street was empty of traffic. The way in front of the taxi was clear. The scene for our escape was set.

"Go!" I said to the driver.

"Where?" the driver said.

"Just drive!" I said.

One of the SSNP guys landed a final blow on the side of Christopher's face through the open window, but the driver sped away and we were free.

I don't remember what we said in the car. I was barely scathed in the punch-up, and Jonathan seemed to be fine. Christopher was still in one piece, though he was clearly in pain. Our afternoon had gone sideways, but it could have been a great deal worse than it was.

"Let's not go back to our hotel yet," I said. I covered my face with my hands and rubbed my eyes with my palms. "In case we're being followed."

"Where do you want to go?" our driver said.

"Let's just drive for a while," Jonathan said.

So our driver took us down to the Corniche that follows the curve of the Mediterranean. He never did ask what happened. Or, if he did, I don't remember him asking. I kept turning around and checking behind us to make sure we weren't being followed.

"Maybe we should go to the Phoenicia," Jonathan said.

The Phoenicia InterContinental Hotel was one of the priciest in the city. Management installed a serious security regime at the door. This was the place where diplomats and senators stayed when they were in town. I doubted the guards would allow thugs from any organization into their lobby.

"He deserves a huge tip," Jonathan said as our driver dropped us off.

"Yes," I said. "He certainly does."

The three of us relaxed near the Phoenicia's front door for a few minutes. We would need to change cars but first had to ensure we hadn't been followed.

"You're bleeding," Jonathan said and lightly touched Christopher's elbow.

Christopher seemed unfazed by the sight of blood on his shirt.

"We need to get you cleaned up," Jonathan said.

"I'm fine, I think," Christopher said.

He seemed to be in pretty good spirits, all things considered.

"The SSNP," I said, "is the last party you want to mess with in Lebanon. I'm sorry I didn't warn you properly. This is partly my fault."

"I appreciate that," Christopher said. "But I would have done it anyway. One must take a stand. One simply must."

⌒

Bashar al-Assad's government in Damascus still wielded some of its occupation instruments inside Lebanon. The Syrian Social Nationalist Party was one of those instruments, and it counted the regime as its friend and ally. The geographic "nationalism" of the SSNP differed from the racialist Pan-Arab Nationalism of the Syrian Baath Party, but it conveniently meshed with al-Assad's imperial foreign policy in the Middle East. It logically followed, then, that the SSNP was also allied with Hezbollah.

The SSNP was first and foremost a Syrian proxy, and Hezbollah was first and foremost an Iranian proxy, but during the previous May when various March 8 militias invaded Beirut, the SSNP established itself simultaneously as a de facto Hezbollah proxy.

I still shudder to think what might have happened to Christopher, Jonathan, and me if we were Lebanese instead of British and American.

"If you were Lebanese," said a longtime Beiruti friend, "you might have disappeared."

The next morning I awoke to find more than a dozen e-mails in my inbox from friends, family, and acquaintances, some of whom I hadn't heard from in a long time, asking me if I was okay.

None of us had written about the incident yet, so I wondered what on earth must have happened while I was asleep. Did another war just break out? Did another car bomb go off? I hadn't heard any explosions or gunshots.

As it turned out, the incident on Hamra Street with the SSNP made the news on at least four continents, and possibly six.

Great, I thought. Now *I'm* the story. Christopher was the nearest thing the journalism world had to a celebrity, so pretty much everything he did was news.

Every single reporter without exception got the details wrong. In one version, we got in a bar fight. In another, we were attacked by foppish shoe shoppers.[4] In almost every version, Christopher was drunk or had been drinking.[5] Not one of the reporters who wrote up the story bothered to ask any of us who were actually there what had happened. Some even claimed they had "confirmed" this or that detail, but all they were doing was publishing rumors. It made me think, not for the first time, that first-person narrative journalism, whatever its faults, was far more reliable than the alternative.

I later sat down with Christopher over coffee in the hotel lobby and asked him to reflect on the recent unpleasantness.

"When I told you that I should have warned you," I said, "that I take partial responsibility, you said. . ."

"It wouldn't have made any difference," he said. "Thank you, though, for giving me a protective arm. I think a swastika poster is partly fair game and partly an obligation. You don't really have the right to leave one alone. I haven't seen that particular symbol since I saw the Syrianization of Lebanon in the 1970s. And actually, the first time I saw it, I didn't quite believe it."

"You saw it when you were here before?" I said.

"Oh, yes," he said. "But it was more toward the Green Line. I did not expect to see it so flagrantly on Hamra. Anyway, call me old-fashioned if you will, but my line is that swastika posters are to be defaced or torn down. I mean, what other choice do you have? I'd like to think I'd have done that if I had known it was being guarded by people who are swastika fanciers. I have done that in my time. I have had fights with people who think that way. But I was surprised first by how violent and immediate their response was, and second by how passive and supine was the response of the police."

The men of the SSNP had to use force to maintain a hold in West Beirut. Many of its members were Orthodox Christians, as was its founder Antun Saadeh, while most West Beirutis were Sunnis. They would hardly be any less welcome in Tel Aviv. If its enforcers didn't jump Christopher in the street, their commemorative sign would not have lasted.

"But I was impressed," Christopher said, "with the response of the café girls."

"What was their response?" I said. "I missed that."

"Well," he said, "when I was thrown to the ground and bleeding from my fingers and elbow, they came over and asked what on earth was going on. How can this be happening to a guest, to a stranger? I don't remember if I was speaking English or French at that time. I said something like '*merde fasciste*,' which I hope they didn't misinterpret."

I did not see the café girls. Or, if I did, I don't remember them. Once the actual violence began, it was over and done with in seconds.

"By then," Christopher said, "I had become convinced that you were right, that we should get the fuck out of there and not, as I had first thought, get the hotel security between them and us. I thought, No, no, let's not do that. We don't want them to know where we are. The harassment might not stop. There was a very gaunt look in the eye of the young man, the first one. And there was a very mad, sadistic, deranged look in the eyes of his auxiliaries. I wish I'd had a screwdriver."

"You know these guys are widely suspected of setting off most or all of the car bombs," I said.

"They weren't ready for that then," he said.

"They weren't," I said, "but they're dangerous."

"Once you credit them like that," he said, "you do all their work for them. They should have been worried about us. Let them worry. Let them wonder if we're carrying a tool or if we have a crew. I'd like to go back, do it properly, deface the thing with red paint so there's no swastika visible. You can't have the main street, a shopping and commercial street, in a civilized city patrolled by intimidators who work for a Nazi organization. It is not humanly possible to live like that. One must not do that. There may be more important problems in Lebanon, but if people on Hamra don't dare criticize the SSNP, well, fuck. That's occupation."

"It is," I said, "in a way. They have a state behind them. They aren't just a street gang; they're a street gang with a state."

"Yes," Christopher said. "They're the worst. And also a Greek Orthodox repressed homosexual wankers organization, I think."

The Syrian Social Nationalist Party spokesman denied the attack ever took place. He lied.

～

Some of my politically connected Lebanese pals were furious when they heard what happened. One friend, whom I'll just call Faisal so he won't get into trouble, said it was time to retaliate.

"They attacked guests in our country," he said as his blood pressure rose, "and they can't get away with it."

I appreciated that my friends were looking out for me, but I felt distinctly uneasy about where he was going with this. A retaliation could easily end badly and might even escalate. Still, I couldn't dissuade him, and he called his bosses and asked for a posse.

Party leaders turned him down, which disappointed him but relieved me. And it occurred to me later that what Faisal had in mind was likely much more serious than tit-for-tat payback.

"What, exactly, did Faisal mean by *retaliate*?" I asked a mutual Lebanese friend.

"He wanted to shoot them, of course," she said.

He wanted to shoot them!

Some Western journalists who lived and worked in Lebanon eventually came to the conclusion that there were no "good guys," that every faction was tribal and brutish and equally to blame for the country's violence and instability. At times I almost agreed, but the March 14 parties did manage to keep their worst instincts in check. They wouldn't use car bombs or death squads or terrorism, not even against car bombers, death squads, and terrorists.

I thought Faisal's party leaders were wise to say no. Killing a man in self-defense is one thing, but if every party responded to each provocation with premeditated extrajudicial gangland-style assassinations, Lebanon would go straight back to the late 1970s.

That was the moment when I understood Beirut's Spring truly was finished.

Sending paramilitaries in the streets to gun down members of the SSNP was a terrible idea, but the police and the army weren't going to stop them or Hezbollah. Damascus, Tehran, and their proxies could continue indefinitely to act with impunity. They may as well have had their names affixed to the title.

"The first duty of all civilizations," foreign policy analyst Lee Harris wrote in *Civilization and Its Enemies*,[6] "is to create pockets of peaceableness in which violence is not used as a means of obtaining one's objective; the second duty is to defend these pockets against those who try to disrupt their peace, either from within or without."

In Lebanon, this had become all but impossible without destroying the country.

"Once you have accepted this reality," Harris continued, "you are faced with the problem of how to fight. If your enemy is composed of men who will stop at nothing, who are willing to die and to kill, then you must find men to fight on your side who are willing to do the same. Only those who have mastered ruthlessness can defend their society from the ruthlessness of others."

March 14's refusal to behave ruthlessly set it apart, in a good way, from most Middle Eastern political movements. That's what made me unashamed to support it against the alternative. Yet it was that very quality that doomed it in the face of the unflinching ruthlessness of its enemies.

A peaceful disarmament of Lebanon's militias was out of the question while the Syrian and Iranian regimes were in place. So was a war of disarmament, at least while the army remained weak and divided. Another war with Israel, then, was looking more and more likely. Short of an unpredictable history-changing Black Swan[7] event in the region, war seemed—again—to be in Lebanon's future no matter what. The only question remaining was what kind of war it was going to be.

⌒

For years the Saudis tried to lead a united Arab front against Syria, but after the U.S. and France announced their intention to engage with Damascus, the Saudis found that they, rather than Bashar al-Assad and his Alawite clique, were the ones who were isolated.

That by itself was untenable. Riyadh also needed to patch things up with Damascus so the two could work together in Iraq, where they had parallel interests. Al-Assad wished to continue promoting instability there for his usual reasons, while the Saudis felt compelled to subvert the Shia-dominated order that emerged after Saddam Hussein's Sunni-led Baath Party government was demolished. The Saudis feared that Iraq, with its Shia majority, might align itself with Iran if the violent Sunni resistance abated. So the Saudis, Michael Young wrote in Beirut's *Daily Star*,[8] "decided that Lebanon was a distraction worth dispensing with."

A month after Barack Obama was sworn in as president of the United States, Saudi King Abdullah met with al-Assad in Kuwait and cut a deal, and the March 14 bloc in Lebanon found itself without backup. The U.S. and France were still its allies on paper, of course, as were the Saudis, but since they were all "reaching out" to the Syrians, their Lebanese allies had little choice but to follow.

The latter, at least, was put on hold until after the election in June of 2009. The anti-Hezbollah side won and even added a seat to its preexisting majority, but almost as soon as the votes were counted, Walid Jumblatt did what his supporters most feared and dreaded— he abandoned the March 14 alliance and declared himself neutral.

He would not dare do that in advance of the election. He needed March 14 to win as much as they needed him, but he could no longer afford to be a partisan for the weak horse.

Some said he feared an internal war between Sunnis and Shias— a distinct possibility—and wanted to step back and out of the way. He himself said compromise with Hezbollah, though undesirable, was necessary because the Lebanese state was too weak to disarm a foreign-sponsored militia, which was true. Most important, however, he believed correctly that Lebanon could not effectively take a hard line while her erstwhile defenders invited Hezbollah's patron regimes in from the cold.

"Four years after the Cedar Revolution," Lee Smith wrote ruefully in *Slate*,[9] "Lebanon is not a functioning democracy but, rather, a state in which a democratic majority is held at gunpoint by a gang of obscurantist fanatics who prize death more than life, and Jumblatt must try to make his peace with them, lest the community he has been tasked to defend since birth is destroyed."

And then it got worse. After months of wrangling and haggling in Beirut and in the wider Middle East, where every major player had a stake in the outcome, Saad Hariri replaced Fouad Siniora as prime minister and was able to form a government, but his prime ministership devolved into little more than a titular figurehead post, at least when it came to foreign policy and internal security. Hassan Nasrallah was not the most popular leader in Lebanon, but he was without a doubt the most powerful.

Hariri was all but forced to surrender to Hezbollah's continuing existence as a militia with its own foreign policy and its ability to defy the Lebanese state. March 14 parliamentarians resisted an extraordinary amount of pressure for months before caving in, but cave in they did. At the end of the day, they had to do what Hezbollah and its allies and now even the Saudis ordered them to do unless someone with an even bigger stick had their back. Yet no one had Hariri's or Lebanon's back, not anymore. And toward the end of the year, in December of 2009, Hariri made headlines all over the world when he spent two days cringing in front of the cameras in Damascus with the man who was suspected of murdering his father.

Walid Jumblatt was next in line to make his own pilgrimage to Damascus and apologize for resisting the regime that also killed *his* father. Al-Assad made the ordeal as humiliating as possible and forced Jumblatt to all but beg for the privilege. Nasrallah made a public show of convincing al-Assad to "let" Jumblatt visit Syria, and Jumblatt was then obliged to publicly "thank" Nasrallah for being his fixer.

So that was it then, or at least almost. Lebanese Forces leader Samir Geagea refused to play along, and Lebanon's President Michel Suleiman—a clear improvement over his predecessor Emile Lahoud—did the best he could to preside as a "consensus" leader over irreconcilable factions. Even these impotent bleats of protest, though, were too much for the increasingly emboldened al-Assad.

"The Syrian regime would love to get rid of these 'thorns,'" Hanin Ghaddar wrote on *NOW Lebanon*.[10] "A national unity government, formed despite the clear majority achieved by March 14 at the polls on June 7, 2009, is apparently not enough. Neither is a ministerial statement that was drafted under duress and that gives legitimacy to Hezbollah's arms. Jumblatt's decision to leave March 14 was also not enough; ditto Hariri's visit to Damascus. The goal, it appears, is to destroy March 14, its leadership and its achievements, including the international resolutions on Lebanon. . . . Until there is another sea change in regional politics, one that hopefully restores Lebanon to the international community's agenda, March 14 faces a bitter fight for survival."

An unsigned editorial at the same website published on February 12, 2010, two days before the five-year anniversary of the assassination of Rafik Hariri, was even more pessimistic.[11] "It's all over. War, blackmail, civil violence, regional horse-trading and even bare-faced hypocrisy have put an end to the dream. Hezbollah is still armed, the drums of war are once again beating, the speaker of parliament was reelected by the very politicians his gunmen tried to topple, the tribunal is going nowhere fast, and, last but not least, the arm of Syrian influence once again reaches into the very heart of Lebanese power. The end came in 2009 when, on polling day, millions of Lebanese voters said 'yes' to prosperity, democracy and sovereignty and 'no' to the forces for whom violence is the final option, only to have these votes ripped up in their faces."

Meanwhile, what the Israeli government called its "Dahiyeh Doctrine" potentially placed all of Lebanon in its crosshairs if and when another war with Hezbollah broke out.

"The only way to deter the other side and prevent the next round," IDF Major General Giora Eiland said,[12] "or if it happens, to win—is to have a military confrontation with the state of Lebanon."

"In the end," Prime Minister Benjamin Netanyahu said in September of 2009,[13] "it is the Lebanese government that is responsible for upholding the cease-fire, and we view it as responsible for any violations and aggression directed at us from Lebanese territory."

A spokesman for his office said essentially the same thing to me personally when I asked, in late January 2010, what Israel intended to do if Hezbollah fired off its missiles again. "Since Hezbollah is now a member of the official Lebanese government," he said, "the government will be held responsible for any belligerence that Nasrallah might instigate."

That was the on-the-record response.

I heard off-the-record talk from credible sources in back channels that the Israelis actually intended to target al-Assad's government instead of Hariri's. Once in a while, this sort of talk even leaked into the public.

"Not only will you lose the war," Israeli Foreign Minister Avigdor Lieberman said to al-Assad in February of 2010,[14] "you and your family will no longer be in power."

Lieberman was publicly chastised in Israel by his own government after he said that—a not uncommon occurrence. He was a polarizing and at times blustering figure who flirted with extremists, and many Israelis thought he was terrible. Perhaps he let his mouth get in front of his head and tipped off al-Assad when he shouldn't have. Maybe what he said was not even true. He may have been ordered to say what he said, knowing in advance that it would be retracted, as part of an Israeli good-cop, bad-cop routine. I don't know. I was never able to nail down the Israeli government's real intentions toward Syria, Iran, and Lebanon, not even off the record.

There was nothing ambiguous about Hezbollah's intentions. Its spokesman and leaders said the same things on the record and off.

In December of 2009, Hassan Nasrallah announced the release of a fresh manifesto, the first since Hezbollah's "Open Letter" in 1985. Its author again displayed reverence for Iran's Islamic Republic founder Ayatollah Ruhollah Khomeini, his Velayat-e Faqih ideology, and his successor Ali Khamenei. He denounced Sunni Arabs who resisted Iranian hegemony—which included nearly every Sunni Arab head of state in the world—as Israeli and American tools.

He vehemently denounced the United States, as usual, along with "global capitalism" and its supposed architects, whom he accused of using Israel as a beachhead. Hezbollah again referred to itself as a "resistance" army rather than a terrorist army, reserving that most perfidious of designations for the United States. "American terrorism," the manifesto said, "is the origin of all terrorism in this world."

And Hezbollah called once again for the destruction of Israel in its typically belligerent language. Jerusalem, the manifesto said, should be "liberated" from "the cantankerous occupying Zionist." (I am quoting here from Hezbollah's own official translation.[15])

"There is not a shred of evidence to suggest that these sentiments are intended for the printed page only," scholar Jonathan Spyer wrote.[16] "Indeed, recent visitors to Lebanon speak of a high, almost delusional state of morale among circles affiliated with Hezbollah. In the closed world around the movement, it is sincerely believed that the next war between Israel and Hezbollah will be part of a greater conflict in which Israel will be destroyed. . . . Current events in Lebanon show its local Shia manifestation to be in a state of rude health. It is brushing aside local foes, marching through the institutions, as tactically agile as it is strategically deluded. Yet its latest manifesto suggests that it remains the prisoner of its ideological perceptions. The recent history of the Middle East, meanwhile, indicates that gaps between reality and perception tend to be decided—eventually—in favor of the former."

Strategically deluded or not, Hezbollah was more capable of wreaking destruction than ever. Israeli and American intelligence sources both claimed Nasrallah had a much bigger and more formidable arsenal than he had during the July War, and Nasrallah concurred. He was now able to hit any and every place in Israel with long-range missiles, meaning that, unlike in 2006, Hezbollah could strike not only the northern cities of Kiryat Shmona and Haifa but also Jerusalem, Tel Aviv, Ben Gurion International Airport, and the Dimona nuclear power plant. So while the Arab states, the Western countries, and the United Nations Security Council fretted over Iran's nuclear weapons program, Ahmadinejad and Khamenei were quietly arming their chief terrorist proxy with more advanced conventional weapons, weapons that by themselves could make the July War look like a bar fight if a new one broke out.

Hezbollah was far more dangerous than any Palestinian terrorist group that had ever been fielded from the West Bank or Gaza, and it was far more dangerous than it had been in the past, when it was already strong enough to wear out the Israelis to a draw. If Israel's nuclear power plant came under fire, if Tel Aviv skyscrapers exploded from missile attacks, if Hezbollah managed to turn all of Israel into a kill zone where there was no place to run, Israelis may well panic like they hadn't since the 1973 Yom Kippur War, when it briefly appeared the Egyptian army might overrun the whole country. If that were to happen, they would likely respond with a determination and fury not seen for a generation.

And what of Iran itself?

In the spring of 2010, Ayatollah Mohammad Bagher Kharrazi, head of the Iranian branch of Hezbollah, boasted that Tehran would soon be the capital of a new "Greater Iran," which he called the

Islamic United States.[17] This new Persian Empire would stretch from Afghanistan to the Mediterranean and would necessitate the destruction of Israel.

His vision was one of apocalypse. The birth of the Islamic United States, he said, would finally trigger the appearance of the Mahdi, the occluded twelfth Shia imam who has been hidden for more than a thousand years and is destined to return, sword in hand, on Judgment Day, with Jesus Christ at his side, to promote peace and justice in the world by smiting all of God's enemies.

It was nonsense, of course, but that didn't mean Kharrazi and his comrades in Hezbollah and the Iranian Revolutionary Guard Corps didn't believe it.

The Israelis, understandably, felt more threatened by a nuclear-armed Iran than anyone else. They were the ones the Iranian leadership threatened to obliterate, whether or not Tehran meant to go through with it. No one could know for sure what the Iranian regime would do with a bomb, nor did anyone know if the Israelis were willing to wait and find out. They hinted that they might destroy the weapons facilities with air strikes, and Hezbollah threatened to retaliate with an epic missile barrage if they did.

A preemptive strike against Iran's nuclear weapons facilities could instantly trigger a regional war engulfing not only Israel and Iran but also Lebanon, Gaza, and Syria. The Iranians might even retaliate in Iraq and drag an unwilling United States into the fight. It has been a long time since the Middle East has experienced a war on so large a scale and involving so many countries at once, but it was shaping up as a real possibility.

Christopher Hitchens still walked with a limp from our run-in with the Syrian Social Nationalist Party when he decided to attend a rally in the *dahiyeh* commemorating Hezbollah's deceased military commander Imad Mughniyeh, who was killed the previous year by a car bomb in Damascus. Our mutual friend and colleague James Kirchick went with him. I was invited to join them, but I had an appointment on Mount Lebanon that I couldn't cancel. What Hitchens and Kirchick saw at that rally gave them the chills.

They told me all about it at the bar in the lobby of the Bristol Hotel, and Hitchens reported it in *Vanity Fair.*[18]

"Try picturing a Shia Muslim mega-church," he wrote, "in a huge downtown tent, with separate entrances for men and women and separate seating (with the women all covered in black). A huge poster of a nuclear mushroom cloud surmounts the scene, with the inscription OH ZIONISTS, IF YOU WANT THIS TYPE OF WAR THEN SO BE IT!"

This was, to the best of my knowledge, the first time Hezbollah, or any other terrorist group for that matter, seconded the Iranian government's threat of nuclear war.

"There is keening and wailing," Hitchens continued, "while the aisles are patrolled by gray-uniformed male stewards and black-chador'd crones. Key words keep repeating themselves with thumping effect: shahid (martyr), jihad (holy war), yehud (Jew). In the special section for guests there sits a group of uniformed and be-medaled officials representing the Islamic Republic of Iran."

Was the Lebanese government aware of just how much trouble Hezbollah was threatening to bring down on everyone's heads? I didn't know, but it didn't matter. Lebanon had come full circle. After temporarily freeing itself from Syrian overlordship, it had been effectively reconquered by proxy.

The idealistic young people and their more cautious elders who descended on Martyrs Square in 2005 set the agenda for a while, but despite their electoral victory, they had been replaced with fanatics and their bloodthirsty cries of *shahid*, *jihad*, *yehud*. Beirut in 2005 wasn't Berlin in 1989. It was Budapest in 1956.

Hitchens sat on his bar stool at the Bristol and told bawdy scotch-soaked jokes to the waitress and a circle of colleagues. She found him charming and laughed heartily, as did I. But when I took a sip from my glass of Johnny Walker Black Label, Lebanon's portentous prewar feeling drowned out the gaiety. I savored the slow alcohol burn as I closed my eyes, slowly exhaled, and wondered how long it would be *this* time before the blood, fire, and mayhem returned, dreading the fact that the next round might be the worst, hoping it would be the last.

death to the dictator

Iran's Shia farm
must be shut down, and
its residents set free.
—ABU KAIS

After Iran's presidential election on June 12, 2009, the Islamic Republic regime vividly revealed itself as an enemy of the people.

The whole thing was a sham from the start. Neither voters nor independent political parties were allowed to choose the four candidates. Supreme Guide Ali Khamenei handpicked them all.

The incumbent, Mahmoud Ahmadinejad, severely damaged Iran's image abroad with his buffoonish Holocaust denial, his sinister threats to annihilate Israel, and even a creepy televised appearance at Columbia University in New York where he absurdly denied that any gay people lived in Iran. The country was in ghastly condition, the economy was on its back, and the religious authorities were bullying and harassing everyday people more than they had in years.

A mass movement of citizens desperate for change rallied behind Ahmadinejad's most viable opponent, Mir Hossein Mousavi. He was

Iran's prime minister during the Iran-Iraq war in the 1980s and a creature of the regime as Ahmadinejad was, but he seemed to have a moderate streak in him, at least by comparison. Many, if not most, of his supporters were considerably more liberal-minded than he was, but they backed him because he seemed the best of a sorry lot and might better their lives by a few increments.

Mousavi branded himself with the color green, and his supporters strung up green ribbons and flags all over Tehran during the campaign's final days. Iran almost looked like a democracy then, even if most in the Green Movement would have rallied behind a different standard-bearer had they been given the chance.

The carefully crafted illusion of a semidemocratic Iran did not last but weeks.

Ahmadinejad was declared the winner without a single vote being counted. Villages, towns, cities, and entire regions of the country that overwhelmingly backed Mousavi were said to have elected Ahmadinejad in a landslide, even in Iranian Kurdistan, where support for him was weakest. The announcement was beyond incredible, as if George W. Bush and Dick Cheney won San Francisco and Berkeley in a rout.

Iran exploded. Millions of furious citizens took to the streets and demanded their votes be counted. Tehran briefly looked a little like Beirut on March 14, 2005, but that didn't last. The government sicced thousands of heavily armed riot policemen and plainclothes Basij militia thugs on the demonstrators. Rumors quickly spread that the authorities even imported Arabic-speaking club-wielders from Hezbollah in Lebanon and Hamas in Gaza.

Foreign correspondents on journalist visas were hardly allowed to leave their hotel rooms, but local people recorded hundreds of videos of enormous crowds of antigovernment protesters with hand-held cameras and uploaded them onto the Internet. Their videos were seen all over the world, first on YouTube and later on news programs like CNN and the BBC. The government organized rallies in support of itself but was caught using software to alter images that made its loyal subjects appear more numerous than they were.[1]

Few in Tehran seriously believed Ahmadinejad won in the capital, but some thought he still had lots of support in the conservative countryside. Even that idea was swiftly debunked, however, by Eric Hooglund at the *Tehran Bureau* website.[2]

"Take Bagh-e Iman, for example," he wrote. "It is a village of 850 households in the Zagros Mountains near the southwestern Iranian city of Shiraz. According to longtime, close friends who live there, the village is seething with moral outrage because at least two-thirds of all people over 18 years of age believe that the recent presidential election was stolen by President Mahmoud Ahmadinejad. When news spread on Saturday (June 13) morning that Ahmadinejad had won more than 60 percent of the vote cast the day before, the residents were in shock."

Foreign journalists were banned outright after their visas expired. I planned to visit myself on a tourist visa, which would have allowed me to work with fewer restrictions if I was careful not to get caught, but I was strongly advised by colleagues who knew Iran better than I did that it would be a terrible idea now that the country was in turmoil. The government was more paranoid and aggressive than it had been in more than a decade.

Nearly lost in all the media coverage was the fact that one faction of the Iranian establishment had just clobbered the others. Journalist and professional Iran watcher Kevin Sullivan at *RealClearPolitics* called it a coup.[3]

"Iran hawks prefer to label the Iranian police state as simply 'The Mullahs,'" he wrote, "but the legitimate clerics in this dispute are the ones standing with Mir Hossein Mousavi against *one* mullah and his secular police apparatus. If the election has been rigged in such a fashion, then what you are in fact seeing is the dropping of religious pretense in the 'Islamic' Republic of Iran. This is a secular police state in action."

Danielle Pletka and Ali Alfoneh at the American Enterprise Institute published a piece in the *New York Times* detailing how Ahmadinejad spent the previous four years placing Revolutionary Guard Corps officers in positions of power all over the country. He and Khamenei heeded warnings by guard commanders that the Islamic Republic might eventually succumb to a "soft regime change" or an "orange revolution" if hard-liners failed to seize firm control of the country.

"In the most dramatic turnabout since the 1979 revolution," they wrote,[4] "Iran has evolved from theocratic state to military dictatorship."

Days passed, demonstrations overwhelmed much of the capital, and the government stepped up its internal repression. Activists were shot dead in the streets and taken to Evin Prison, where they were tortured, raped, and sometimes executed. Civilians on the streets, even women, fought back against the riot police and Basij militiamen with their hands.

The country was paralyzed, and the longer it dragged on, the less it looked like a mere series of protests. "We can say," Iran expert Michael Ledeen wrote,[5] "at least for the moment, there is a revolutionary mass in the streets of Tehran."

Ahmadinejad and Khamenei must have been terrified. Ever since 1979, "Death to America" was the Iranian rallying cry. Not all Iranians felt such antipathy to the "Great Satan," of course, and fewer felt this way over time. Many younger Iranians weren't old enough to remember the heady days of the revolution and the anger at America for supporting the Shah, and they never felt particularly hostile toward the United States. "Death to America" remained the rallying cry even so, even after the fire had mostly gone out.

But now the government—or at least one part of the government—brazenly and contemptuously defied the wishes of the Iranian people and proved, once and for all, that *it*, not the United States, was the enemy.

Thousands climbed onto the roofs of their houses and apartment buildings and screamed "Allahu Akbar," the war cry of 1979, and "Marg bar diktator," or *Death to the dictator*. Somebody uploaded a chilling video to YouTube showing the skyline of Tehran at three o'clock in the morning. You could hear the whole city screaming, the sound like a stadium roar, in defiance and rage at the state.

⌢

Suddenly, an alternative future presented itself, one that was not clear from Beirut as Hezbollah dug in for war. Another horrific round of armed conflict in the Levant might not be inevitable after all if Iranian citizens could replace their regime with something more moderate, more civilized, and perhaps even democratic and liberal. A new regime in Iran could radically transform the region by kneecapping terrorist armies created and funded by the Islamic Republic.

Walid Jumblatt understood perfectly well that his country's Hezbollah problem could not be resolved in Beirut. "The solution is not in Lebanon," he told me before he was forced to surrender. "The solution is in Tehran."

There would be no solution, however, while Khamenei and Ahmadinejad ruled. Islamic Republic officials spent years and millions of dollars acquiring hard power assets in the Middle East, and they were on the brink of acquiring the greatest hard power asset of all—a nuclear weapon. And in October 2010, Ahmadinejad visited South Lebanon and was treated to a hero's welcome by Hezbollah officials and cheering local residents, symbolically affirming what had been true for some time—Fatima Gate was no longer "The Good Fence." It was effectively the Iranian border with Israel.

Western engagement wouldn't likely lead anywhere. Offers of economic incentives and normal relations with this gang in return for their voluntary amputation of overseas instruments like Hezbollah was a fool's quest. For thirty years they made it abundantly clear that they would rather rule a poor but powerful and confrontational nation than a prosperous and moderate one.

President Barack Obama had his choice of bad and worse options with the current regime, but an internal overthrow of the leadership would cut the Gordian Knot and resolve a host of problems all by itself.

A Resistance Bloc without an Iranian head might violently thrash out its death in the bush for a while, but it would become, over time, significantly less dangerous than it was. Diplomatic engagement with Syria could be worthwhile at that point. Bashar al-Assad, assuming Ahmadinejad and Khamenei fell first, would have to recalculate his interests all over again. It would no longer be necessary to lure Damascus away from Tehran if a liberal or moderate Iran pushed al-Assad away first.

A new government would almost certainly reestablish ties with the United States in short order and would most likely open up to Israel, too, even if the latter took a bit longer.

Iranian author Amir Taheri explained in his book *The Persian Night* that Israel and Iran had no logical reason at all to be enemies. "There is no history of enmity between Iranians and Jews," he wrote.[6] "On the contrary, most historical narratives on both sides radiate with genuine warmth and affection. Ancient Persians helped save the Jews from extermination in Babylon. Jews always remained loyal to Iran, fighting and dying for it whenever given an opportunity. Even when Israel was reborn as a state, few Iranian Jews were prepared to choose it over Iran. Iran and Israel do not face any of the problems that set one nation-state against another. There is no border dispute between them. They are not competing over access to rare natural resources or markets. They do not suffer from a collective memory of hatred and war. Any Western visitor to Iran would quickly realize that Iranians do not hate Jews and would not be prepared to sacrifice them for the Arabs."

Hezbollah would find itself terribly vulnerable if its patrons and armorers were jailed, exiled, or killed. A post-Khomeinist Iran would be no more likely to support the Party of God than post-communist Russia was willing to sponsor insurgencies in Asia and Latin America. A moderate or even merely different regime in Iran may well act directly *against* Hezbollah, first by cutting off the arms and largesse, and second by throwing its diplomatic weight, for the first time in decades, behind Lebanon's legal authorities. Hezbollah would suddenly realize that, like it or not, Beirut, not Tehran, is its capital. Eventually, the party would come up short on money and guns like Fidel Castro did when Moscow abruptly cut off aid shipments to Cuba after its communist empire burst.

Nasrallah might try to maintain an alliance with al-Assad in Damascus, but their partnership was never anything but cold and tactical anyway. Hezbollah's ideology wasn't Pan-Arabist as al-Assad's was, nor did Syria's secular Alawite government have any interest whatsoever in radical Islam or violent Shia sectarianism.

A huge number of Lebanese Shia children—though fortunately not all of them—were raised on Hezbollah's toxic education curriculum, and it might take a generation or longer to undo the psychological damage. Eventually, though, Lebanon's Shias would have little choice but to come to terms with their countrymen and recognize the authority of the state, just as the Sunnis and Druze finally did after their own radical causes proved as destructive as they were impossible.

Messy as it was, Lebanon's system worked, more or less, when it was not being assaulted and undermined from countries on the outside and by their proxies on the inside. Just as Eastern European nations quickly and naturally turned democratic after the fall of the Soviet Union, despite still having powerful communist parties at home, Lebanon might finally be sort of okay in a world without a Khomeinist Iran and its partner in Damascus that used terrorism and war as tools of imperial destabilization.

One day, eventually, Hezbollah's state within a state will wither away or be smashed like Yasser Arafat's was, even if Lebanon is torn to pieces and succumbs to authoritarian rule again in the meantime. Lebanon has a terrible and sometimes frightening dark side, but its liberal and democratic ethos is real and resilient. It can be forced underground for a while, but no one has ever been able to drive it from the country entirely.

Iran likewise has a liberal and democratic ethos that never quite goes away.

By the time the Constitutional Revolution was finished in 1911, Iran, for the first time, established a parliament. The 1979 revolution tragically led to the establishment of a fascist-like state, but the revolution itself was not fascist. Khomeini was only able to lead a revolt of leftists, Islamists, and liberals against the Shah because he promised that clerics would be absent in the chambers of power and that Iran would be a democracy with freedom for all its citizens. And he only managed to make himself the head of the new state by using brute force to bludgeon his liberal and leftist former allies into submission.

The spirit not of Khomeinism but of 1979 itself came roaring back strong as ever after Ahmadinejad and Khamenei mounted their coup. Iranian liberalism may have finally reached maturation during the radical ferment against the most tyrannical government in its people's memory. One day the activists are bound to prevail. Totalitarian regimes are always self-defeating and temporary, and Islamism, once discredited, will have a hard time returning as a governing force.

Iranian writer Reza Zarabi said the regime not only destroyed its own legitimacy but also the religion it professed to practice. "The name *Iran*," he wrote,[7] "which used to be equated with such things as luxury, fine wine, and the arts, has become synonymous with terrorism. When the Islamic Republic government of Iran finally meets its demise, they will have many symbols and slogans as testaments of their rule, yet the most profound will be their genocide of Islam, the black stain that they have put on this faith for many generations to come."

When Iran's incomplete revolution is finally finished, Lebanon's will stand a chance again, too. While there aren't many reasons for optimism in the short run, the Resistance Bloc—like every other Middle Eastern empire in history—will one day be destroyed by a more vital force. There may be real peace at last in the Eastern Mediterranean when the citizens of Iran seize the levers of power, when al-Assad's family loses its control over Syria, and when Lebanon is the final home for all her children.

ACKNOWLEDGMENTS

I would first like to thank everyone at Encounter for turning my manuscript into a book, especially Roger Kimball, Heather Ohle, Nola Tully, Lauren Miklos, Sam Schneider, Emily Pollack, and Elissa Englund. Thanks also to my agent, John Mason, who helped this book find a home, and to Rita el-Haddad, Faerlie Wilson, and Charles Chuman for fact-checking my first draft. I take sole responsibility for any mistakes that remain, but there are fewer now thanks to their efforts.

Thanks are also due to a number of newspaper and magazine editors who published my work from the Middle East before I even thought of writing this book: Barry Gewen at the *New York Times*; James Taranto at the *Wall Street Journal*; Marc Cooper at the *LA Weekly*; Brian Anderson at *City Journal*; Nick Gillespie at *Reason*; David Hazony at *Azure*; Michael Young at Beirut's *Daily Star*; Josh

Greenman at the *New York Daily News*; Jonathan Foreman at *Standpoint*; John Podhoretz, Sam Munson, Abe Greenwald, and Kejda Gjermani at *Commentary*; and Roger L. Simon at *Pajamas Media*.

I will always be grateful to Glenn Reynolds, Andrew Sullivan, Charles Johnson, Matt Welch, and Ken Layne for bringing me out of obscurity long ago. Without them, even my early freelance writing career may not have been possible. Thanks also to Joe Katzman and Marc Danziger for letting me write at *Winds of Change* once in a while and to Michael Yon for inspiring me with his unique and outstanding war correspondence.

My friends, colleagues, and comrades in Lebanon deserve an especially warm thanks: Faerlie Wilson, Lee Smith, Charles Chuman, Eli Khoury, Elie Fawaz, Michael Young, Tony Badran, Toni Nissi, Abu Kais, Anssi Kullberg, Hassan Mohanna, Wissam Youssef, Makram Rabah, Hanin Ghaddar, and Andrew Tabler.

The same goes for my friends, colleagues, and comrades in Israel: Noah Pollak, Benjamin Kerstein, Lisa Goldman, Allison Kaplan Sommer, Martin Kramer, Stefanie Pearson, Yaacov Lozowick, Richard Landes, Aliza Landes, and Michael Oren.

I also appreciate assistance, advice, and encouragement from Christopher Hitchens, Paul Berman, Jason Epstein, Jim Hake, Jamie Kirchick, and Andrew Apostolou.

Many thanks to all the readers of my website who donated money for travel and equipment expenses, and thanks especially to Kevin Hassinger, Patrick M. Neeley, Carl Hoffman, Philippe Kalaf, Asher Abrams, John Maloney, Virginia Pigot, and James D. Woolery for extremely generous donations.

Closer to home, I'd like to thank Scott William Carter for twenty years of mutual support sessions over coffee while we learned to write professionally together, and Nancy Rommelmann for her invaluable feedback and advice.

My parents, John and Gena, and my brother, Scott, have been fantastically supportive through my entire life and I can hardly thank them enough.

Last and most important of all, thanks to my lovely wife, Shelly, for ten wonderful years and counting, for putting up with so many of my long and sometimes dangerous trips abroad, for patience while I spent the better part of a year holed up in my office writing this book, and to Dean Wesley Smith and Kristine Kathryn Rusch for teaching me how.

ENDNOTES

INTRODUCTION: THE BEIRUT SPRING

1. "Record Protest Held in Beirut," BBC News, March 14, 2005.

2. "Hama," GlobalSecurity.org, http://www.globalsecurity.org/wmd/world/syria/hama.htm.

3. Thomas Friedman, "When Camels Fly," *New York Times*, February 20, 2005.

4. Central Intelligence Agency, *The World Factbook*, October 27, 2010.

5. Eli Reed and Fouad Ajami, *Beirut: City of Regrets* (W. W. Norton and Company, 1988), p. 31.

6. Robert Fisk, "Lebanon Does Not Want Another War. Does It?" *The Independent*, May 11, 2008.

7. Alice Fordham, "Talking To: Christopher Hitchens," *NOW Lebanon*, February 21, 2009.

8. William Harris, *The New Face of Lebanon: History's Revenge* (Markus Wiener Publishers, 2006), p. 281.

9. *The Beirut Spring* (Quantum, 2005), p. 52.

10. Nicholas Blanford, *Killing Mr. Lebanon: The Assassination of Rafik Hariri and Its Impact on the Middle East* (Palgrave Macmillan, 2009), p. viii.

11. William Harris, *The New Face of Lebanon: History's Revenge* (Markus Wiener Publishers, 2006), p. 291.

12. http://www.fas.org/asmp/resources/govern/108th/pl_108_175.pdf.

13. Omar Raad, "No Stability for Lebanon Says Syria's President," *Ya Libnan*, October 11, 2007.

14. Nicholas Blanford, *Killing Mr. Lebanon: The Assassination of Rafik Hariri and Its Impact on the Middle East* (Palgrave Macmillan, 2009), p. 101.

15. http://www.unhcr.org/refworld/docid/41516a7e4.html.

16. "Kansou Vows to 'Crucify Jumblat above History's Garbage Dump,'" *Naharnet*, February 4, 2005.

17. *The Beirut Spring* (Quantum, 2005), p. 61.

18. Nicholas Blanford, *Killing Mr. Lebanon: The Assassination of Rafik Hariri and Its Impact on the Middle East* (Palgrave Macmillan, 2009), p. 81.

19. William Harris, *The New Face of Lebanon: History's Revenge* (Markus Wiener Publishers, 2006), p. 302.

20. *The Beirut Spring* (Quantum, 2005), p. 55.

21. "Lebanese Ministers Forced to Quit," BBC News, February 28, 2005.

22. "Huge Beirut Protest Backs Syria," BBC News, March 8, 2005.

23. *The Beirut Spring* (Quantum, 2005), p. 61.

24. Joe Klein, "Appointment in Damascus," *Time*, March 6, 2005.

25. Charles Glass, *Tribes With Flags* (Atlantic Monthly Press, 1990).

26. Michael Young, "Thanks So Much but It's Time to Leave," *Daily Star*, February 17, 2005.

27. Lee Smith, "A Talking Tour of Beirut," *Slate*, March 10, 2005.

28. Charles Krauthammer, "Three Cheers for the Bush Doctrine," *Time*, March 7, 2005.

29. Tony Badran, "Thanks So Much but It's Time to Leave," *Across the Bay*, February 17, 2005.

30. Tony Badran, "The Wrong Nationalism," *Across the Bay*, February 20, 2005.

31. Samir Kassir, "Beirut Is the Arab Spring," *An-Nahar*, March 4, 2005.

32. Michael Young, "Republic of Fearlessness?" *Reason*, June 8, 2004.

33. Joshua Landis, "Syria Will Have to Withdraw from Lebanon," *Syria Comment*, February 16, 2005.

34. Sandra Mackey, *Lebanon: A House Divided* (W. W. Norton and Company, 1989) p. 18.

CHAPTER ONE: STATE WITHIN A STATE

1. http://www.standwithus.com/pdfs/flyers/hezbollah_program.pdf.

2. Hassan Krayem, "The Lebanese Civil War and the Taif Agreement," American University of Beirut, http://ddc.aub.edu.lb/projects/pspa/conflict-resolution.html.

3. "Hezbollah Warns against Disarmament," *Washington Times*, May 25, 2005.

4. Eric Hammel, *The Root: The Marines in Beirut, August 1982–February 1984* (Zenith Press, 2005), p. 148.

5. Eli Reed and Fouad Ajami, *Beirut: City of Regrets* (W. W. Norton and Company, 1988), p. 23.

6. Vali Nasr, "The Shia Revival: How Conflicts within Islam Will Shape the Future," Carnegie Council, October 18, 2006, http://www.carnegiecouncil.org/resources/transcripts/5400.html.

7. Fouad Ajami, *The Vanished Imam* (Cornell University, 1986), p. 22.

CHAPTER TWO: HANGING WITH HEZBOLLAH

1. Marylin Raschka, "Body Dumped in Beirut Identified as Buckley's," *Los Angeles Times*, December 28, 1991.

2. Augustus Richard Norton, *Hezbollah: A Short History* (Princeton University Press, 2007), p. 74.

3. Ibid.

4. Ibid., p. 79

5. John Mintz, "U.S. Bans Al-Manar, Says TV Network Backs Terror," *Washington Post*, December 22, 2004.

6. David Aaronovitch, "We Can't Bear Pictures of the Dead. Hezbollah Want to See Nothing Else." *The Times* of London, August 1, 2006.

7. Jeffrey Goldberg, "In the Party of God (Part I)," *The New Yorker*, October 24, 2002.

CHAPTER THREE: WE KNOW WHERE YOU LIVE

1.   Michael J. Totten, "Meeting Hezbollah," October 7, 2005, http://www.michaeltotten.com/archives/000963.html.

2.   Daniel Byman, "Should Hezbollah Be Next?" *Foreign Affairs*, November/December 2003.

3.   Herbert I. London, "Why the U.S. Is Silent," Hudson Institute, October 11, 2006, http://www.hudson.org/index.cfm?fuseaction=publication_details&id=4241.

CHAPTER FOUR: THE SHATTER ZONE

1.   Robert D. Kaplan, "The Revenge of Geography," *Foreign Policy*, May/June 2009.

2.   "The Cairo Agreement," *Daily Star* (Beirut), Research Index, http://www.dailystar.com.lb/researcharticle.asp?article_id=42.

3.   http://www.un.org/en/peacekeeping/missions/unifil/.

4.   Thomas L. Friedman, *From Beirut to Jerusalem*, rev. ed. (Farar, Straus, and Giroux, September 1, 1991), p. 155.

5.   Ibid., p. 158.

6.   http://tinyurl.com/e3wt8.

7.   Magnus Ranstorp, *Hizb'Allah in Lebanon: The Politics of the Western Hostage Crisis* (Macmillan Press, 1997), p. 114.

8.   http://www.4mothers.org.il/.

9.   James J.F. Forest (ed.), *The Making of a Terrorist: Training and Root Causes* (Praeger, November 30, 2005), pp. 254-255.

CHAPTER FIVE: WELCOME TO HEZBOLLAHLAND

1.   Uri Ash, "Ghajar Says 'Don't Fence Me In,'" *Haaretz*, June 4, 2002.

2.   Azi Bar'el, "Getting Rid of Ghajar," *Haaretz*, May 10, 2009.

3.   Abbas William Samii, "Syria and Iran: An Enduring Axis," *Mideast Monitor*, April/May 2006.

4.   Thomas L. Friedman, *From Beirut to Jerusalem*, rev. ed. (Farar, Straus, and Giroux, September 1, 1991), p. 77.

5.   Joshua M. Landis, "Islamic Education in Syria: Undoing Secularism," Prepared for Constructs of Inclusion and Exclusion: Religion and Identity Formation in Middle Eastern School Curricula, Watson Institute

for International Studies, Brown University, November 2003, http://fac-ulty-staff.ou.edu/L/Joshua.M.Landis-1/Islamic%20Education%20in%20 Syria.htm.

6.   James Minahan, *Encyclopedia of the Stateless Nations: Ethnic and National Groups around the World, Volume IV, S-Z* (Greenwood, April 30, 2002), p. 82.

CHAPTER SIX: SOMETHING DARK IS COMING

1.   "Border Fighting after Mehlis Rejects Syria Offer," *Daily Star* (Beirut), November 22, 2005.

2.   Abu Kais, "Hizbullah and Israel Meet in Arrogance," *From Beirut to the Beltway*, November 23, 2005.

3.   "Security Council Endorses Secretary-General's Conclu-sion on Israeli Withdrawal from Lebanon as of 16 June," United Nations press release, June 18, 2000, http://www.un.org/News/Press/ docs/2000/20000618.sc6878.doc.html.

4.   "Iran: U.S., Israel Destroyed Iraqi Shrine," Associated Press, Feb-ruary 23, 2006.

5.   Amir Taheri, *The Persian Night: Iran Under the Khomeinist Revolu-tion* (Encounter, March 25, 2009), p. 155.

6.   Foaud Ajami, *The Foreigner's Gift: The Americans, the Arabs, and the Iraqis in Iraq* (Free Press, July 4, 2006), p. 153.

7.   Lisa Goldman, "How Lisa Came to Israel (Part Four)," *On the Face*, January 26, 2005.

CHAPTER SEVEN: EVERYTHING COULD EXPLODE AT ANY MOMENT

1.   Con Coughlin, "Iran's Spies Watching Us, Says Israel," *Daily Tele-graph* (London), April 4, 2006.

2.   Andrew J. Tabler, "Solomon's Baby in the Middle East," *Foreign Policy*, February 2, 2010.

CHAPTER EIGHT: THE JULY WAR

1.   "Kidnapped Soldiers: Ehud Goldwasser, Eldad Regev," *Ynet News*, July 13, 2006.

2.   Chris McGreal, "Capture of Soldiers Was 'Act of War' Says Israel," *The Guardian*, July 13, 2006.

3. Lisa Goldman, "Welcome to the Shooting Gallery," *On the Face*, August 13, 2006.

4. Michael Oren, *Six Days of War: June 1967 and the Making of the Modern Middle East* (Oxford University Press, June 6, 2002).

5. "Map of Israeli Bombings of Lebanon," Samidoun Media Team, http://upload.wikimedia.org/wikipedia/commons/8/8a/Locations_bombed_Aug13_no_fact_box.jpg.

6. "Lebanese Hospital: Number of Casualties from Qana Air Strike Is 28, not 52," *Haaretz*, August 3, 2006.

7. "Operation Grapes of Wrath (2006)," *Ynet News*, August 1, 2006.

8. Chris Link, "Photos That Damn Hezbollah," *Sunday Herald Sun* (Melbourne), July 30, 2006.

9. Law of Armed Conflict, http://usmilitary.about.com/cs/wars/a/loac.htm.

10. Robert Kennedy, *Of Knowledge and Power: The Complexities of National Intelligence* (Praeger, August 30, 2008), p. 93.

11. Ze'ev Ben-Yechiel and Hillel Fendel, "Two Funerals Draw Thousands as Nation Mourns," *Israel National News*, July 17, 2008.

12. Kathryn Petras and Ross Petras, *World Access: The Handbook for Citizens of the Earth* (Fireside, June 11, 1996), p. 374.

CHAPTER NINE: HEZBOLLAH'S PUTSCH

1. Emily Dische-Becker, "Tony the Killer Mechanic and Lebanon against Itself (Again)," *Anecdotes from a Banana Republic*, July 20, 2006.

2. "Lebanese Christian Leader Killed," BBC News, November 21, 2006.

3. Tony Badran, "A Puzzling Run for President in Lebanon," *Los Angeles Times*, December 6, 2006.

4. Iraq Study Group, *The Iraq Study Group Report* (General Books, LLC, March 7, 2010).

5. Michael Young, "The Lebanon Opposition's First Casualty," *Daily Star* (Beirut), December 14, 2006.

6. Christopher Allbritton, "Tales from the South, Sort Of," *Back to Iraq*, July 26, 2006.

7. Charles Levinson, "Difficult Dealings with Hezbollah," *Conflict Blotter*, August 6, 2007.

CHAPTER TEN: FROM JERUSALEM TO BEIRUT

1. Noah Pollak, "Hope over Hate: A Lebanon Diary," *Azure*, Spring 2007.

CHAPTER ELEVEN: SO THIS IS OUR VICTORY

1. http://www.un.org/News/Press/docs/2006/sc8808.doc.htm.

2. Jonathan Chait, "Who Says War Has to Be Proportional?" *Los Angeles Times*, July 23, 2006.

3. Thomas L. Friedman, *From Beirut to Jerusalem*, rev. ed. (Farar, Straus, and Giroux, September 1, 1991), p. 219.

4. Noah Pollak, "Hope over Hate: A Lebanon Diary," *Azure*, Spring 2007.

5. "Israel-Hizbullah Conflict: Victims of Rocket Attacks and IDF Casualties," Israel Ministry of Foreign Affairs.

6. "Lebanon Sees More Than 1,000 War Deaths," Associated Press, December 28, 2006.

CHAPTER TWELVE: THE SIEGE OF AIN EBEL

1. "Free Ain Ebel from Hezbollah Invasion," *The Ouwet Front*, July 28, 2006.

2. Ibid.

3. Sabrina Tavernise, "Christians Fleeing Lebanon Denounce Hezbollah," *New York Times*, July 28, 2006.

CHAPTER THIRTEEN: THE SOLUTION IS IN TEHRAN

1. Francis Kraft, "Radical Islam the Problem, Moderate the Solution, Says Pipes," *Canadian Jewish News*, April 6, 2005.

2. Matt Nash, "Party of Odd," *NOW Lebanon*, January 27, 2009.

3. Lee Smith, *The Strong Horse: Power, Politics, and the Clash of Arab Civilizations* (Doubleday, 2010), p. 218.

4. David Samuels, "The Year of the Elephant: Our Cold War with Iran Unfolds in Lebanon," *The New Republic*, May 11, 2009.

5. William Wallis, "Fighting 'Has Sunk Hope of a Free Lebanon,'" *Financial Times*, August 1, 2006.

6. Abu Kais, "Hizbullah, Aoun Unleash Terror on Lebanon," *From Beirut to the Beltway*, January 23, 2007.

7.   Nicholas Blanford, "Beirut Arms Itself against a Shaky Future," *The Sunday Times* (London), January 5, 2008.

8.   Michael Young, "Next Time Around, Lebanon Will Be in a Civil War," *Daily Star* (Beirut), January 25, 2007.

CHAPTER FOURTEEN: GUNS IN THE CAPITAL

1.   "Lebanon's Army Announces Its Nahr al-Bared Death Toll," *Ya Libnan*, September 4, 2007.

2.   Hussein Abdallah, "Jumblatt Accuses Hizbullah of Bid to Take Over Beirut Airport," *Daily Star* (Beirut), May 5, 2008.

3.   David Schenker, "Showdown between Hezbollah and Beirut," *NOW Lebanon*, May 16, 2008.

4.   "Lebanese MP: Expel Iranian Ambassador," *Jerusalem Post*, May 3, 2008.

5.   Ibid.

6.   "Hezbollah Fighters Overrun West Beirut and Media HQ," *Times Online*, May 9, 2008.

7.   Massoud A. Derhaly, "Lebanon Jews Tap Diaspora to Rebuild Beirut's Shelled Synagogue," *Bloomberg*, September 17, 2008.

8.   Andrew Exum, "Fighting Continues in Lebanon; Policy Options for the U.S.?" *Abu Muqawama*, May 12, 2008.

9.   "Nasrallah Justifies Lebanon Riots [Full Transcript]," *Ya Libnan*, May 8, 2008.

10. Abu Kais, "Jumblatt Calls for an End to Bloodshed," *From Beirut to the Beltway*, May 8, 2008

11. "Hezbollah Secretary General Hassan Nasrallah in Live Press Conference," *NOW Lebanon*, May 8, 2008.

12. "Geagea Compares Hezbollah to Mehdi Army," *NOW Lebanon*, May 7, 2008.

13. "Lest It Be Forgotten: Syrian Social Nationalist (SSNP) Fighters Take the Streets," *NOW Lebanon*, May 9, 2008.

14. Noah Pollak, "The Lesson of Lebanon," *Commentary*, May 9, 2008.

15. "40 Army Officers Submitted their Resignation, Suleiman Rejected," *Naharnet*, May 8, 2008.

16. Ibid.

17. "Minister Ahmed Fatfat to Al-Arabiya," *NOW Lebanon*, May 9, 2008.

18. "Franjieh Vows Escalation, Says Demos Will Continue," *Naharnet*, May 8, 2008.

19. Michael Young, "Pity Lebanon's Shia Community," *NOW Lebanon*, May 15, 2008.

20. Andrew Exum, "The Resistance as Oppressor," *Abu Muqawama*, May 18, 2008.

21. Mustapha, "Resisting the Resistance," *Beirut Spring*, May 9, 2008.

22. Mustapha, "Beware of Al-Qaeda," *Beirut Spring*, May 9, 2008.

23. Thomas L. Friedman, *From Beirut to Jerusalem*, rev. ed. (Farar, Straus, and Giroux, September 1, 1991), p. 30.

CHAPTER FIFTEEN: GÖTTERDÄMMERUNG

1. Tony Badran, "Hezbollah's Third Botched Coup Attempt," *Across the Bay*, May 14, 2008.

2. Lee Smith, "Jumblatt's Men Set Back Iran's Militia in Lebanon," *MichaelTotten.com*, May 12, 2008.

3. Ibid.

4. "Lebanon Politics: Square One?" *Economic Intelligence Unit*, May 15, 2008.

5. Andrew Lee Butters, "Surrendering to Hizballah," *Time*, May 12, 2008.

6. Abu Kais, "The Dark Age of Hizbullah Is upon Us," *From Beirut to the Beltway*, May 9, 2008.

7. MP Khaled Al-Dhaher, interview, *Lebanese Broadcasting Corporation (LBC)*, May 12, 2008.

8. Roee Nahmias, "Saudi FM Says Both Nasrallah, Ariel Sharon Invaded Beirut," *Ynet News*, May 13, 2008.

9. "The Doha Agreement," *NOW Lebanon*, May 21, 2008, http://www.nowlebanon.com/NewsArchiveDetails.aspx?ID=44023.

10. Jesse Aizenstat, "Threatening Israel Isn't Enough Anymore (Comment)," *MichaelTotten.com*, January 29, 2010.

CHAPTER SIXTEEN: THE MYSTIC IN HIS BUNKER

1. Lee Smith, *The Strong Horse: Power, Politics, and the Clash of Arab Civilizations* (Doubleday, 2010).

2. Thomas L. Friedman, *From Beirut to Jerusalem*, rev. ed. (Farar, Straus, and Giroux, September 1, 1991), p. 158.

3. Yitschak Ben Gad, *Politics, Lies, and Videotape* (S.P.I. Books, March 1991), p. 203.

4. David S. Sorenson, *Global Security Watch – Lebanon: A Reference Handbook* (Praeger, November 12, 2009), p. 172.

5. *Free in a Prison Cell*, three-volume DVD set (Samir Geagea, 2006).

6. Lee Smith, *The Strong Horse: Power, Politics, and the Clash of Arab Civilizations* (Doubleday, 2010), p. 6.

7. Ibn Khaldun, *Al-Muqaddimah*, three-volume set (Bollingen, August 1, 1967).

8. *Free in a Prison Cell*, three-volume DVD set (Samir Geagea, 2006).

9. Ibid.

CHAPTER SEVENTEEN: THE ARABIST IN HIS PALACE

1. Michael Young, *The Ghosts of Martyrs Square: An Eyewitness Account of Lebanon's Life Struggle* (Simon and Schuster, April 13, 2010), p. 109.

2. David Samuels, "Why Israel Will Bomb Iran," *Slate*, April 9, 2009.

3. Uzi Mahnaimi and Sarah Baxter, "Saudis give nod to Israeli raid on Iran," *The Sunday Times* (London), July 5, 2009.

4. Ibid.

5. Digby Lidstone, "Iran Woos Arab States as Sanctions Loom," *Financial Times*, December 14, 2009.

6. David Pollock, "Saudi Public Backs Iran Sanctions but Split on Military Action," The Washington Institute for Near East Policy, January 12, 2010.

CHAPTER EIGHTEEN: THE WARLORD IN HIS CASTLE

1. David Schenker, "The Murdered Fathers Club," *The Weekly Standard*, December 19, 2009.

2. Lee Smith, *The Strong Horse: Power, Politics, and the Clash of Arab Civilizations* (Doubleday, 2010), p. 197.

3. Abu Kais, "An Irreparable Damage," *From Beirut to the Beltway*, May 10, 2008.

CHAPTER NINETEEN: A HURRICANE IN THE LAND OF THE CEDARS

1. Ehud Ya'ari, "Behind the Terror," *Atlantic*, June 1987.

2. Rym Ghazal, "Lebanese Police Arrest 7 Members of Pro-Syrian Party, Seize Explosives," *Daily Star* (Beirut), December 22, 2006.

3. Rita Barotta, "Lebanon's Media War Revived after Assault on Future TV Reporter," *Menassat*, November 28, 2008.

4. Marcus Baram, "Christopher Hitchens Beat Up by Lebanese Thugs during Street Brawl," *Huffington Post*, February 18, 2009.

5. James Robinson, "Christopher Hitchens on Beirut Attack: 'They Kept Coming. Six or Seven at First,'" *The Guardian*, February 19, 2009.

6. Lee Harris, *Civilization and Its Enemies: The Next Stage of History* (Free Press, February 3, 2004), p. xv.

7. Nassim Nicholas Taleb, *The Black Swan: The Impact of the Highly Improbable* (Random House, April 17, 2007).

8. Michael Young, "Power Plays between Friends in Beirut," *Daily Star* (Beirut), April 1, 2010.

9. Lee Smith, "Walid Jumblatt Is No Weather Vane," *Slate*, August 7, 2009.

10. Hanin Ghaddar, "Syria's War on March 14," *NOW Lebanon*, March 20, 2010.

11. "The Magic Has Gone," *NOW Lebanon*, February 12, 2010.

12. Howard Schneider, "Hezbollah's Relocation of Rocket Sites to Lebanon's Interior Poses Wider Threat," *Washington Post*, January 23, 2010.

13. "Netanyahu: Lebanon Accountable for Rocket on Israel," *Haaretz*, September 13, 2009.

14. "Lieberman Warns Assad War Will Drive Him from Power," *The Jerusalem Post*, February 4, 2010.

15. http://english.moqawama.org/essaydetails.php?eid=9632&cid=214.

16. Jonathan Spyer, "Hezbollah's Delusions," GLORIA Center, December 9, 2009.

17. "Muslim Cleric Calls for 'Greater Iran,'" Associated Press, May 15, 2010.

18. Christopher Hitchens, "The Swastika and the Cedar," *Vanity Fair*, May 2009.

EPILOGUE: DEATH TO THE DICTATOR

1. Julie Steinberg, "Iran's Lame Attempt at Photoshop," *Wall Street Journal*, June 20, 2009.

2. Eric Hooglund, "Iran's Rural Vote and Election Fraud," *Tehran Bureau*, June 17, 2009.

3. Kevin Sullivan, "Not a Theocracy," *RealClearPolitics*, June 13, 2009.

4. Danielle Pletka and Ali Alfoneh, "Iran's Hidden Revolution," *New York Times*, June 16, 2009.

5. Michael Ledeen, "So How's It Going in Iran?" *Pajamas Media*, June 15, 2009.

6. Amir Taheri, *The Persian Night: Iran under the Khomeinist Revolution* (Encounter, March 25, 2009), p. 160.

7. Reza Zarabi, "The Persian Abyss: Our Dying Islam," *The Jerusalem Post*, May 13, 2007.

INDEX